SCENES FROM ISOLATION

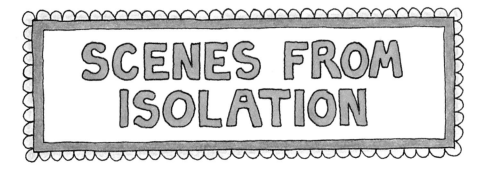

Cathy Guisewite

Andrews McMeel
PUBLISHING®

Introduction

I've worn the same pair of sweatpants for fourteen months.

I've binge-watched, binge-eaten, binge-shopped, binge-prayed. I've Zoomed. Streamed. Screamed. Googled how to get hot fudge out of a duvet cover. Googled how to chop my insulting blue jeans into face masks. Googled how to permanently delete my Google search history. I've meditated, looked within, and asked the big questions—"If no one's allowed in my house for months, what's the point of vacuuming?"

In the beginning, I took my temperature fifty times a day and vowed that if I lived, I would use my lockdown time to write my novel! Clean the basement! Get in shape! Do unto others! Empty my e-mail inbox! I didn't write, clean, exercise, or do unto anyone, and every time I peeked at my e-mail, a clothing store popped up, said it missed me so much it was offering 30 percent off, and I bought another new outfit to wear when I took out the trash.

I've cried at the huge life celebrations that were reduced to yard signs— "Congratulations, Class of 2020!" Sobbed at the tragic, lonely goodbyes. I've cheered the heroic health care workers and fallen to my knees in gratitude for all the essential workers who have kept the country running so the rest of us could stay safe at home.

I started drawing *Scenes from Isolation* because I could only cope with our new normal by reverting to my old normal: dumping angst on paper. I thought I'd be doing it for a few weeks. How long could a pandemic last? And here we are. I couldn't wait until 2020 was over and then 2021 was worse. Fears grew. Rears grew. Lists grew. Impatience grew. Hair fell out. The dog that was so excited to have me home started giving me the stink eye.

Today we have vaccines but variants, reopenings but resurges. Will it ever really be over and when it is, will it ever feel safe to hug someone without wearing a hazmat suit? Will we remember where we were when life screeched to a halt because of droplets?

I hope we'll remember that as lonely as it's felt sometimes, we got through this time together. Maybe we didn't clean our basements, but a lot of us did a deep dive into who we are. We found a powerful reappreciation for who we love. We reconnected to what's important. We should all be proud of whatever we did to get through even one day in lockdown, whatever the day was, which no one could ever figure out.

I hope we'll remember the hope that's sustained us—that the time will finally come when we can all wash our hands of the pandemic. While singing the "Happy Birthday" song, of course. With antibacterial soap, two times in a row, for a full twenty seconds.

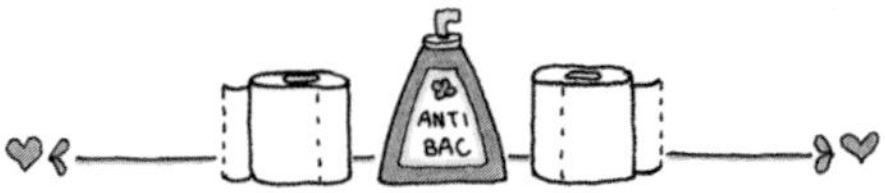
ANTI
BAC

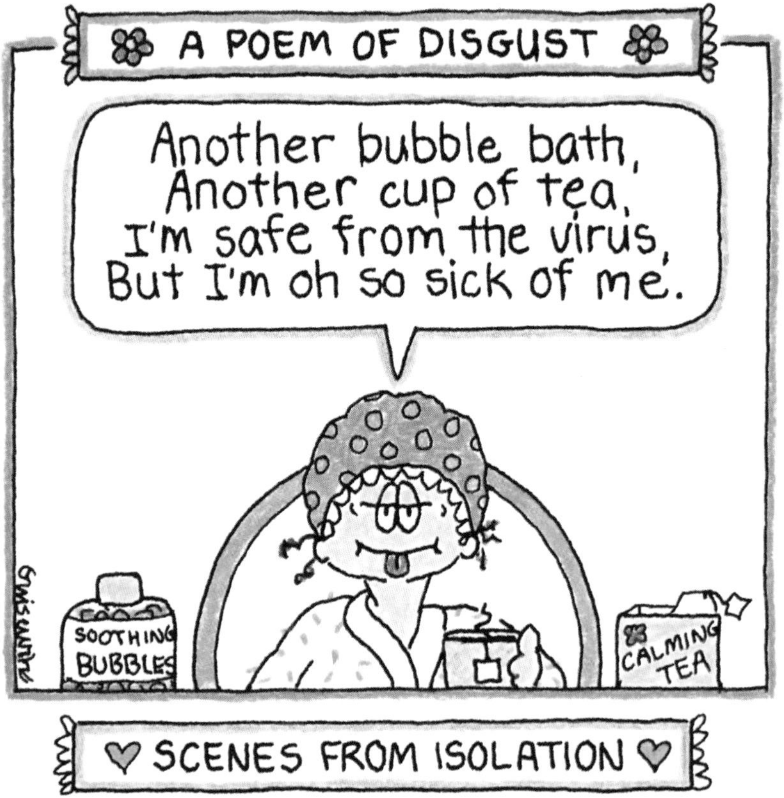
A POEM OF DISGUST
Another bubble bath,
Another cup of tea,
I'm safe from the virus,
But I'm oh so sick of me.
SOOTHING BUBBLES
CALMING TEA
SCENES FROM ISOLATION

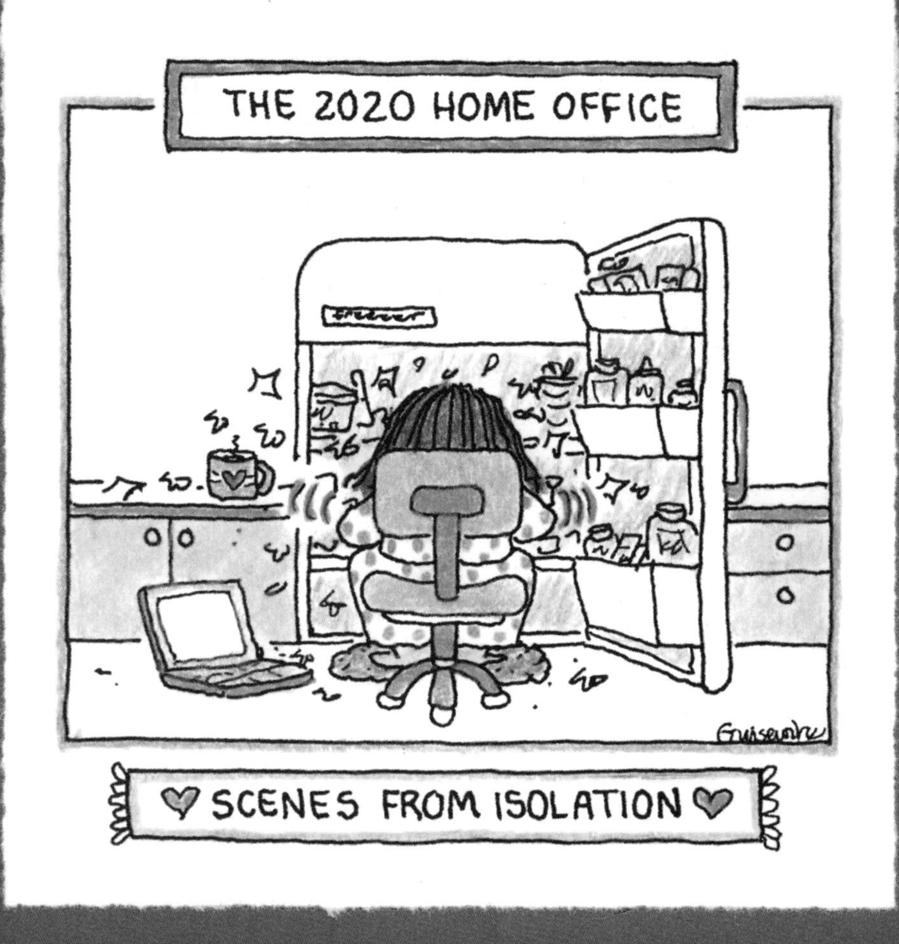
THE 2020 HOME OFFICE
SCENES FROM ISOLATION

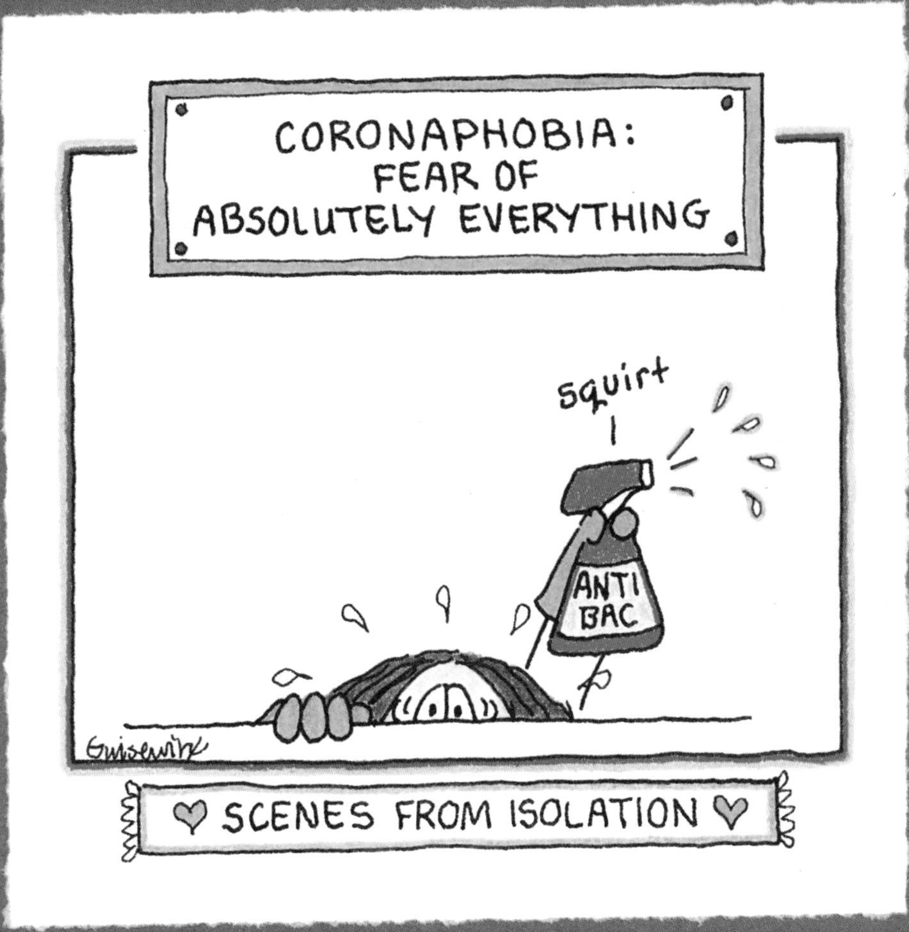
CORONAPHOBIA: FEAR OF ABSOLUTELY EVERYTHING
squirt
ANTI BAC
SCENES FROM ISOLATION

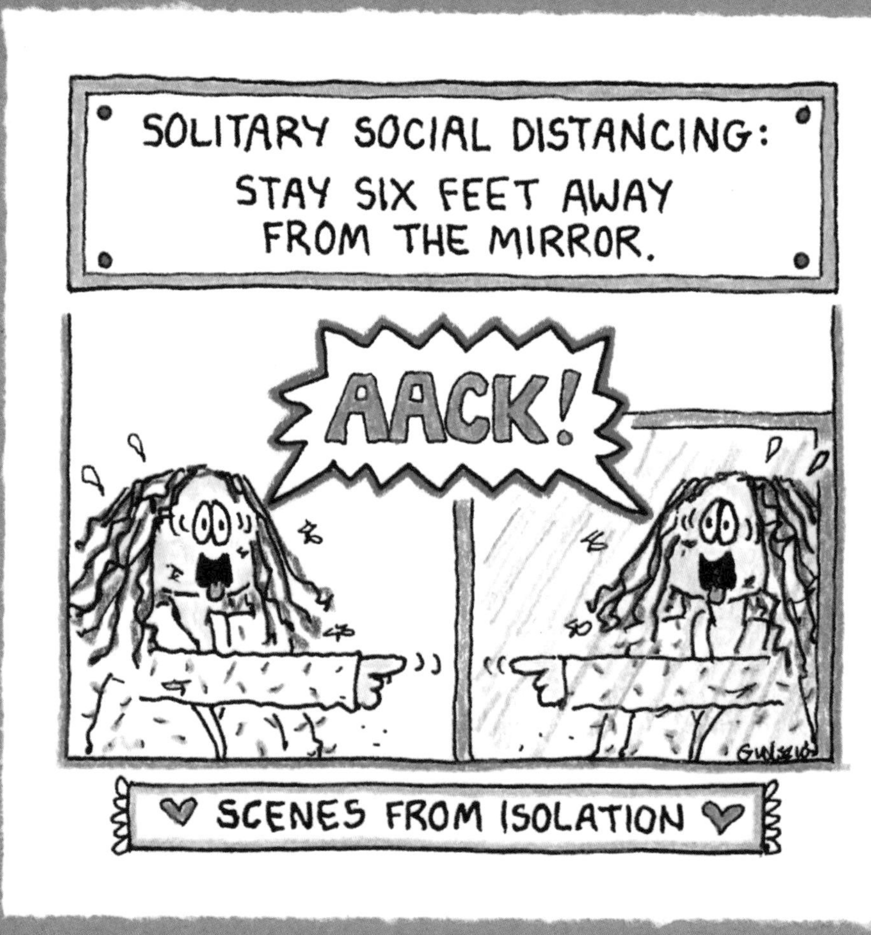
SOLITARY SOCIAL DISTANCING:
STAY SIX FEET AWAY FROM THE MIRROR.
AACK!
SCENES FROM ISOLATION

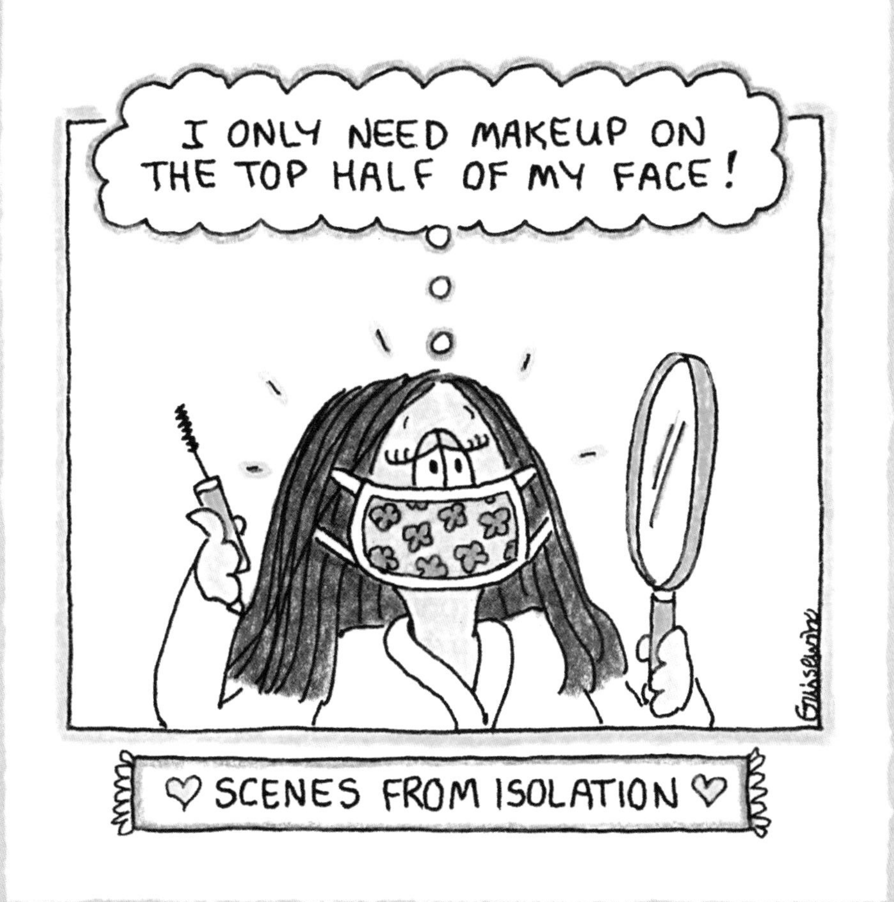
I ONLY NEED MAKEUP ON THE TOP HALF OF MY FACE!
SCENES FROM ISOLATION

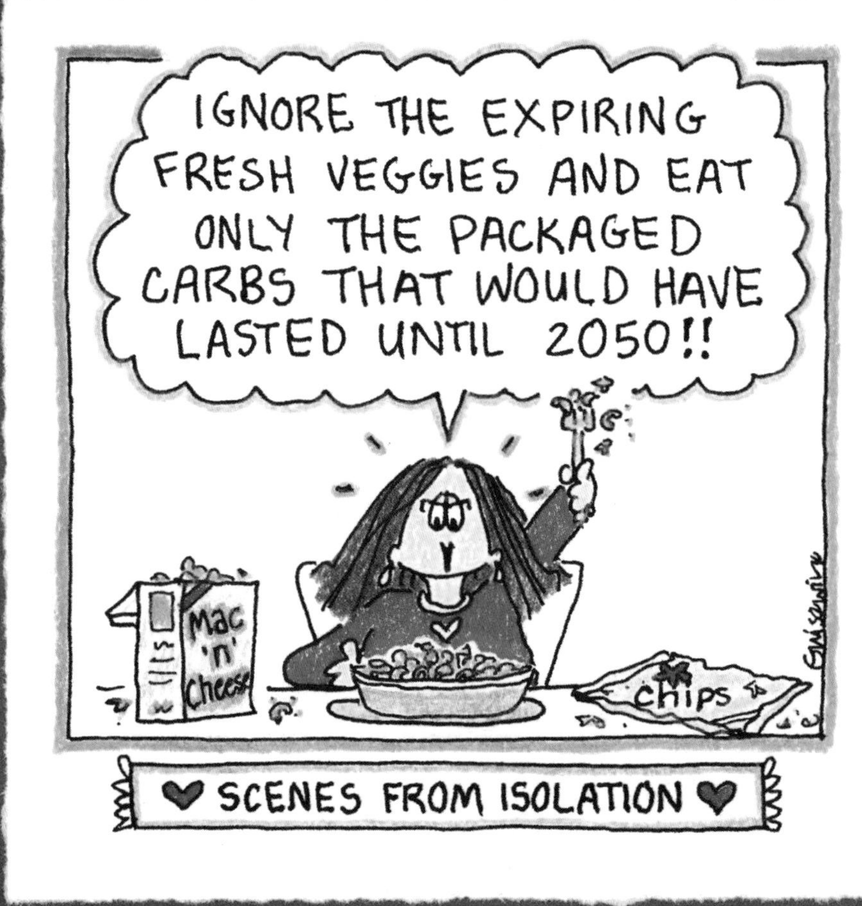
IGNORE THE EXPIRING FRESH VEGGIES AND EAT ONLY THE PACKAGED CARBS THAT WOULD HAVE LASTED UNTIL 2050!!
Mac 'n' Cheese
chips
SCENES FROM ISOLATION

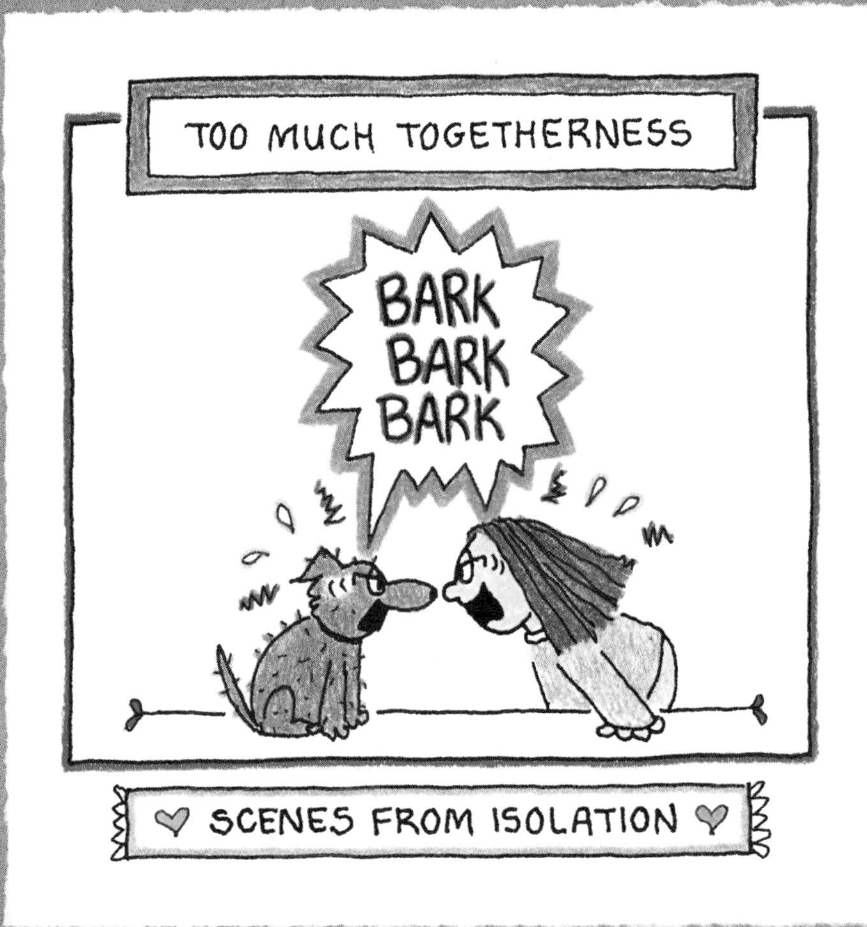
TOO MUCH TOGETHERNESS
BARK
BARK
BARK
SCENES FROM ISOLATION

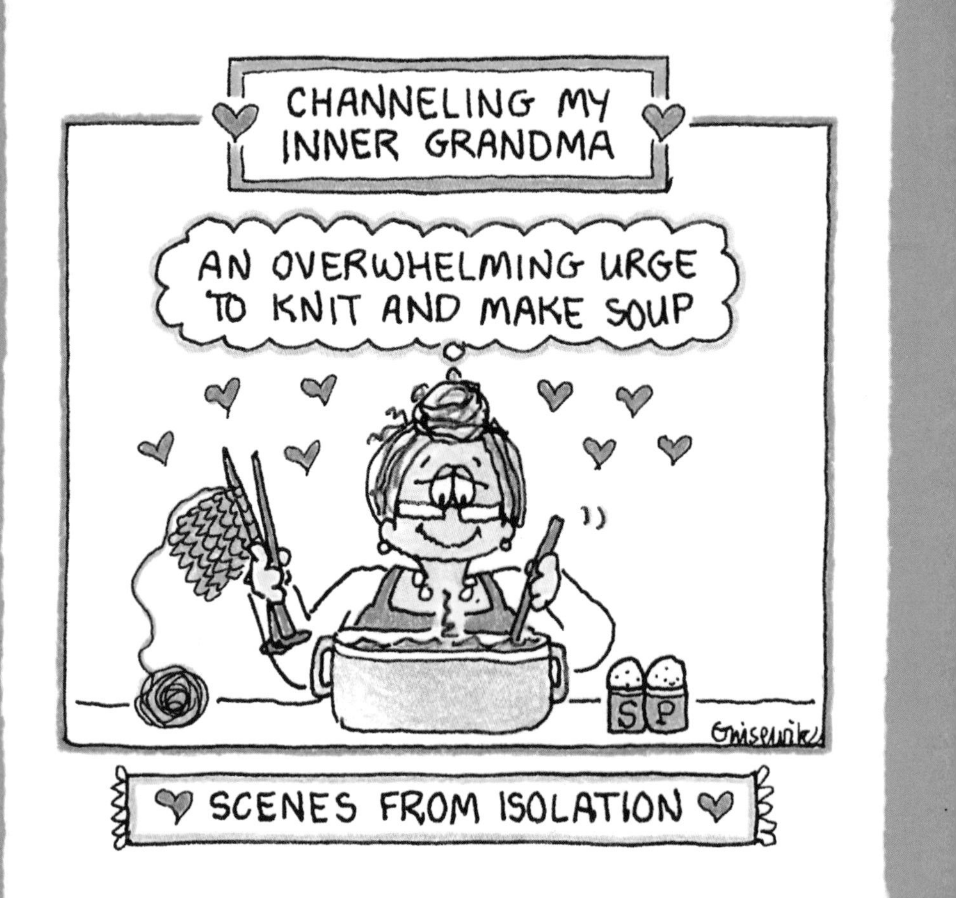
CHANNELING MY INNER GRANDMA
AN OVERWHELMING URGE TO KNIT AND MAKE SOUP
S
P
SCENES FROM ISOLATION

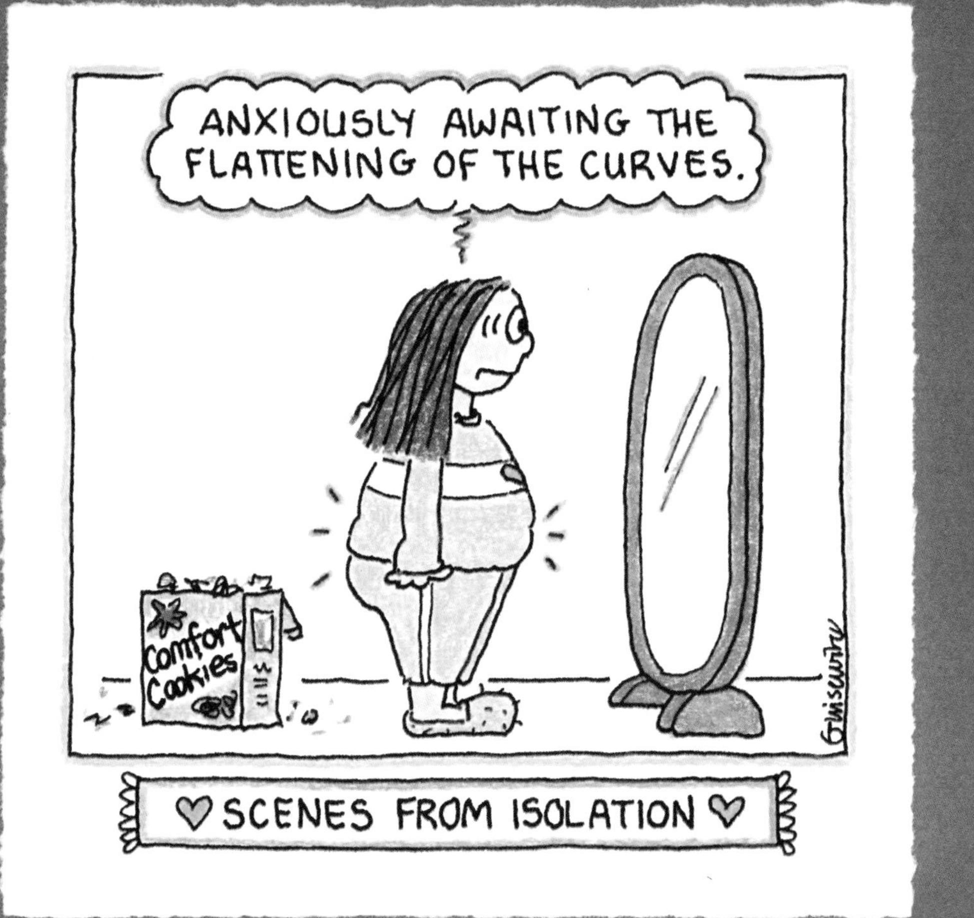
ANXIOUSLY AWAITING THE FLATTENING OF THE CURVES.
Comfort Cookies
SCENES FROM ISOLATION

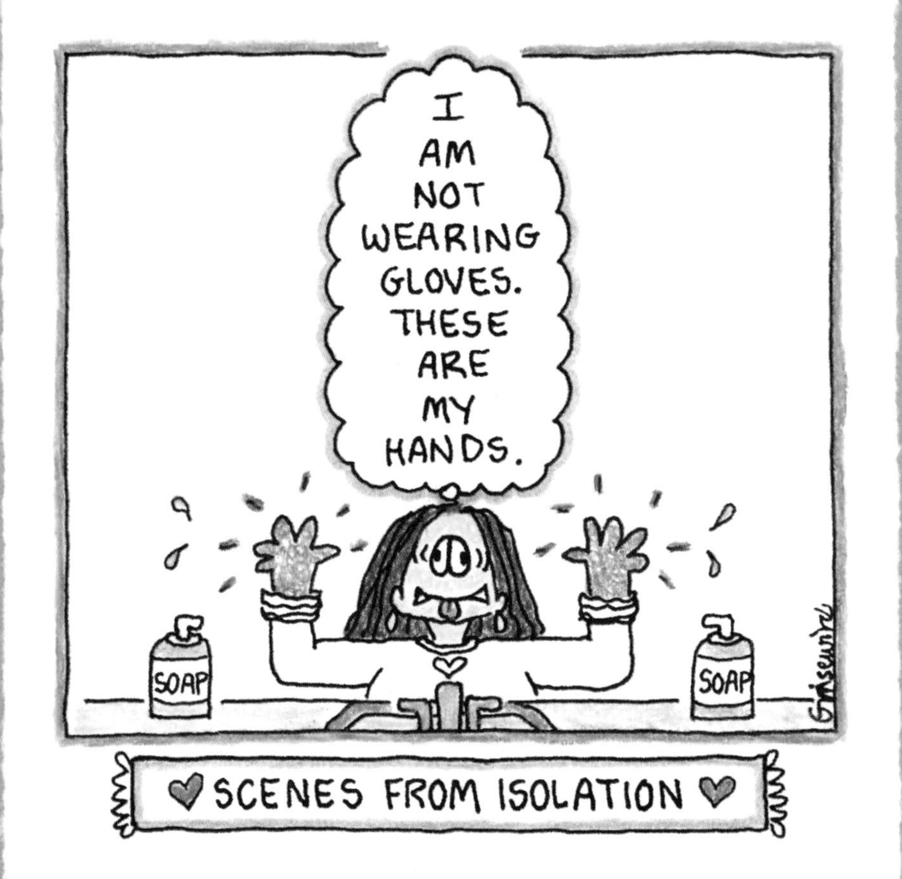
I AM NOT WEARING GLOVES. THESE ARE MY HANDS.
SOAP
SOAP
Guisewite
SCENES FROM ISOLATION

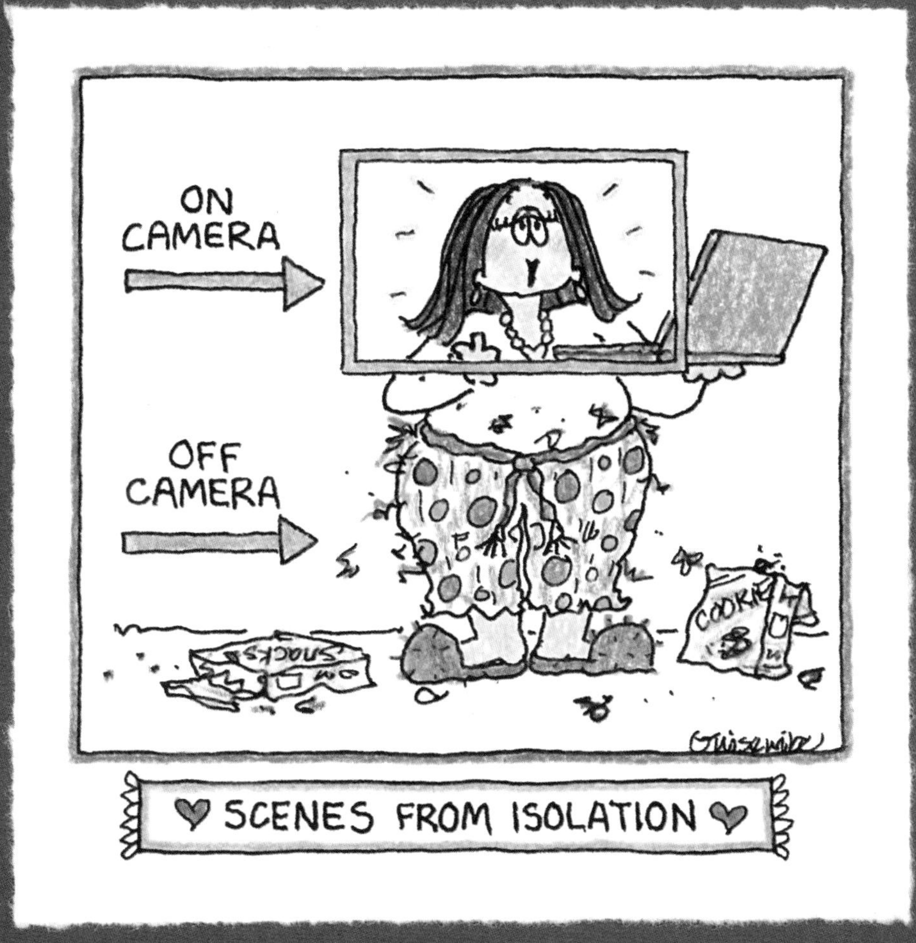
ON CAMERA
OFF CAMERA
SNACKS
COOKIES
SCENES FROM ISOLATION

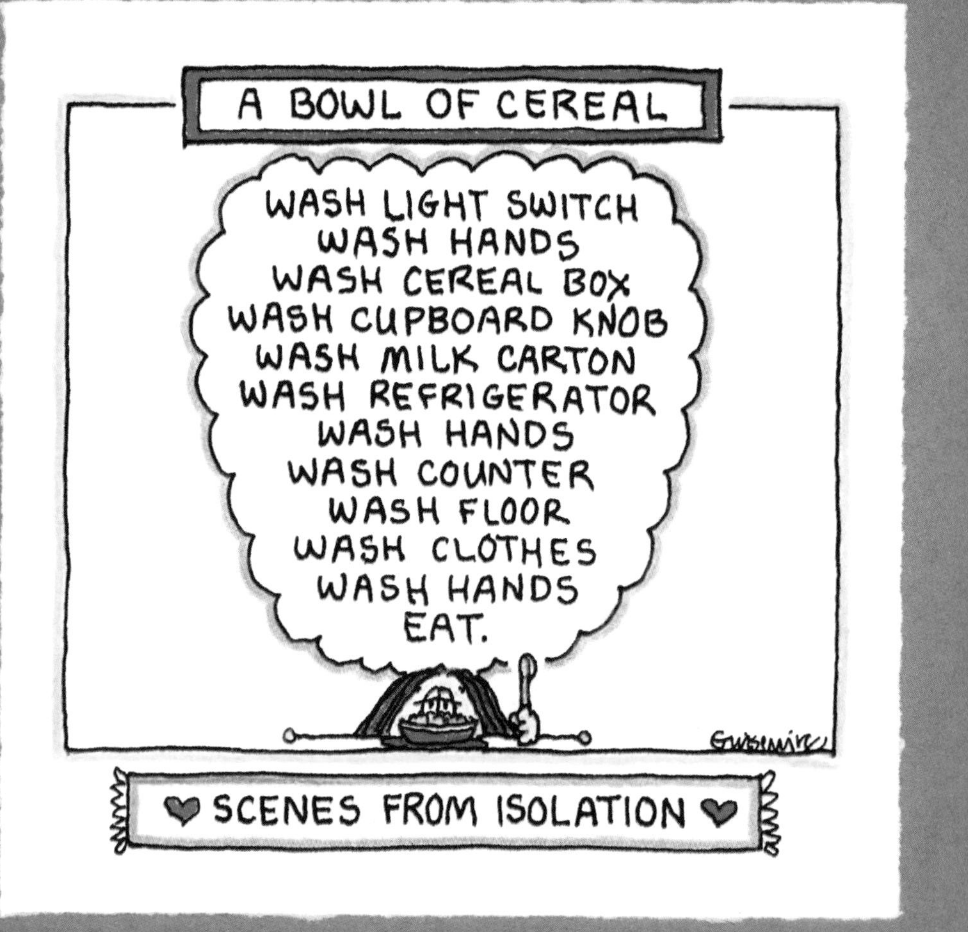
A BOWL OF CEREAL
WASH LIGHT SWITCH
WASH HANDS
WASH CEREAL BOX
WASH CUPBOARD KNOB
WASH MILK CARTON
WASH REFRIGERATOR
WASH HANDS
WASH COUNTER
WASH FLOOR
WASH CLOTHES
WASH HANDS
EAT.
SCENES FROM ISOLATION

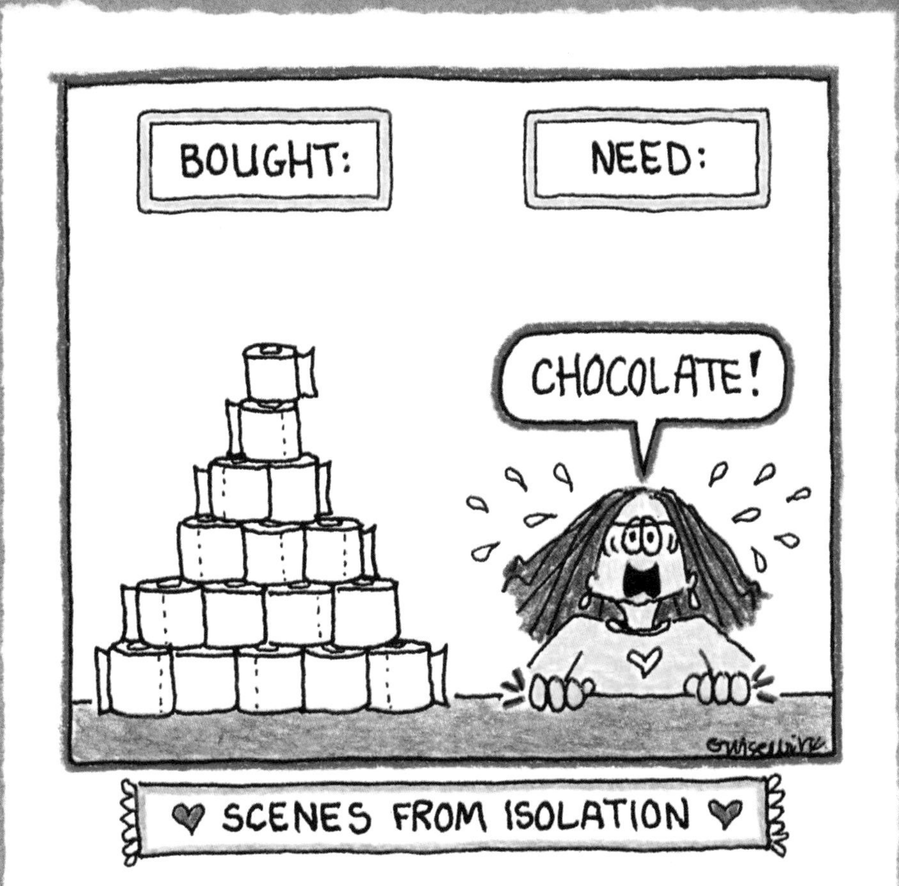
BOUGHT:
NEED:
CHOCOLATE!
SCENES FROM ISOLATION

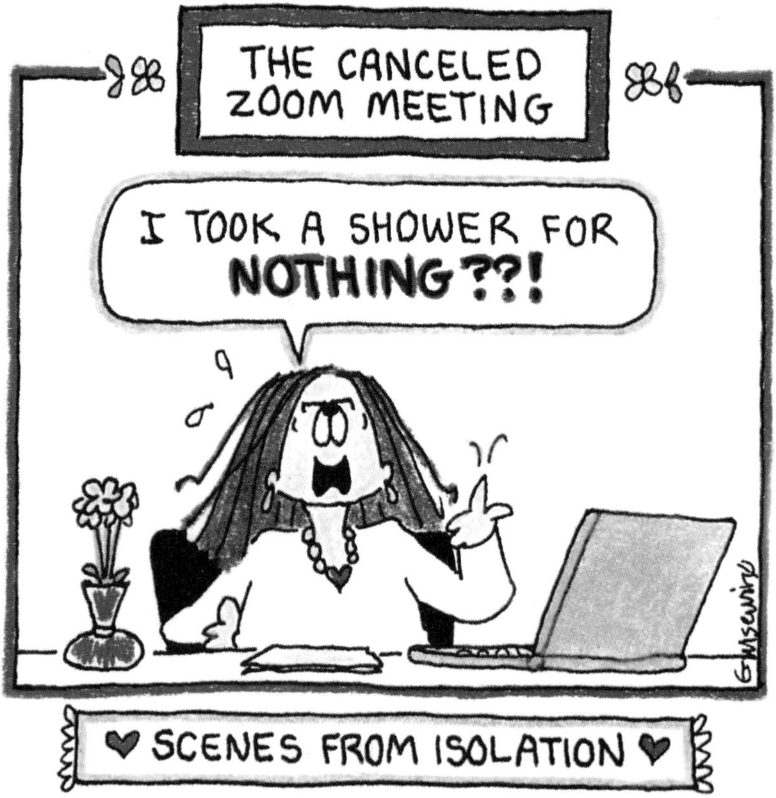
THE CANCELED ZOOM MEETING
I TOOK A SHOWER FOR NOTHING??!
SCENES FROM ISOLATION

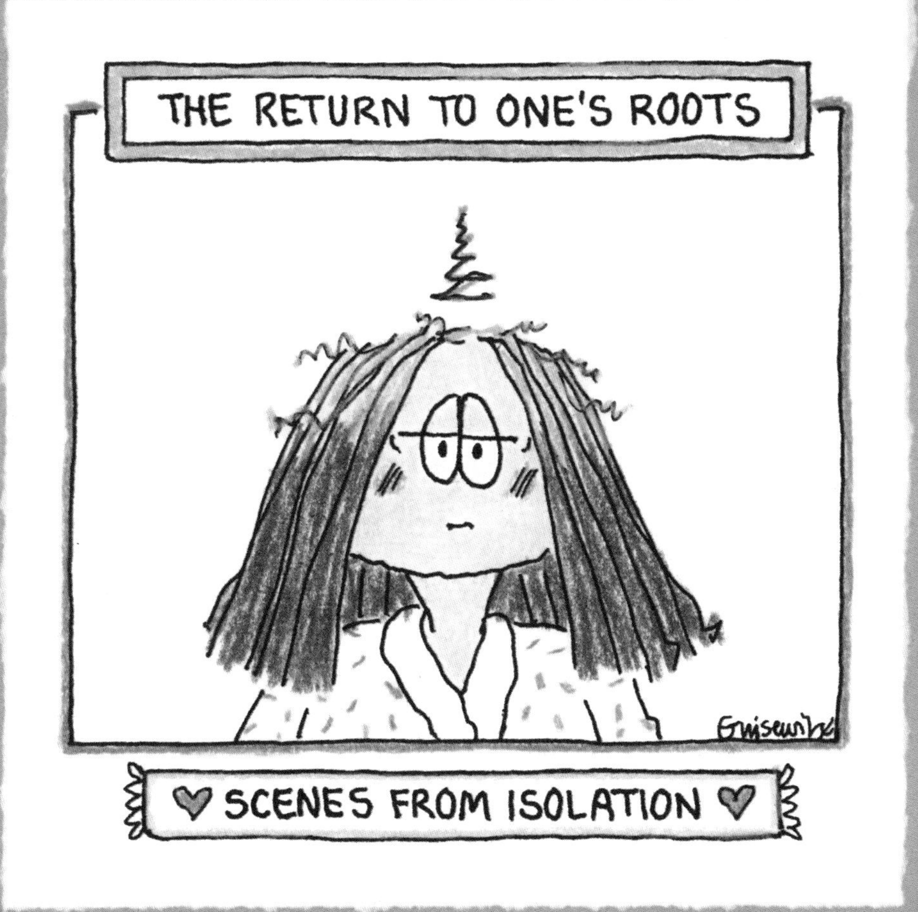
THE RETURN TO ONE'S ROOTS
Guisewite
♥ SCENES FROM ISOLATION ♥

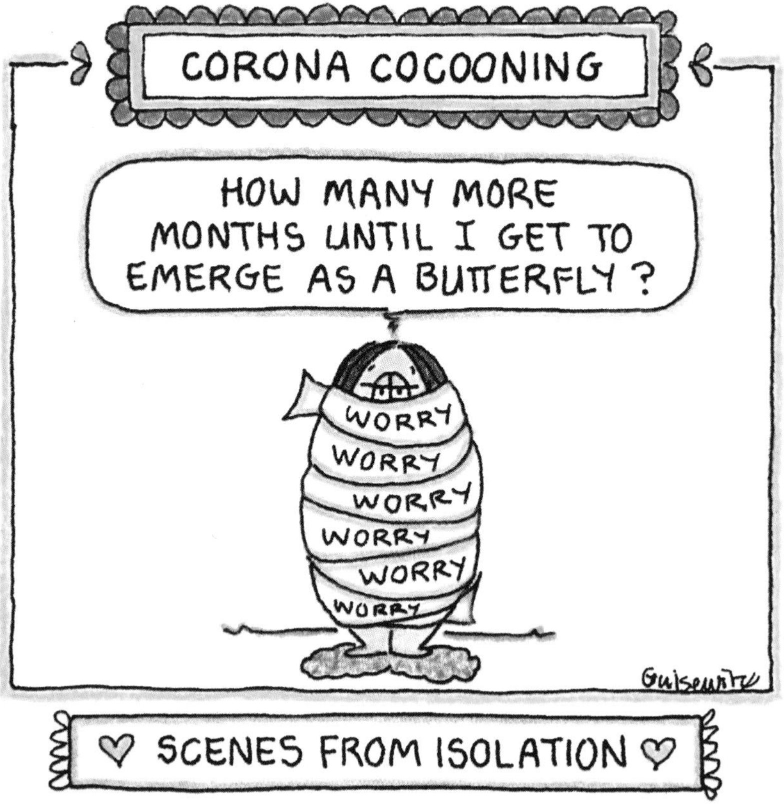
CORONA COCOONING
HOW MANY MORE MONTHS UNTIL I GET TO EMERGE AS A BUTTERFLY?
WORRY
WORRY
WORRY
WORRY
WORRY
WORRY
Guisewite
SCENES FROM ISOLATION

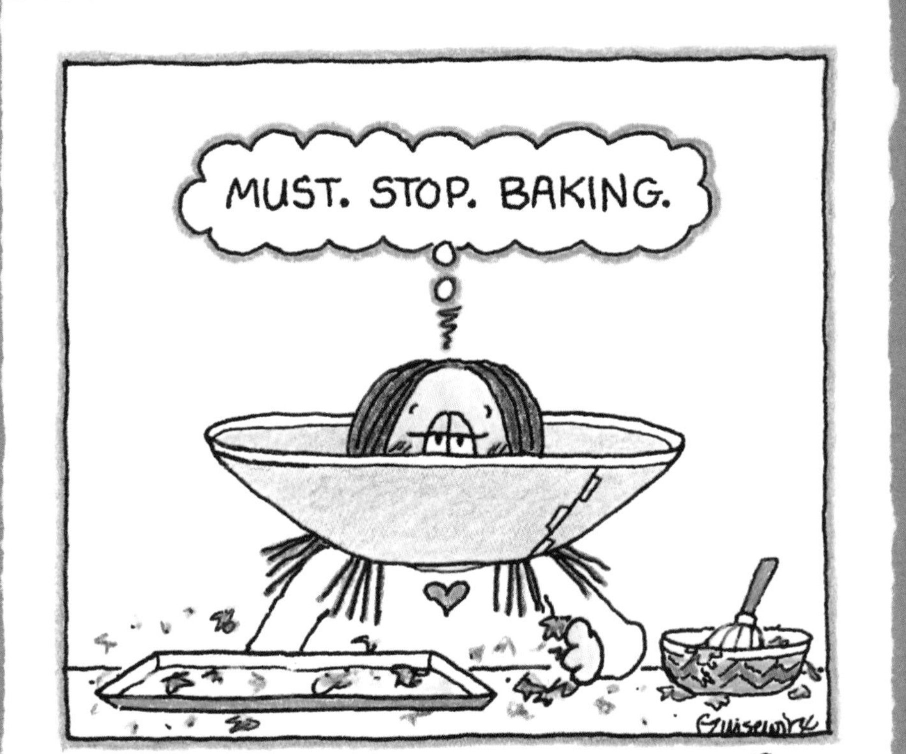
MUST. STOP. BAKING.
SCENES FROM ISOLATION

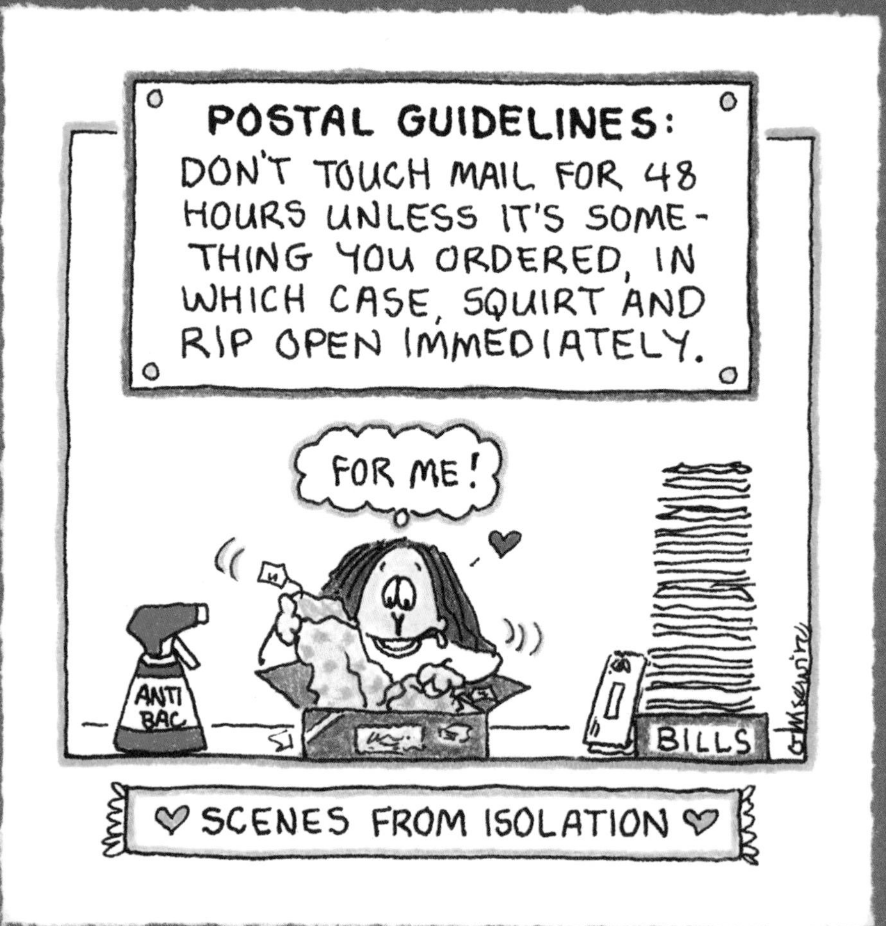
POSTAL GUIDELINES:
DON'T TOUCH MAIL FOR 48 HOURS UNLESS IT'S SOME-THING YOU ORDERED, IN WHICH CASE, SQUIRT AND RIP OPEN IMMEDIATELY.
FOR ME!
ANTI BAC
BILLS
SCENES FROM ISOLATION

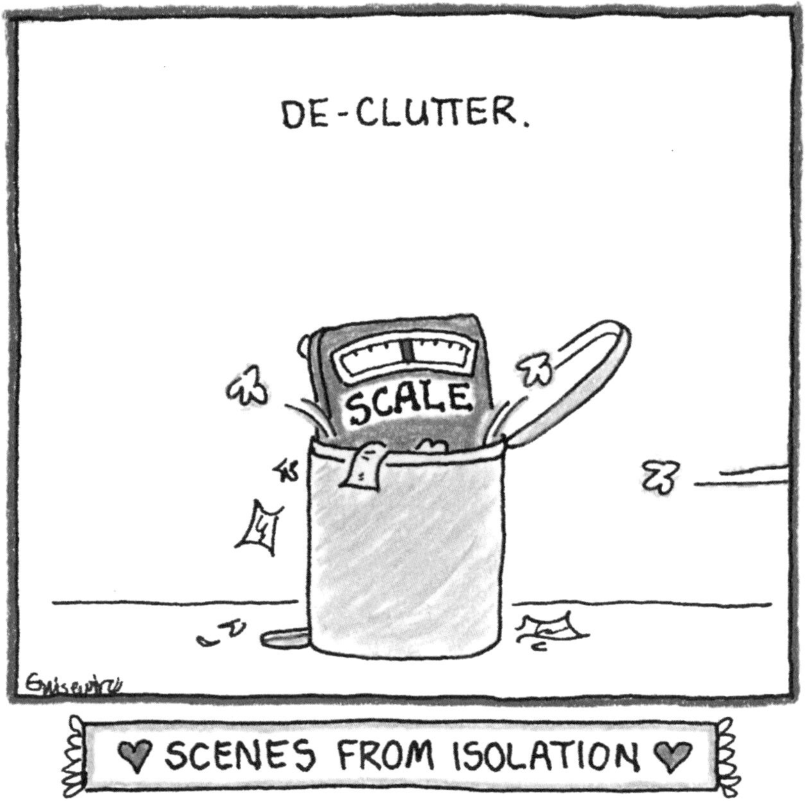
DE-CLUTTER.
SCALE
SCENES FROM ISOLATION

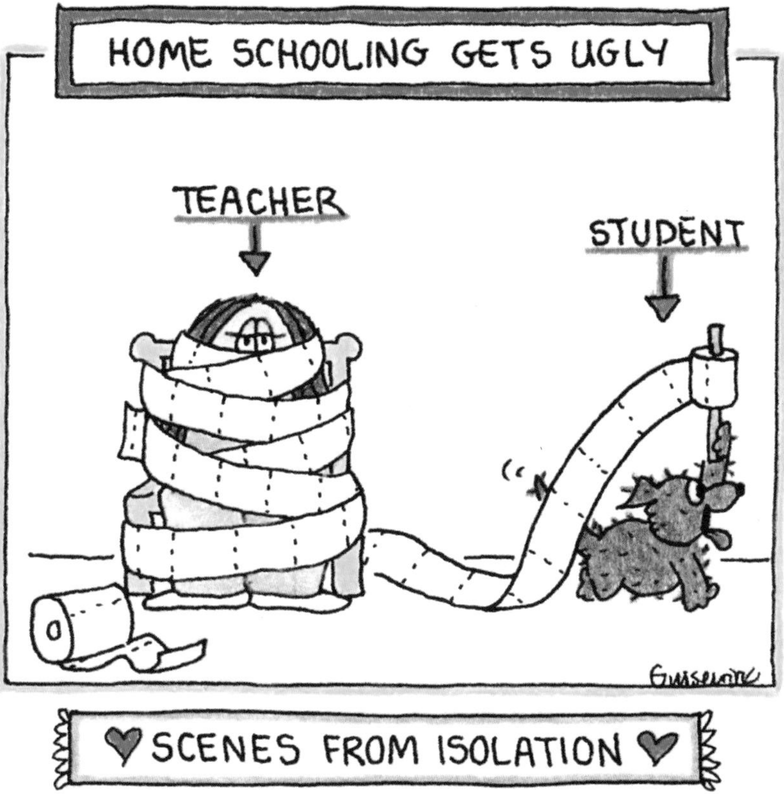
HOME SCHOOLING GETS UGLY
TEACHER
STUDENT
SCENES FROM ISOLATION

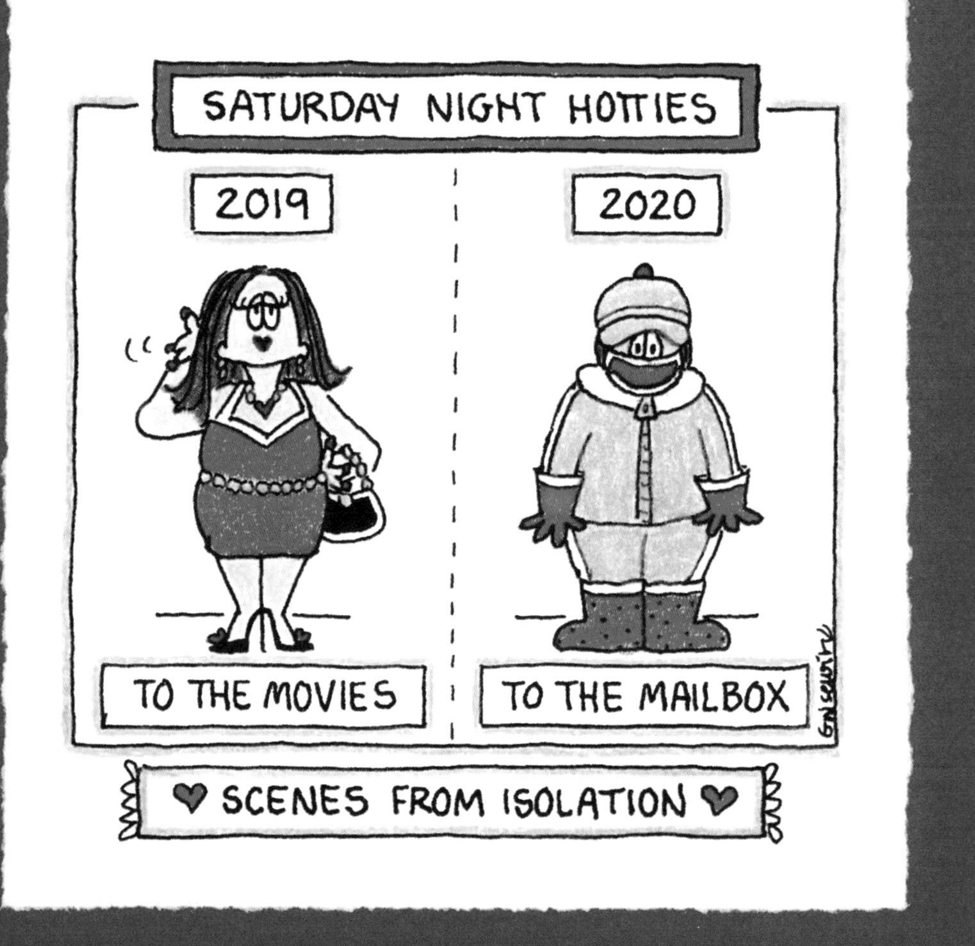
SATURDAY NIGHT HOTTIES
2019
2020
TO THE MOVIES
TO THE MAILBOX
SCENES FROM ISOLATION

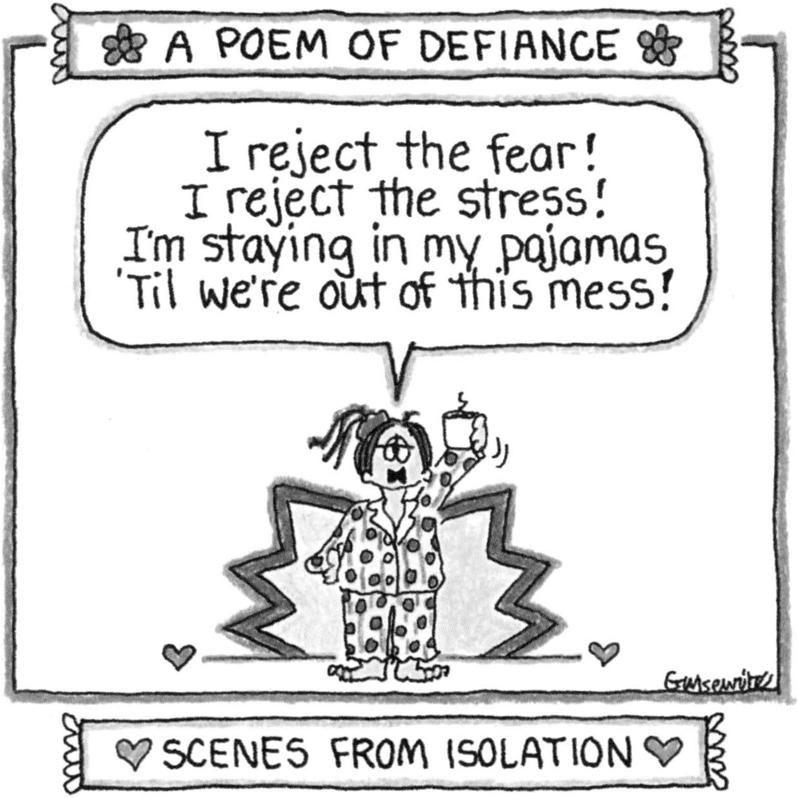
A POEM OF DEFIANCE
I reject the fear! I reject the stress! I'm staying in my pajamas 'Til we're out of this mess!
SCENES FROM ISOLATION

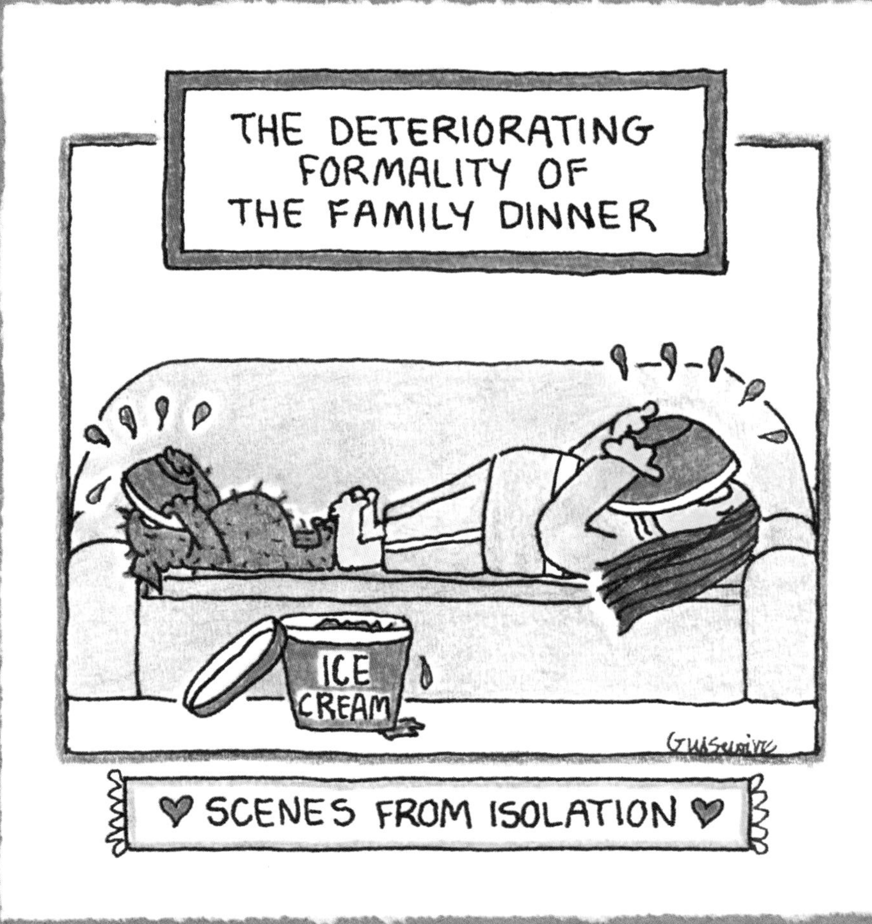
THE DETERIORATING FORMALITY OF THE FAMILY DINNER
ICE CREAM
♥ SCENES FROM ISOLATION ♥

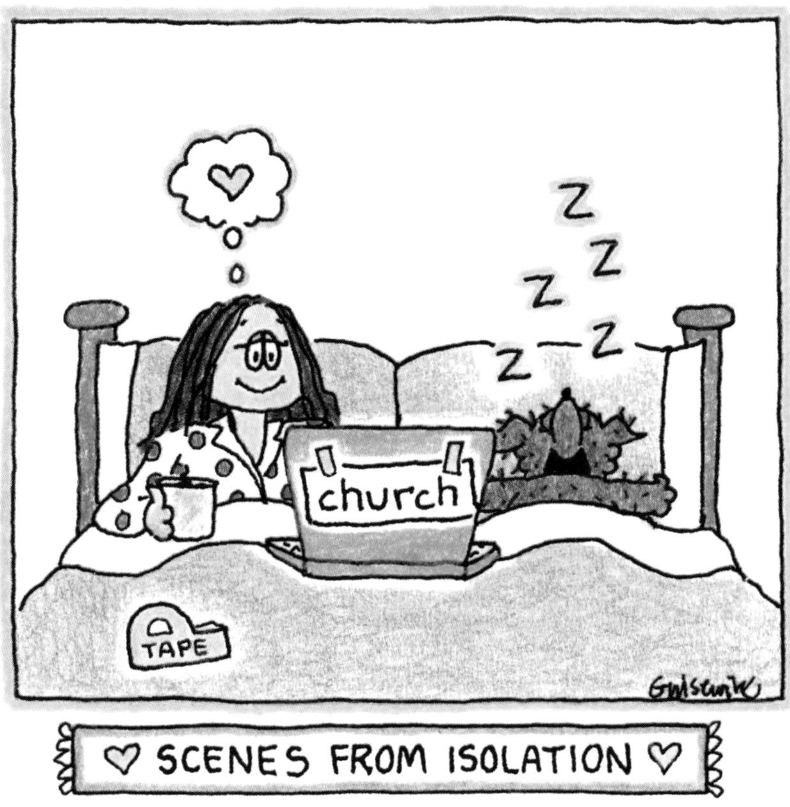
church
TAPE
Z Z Z Z Z Z
♡ SCENES FROM ISOLATION ♡

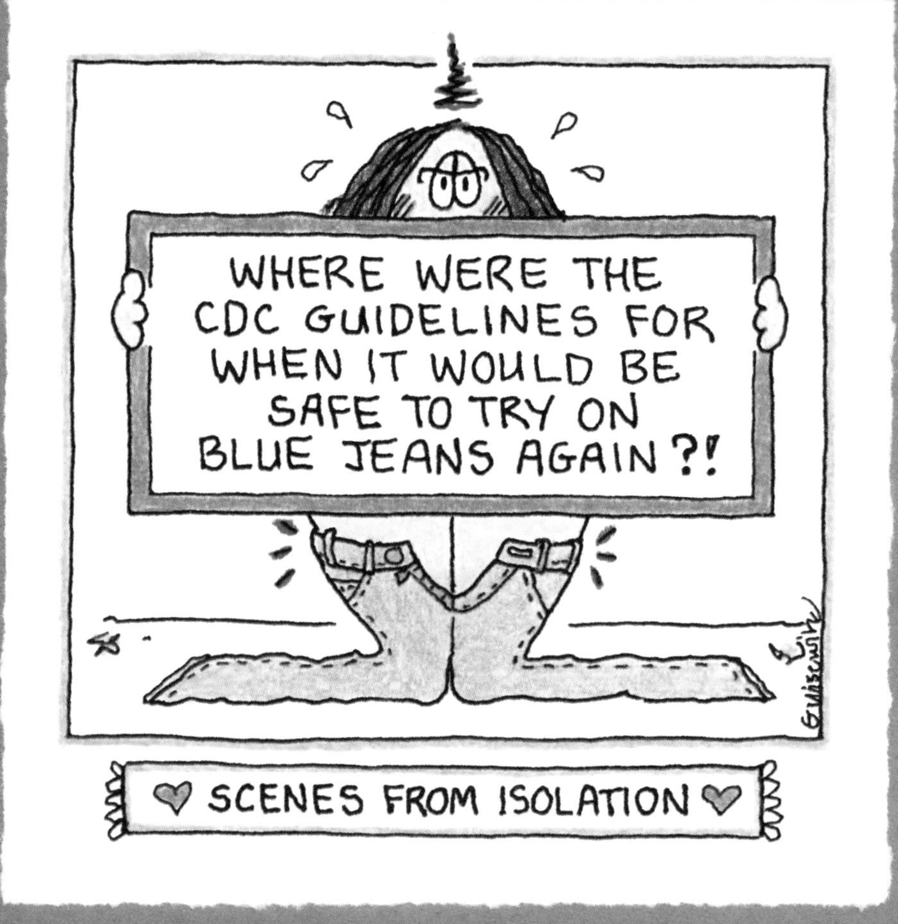
WHERE WERE THE CDC GUIDELINES FOR WHEN IT WOULD BE SAFE TO TRY ON BLUE JEANS AGAIN?!
SCENES FROM ISOLATION
Guisewite

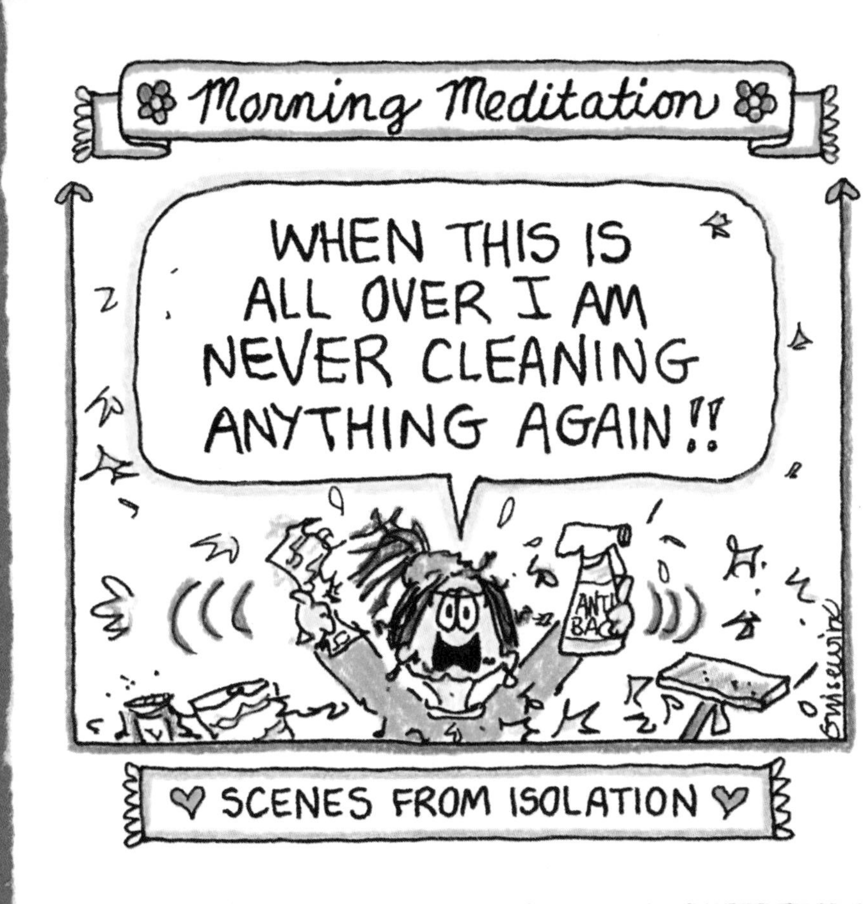
Morning Meditation
WHEN THIS IS ALL OVER I AM NEVER CLEANING ANYTHING AGAIN!!
ANTI BAC
SCENES FROM ISOLATION

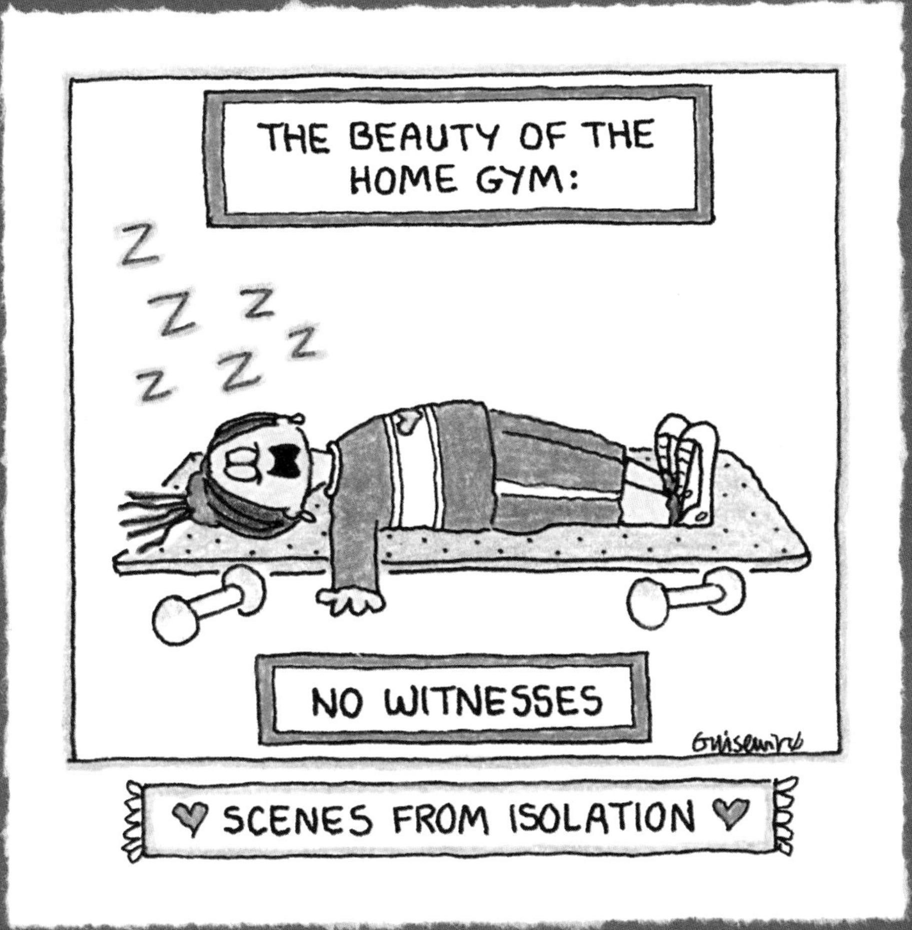
THE BEAUTY OF THE HOME GYM:
Z Z Z Z Z Z
NO WITNESSES
Guisewite
SCENES FROM ISOLATION

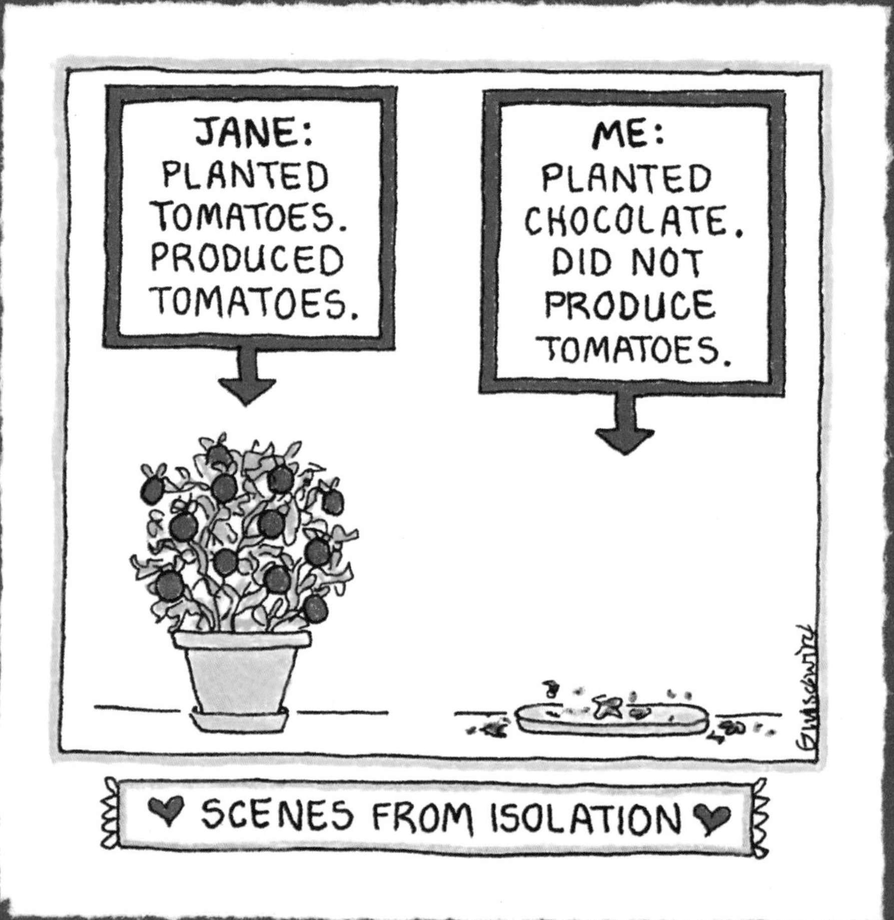
JANE: PLANTED TOMATOES. PRODUCED TOMATOES.
ME: PLANTED CHOCOLATE. DID NOT PRODUCE TOMATOES.
SCENES FROM ISOLATION

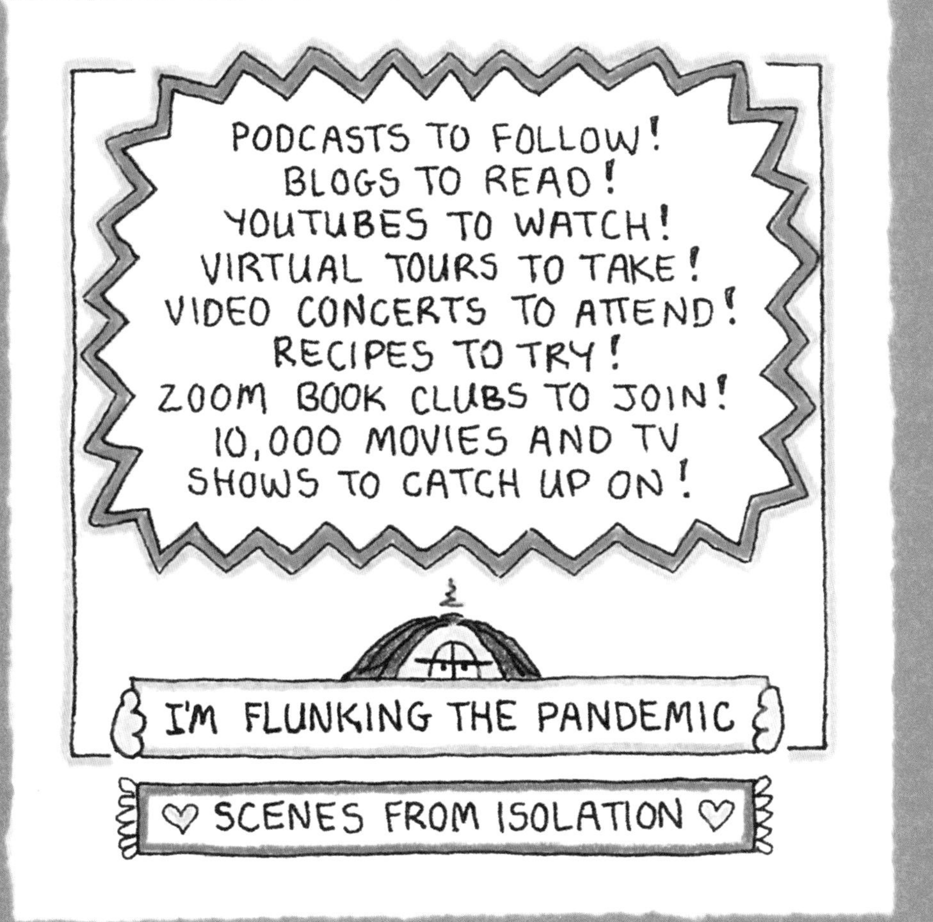
PODCASTS TO FOLLOW!
BLOGS TO READ!
YOUTUBES TO WATCH!
VIRTUAL TOURS TO TAKE!
VIDEO CONCERTS TO ATTEND!
RECIPES TO TRY!
ZOOM BOOK CLUBS TO JOIN!
10,000 MOVIES AND TV SHOWS TO CATCH UP ON!
I'M FLUNKING THE PANDEMIC
♡ SCENES FROM ISOLATION ♡

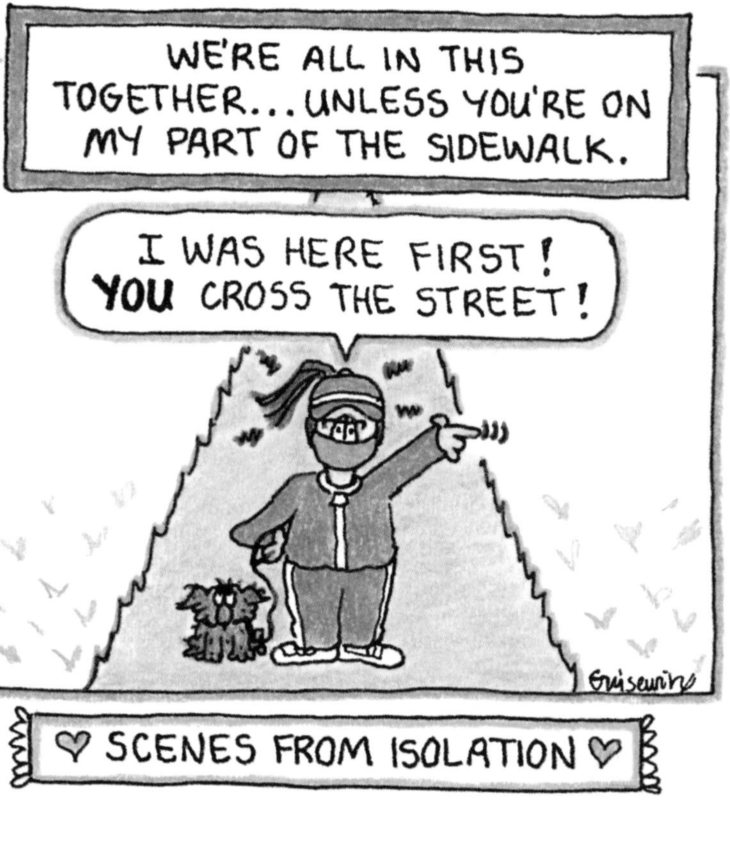
WE'RE ALL IN THIS TOGETHER...UNLESS YOU'RE ON MY PART OF THE SIDEWALK.
I WAS HERE FIRST! **YOU** CROSS THE STREET!
Guisewite
SCENES FROM ISOLATION

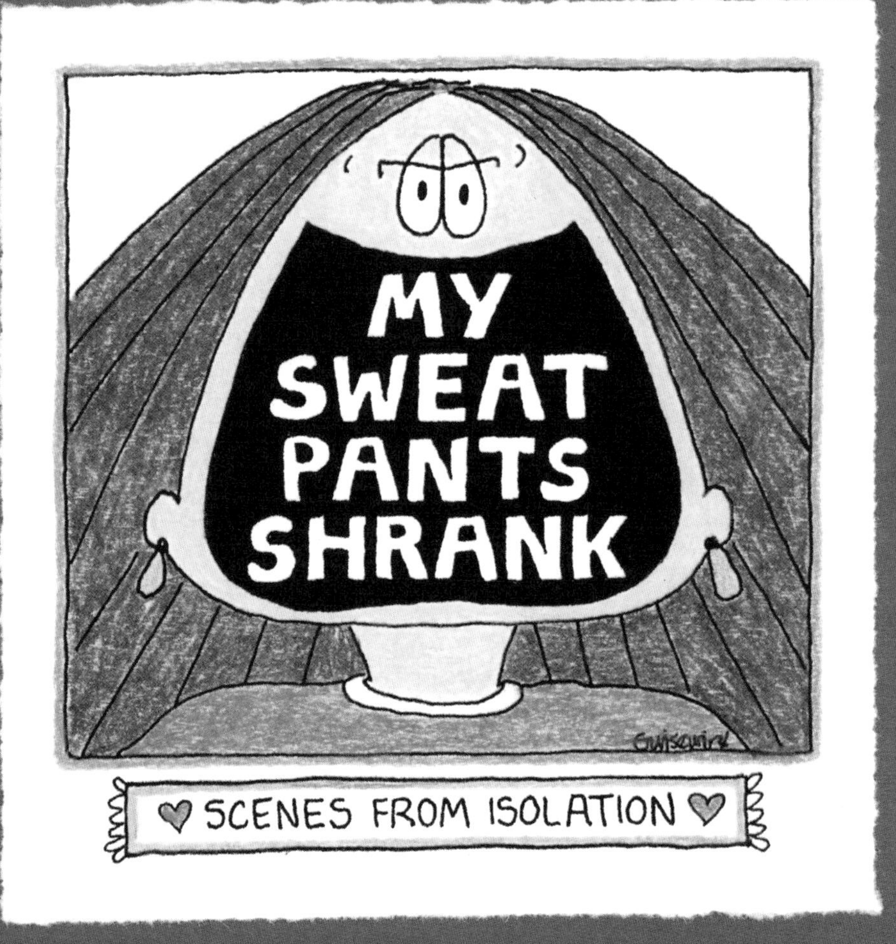
MY SWEAT PANTS SHRANK
SCENES FROM ISOLATION

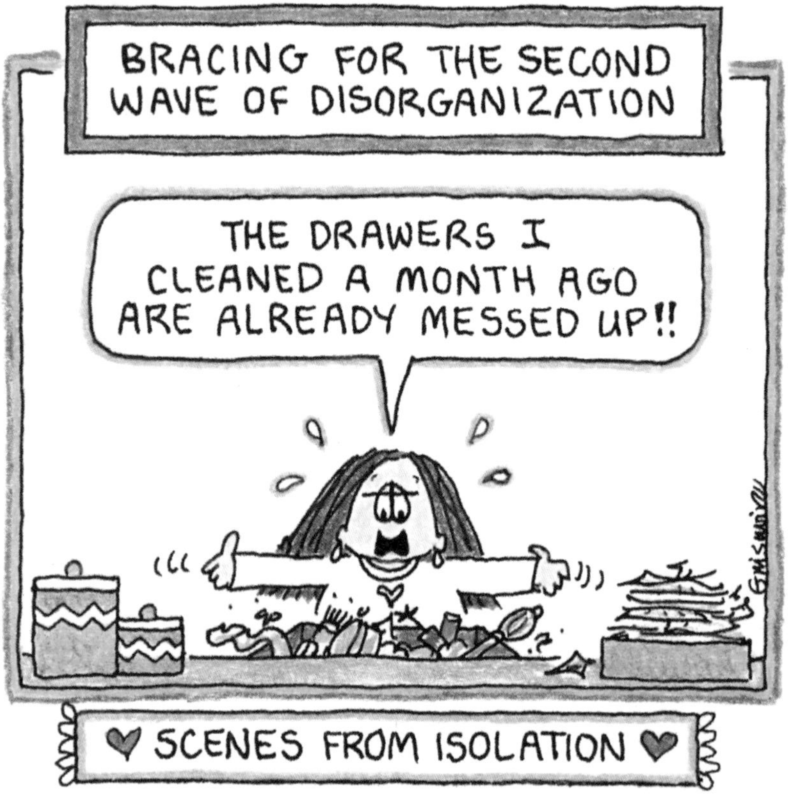
BRACING FOR THE SECOND WAVE OF DISORGANIZATION
THE DRAWERS I CLEANED A MONTH AGO ARE ALREADY MESSED UP!!
SCENES FROM ISOLATION

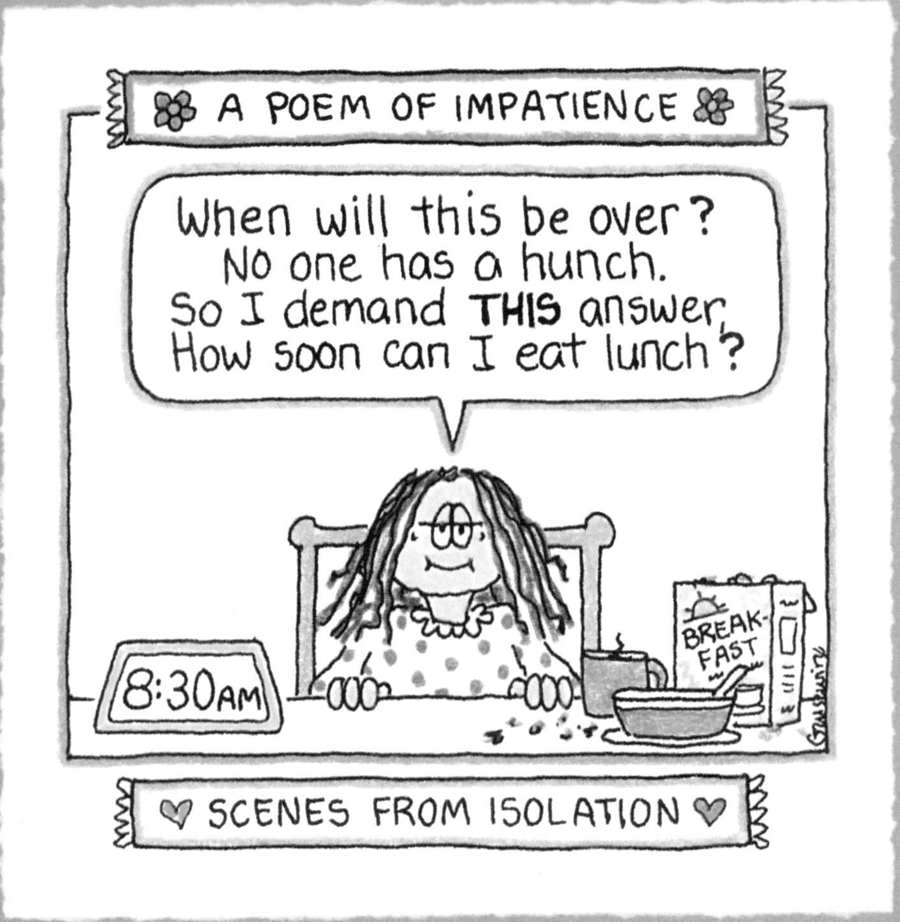
A POEM OF IMPATIENCE
When will this be over? No one has a hunch. So I demand THIS answer, How soon can I eat lunch?
8:30AM
BREAK-FAST
SCENES FROM ISOLATION

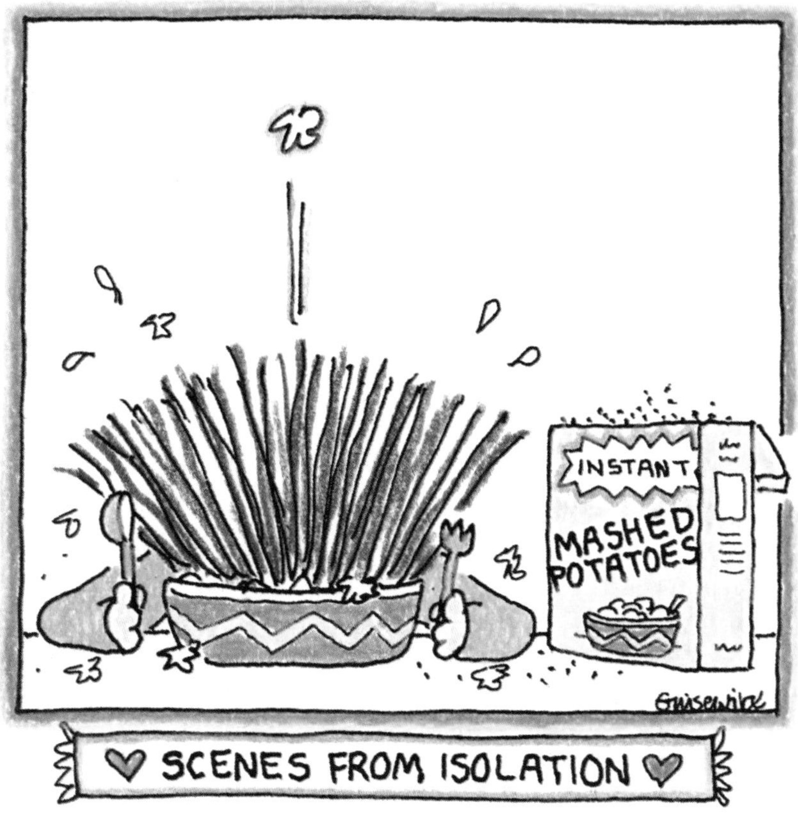
INSTANT
MASHED POTATOES
Guisewite

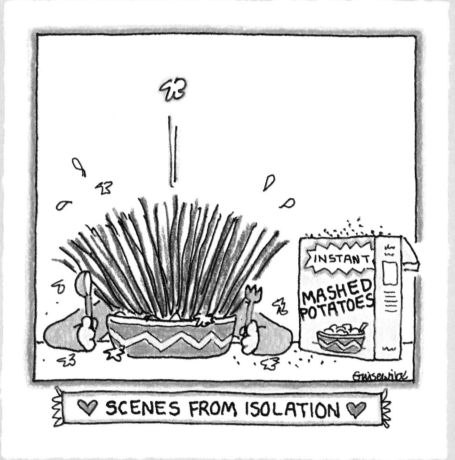

♥ SCENES FROM ISOLATION ♥

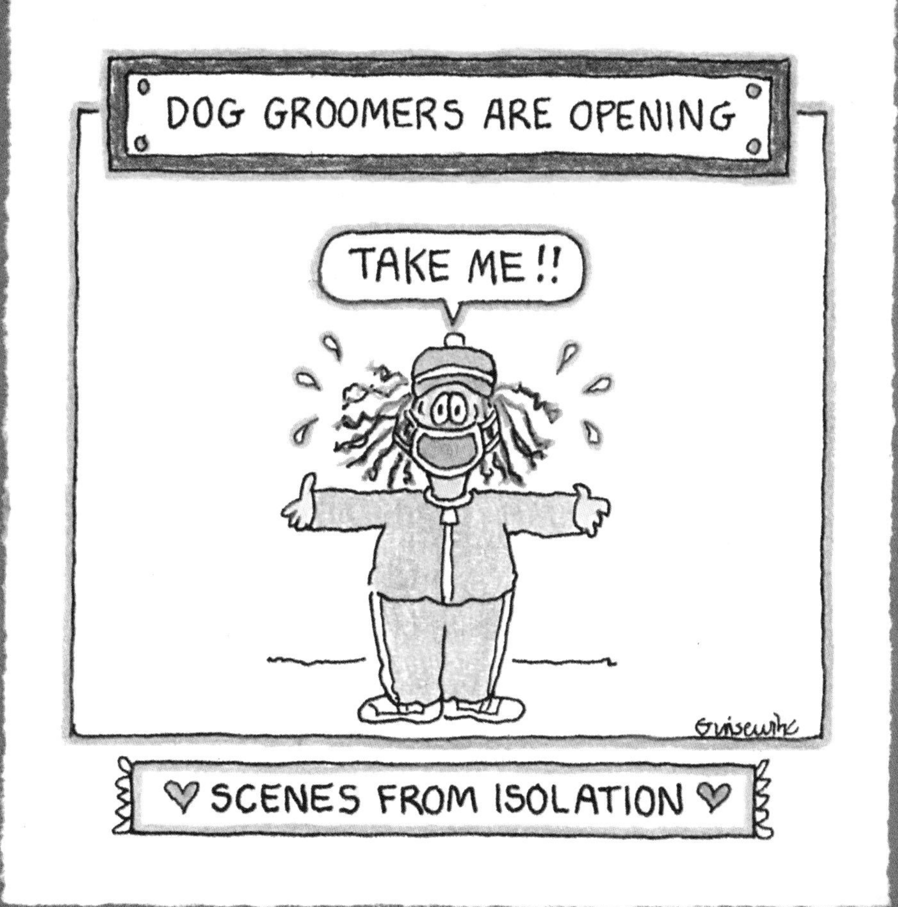
DOG GROOMERS ARE OPENING
TAKE ME!!
SCENES FROM ISOLATION

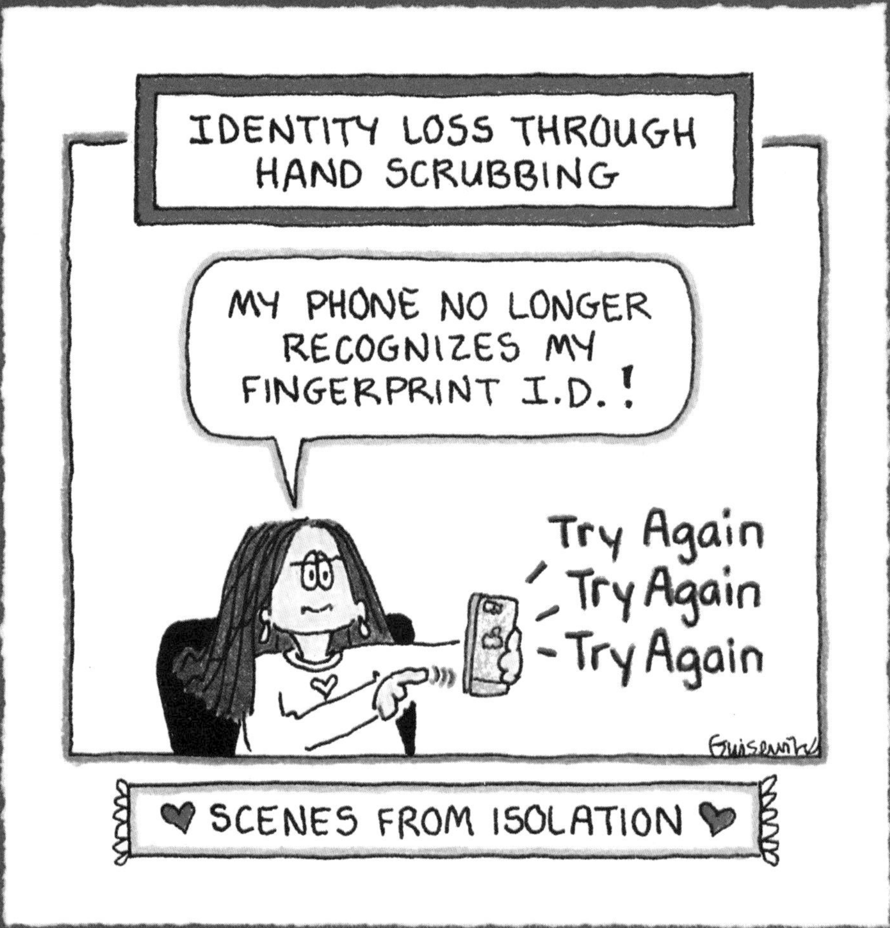
IDENTITY LOSS THROUGH HAND SCRUBBING
MY PHONE NO LONGER RECOGNIZES MY FINGERPRINT I.D.!
Try Again
Try Again
Try Again
SCENES FROM ISOLATION

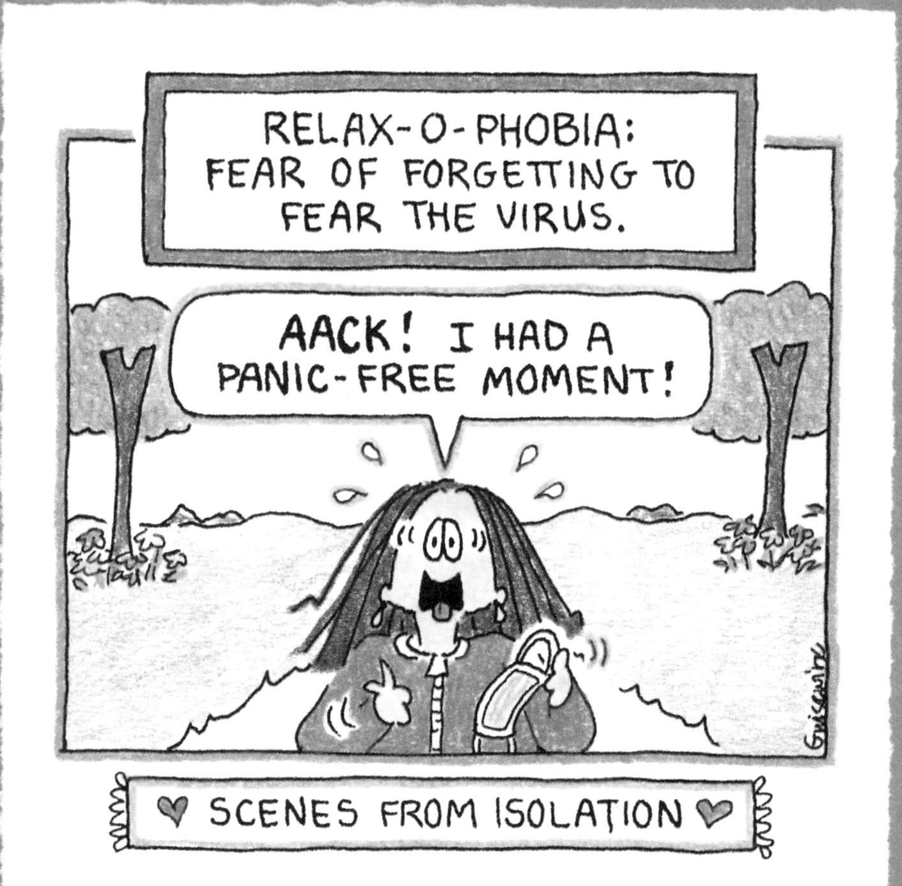
RELAX-O-PHOBIA: FEAR OF FORGETTING TO FEAR THE VIRUS.
AACK! I HAD A PANIC-FREE MOMENT!
SCENES FROM ISOLATION

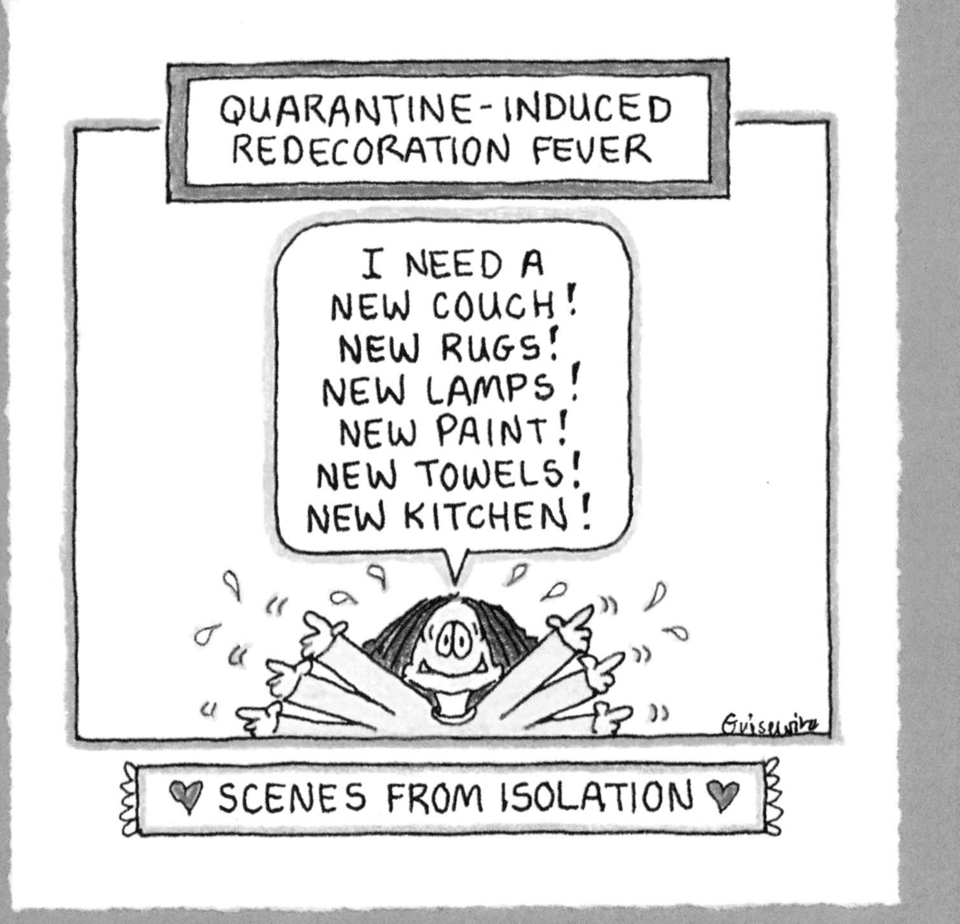
QUARANTINE-INDUCED REDECORATION FEVER
I NEED A NEW COUCH! NEW RUGS! NEW LAMPS! NEW PAINT! NEW TOWELS! NEW KITCHEN!
SCENES FROM ISOLATION

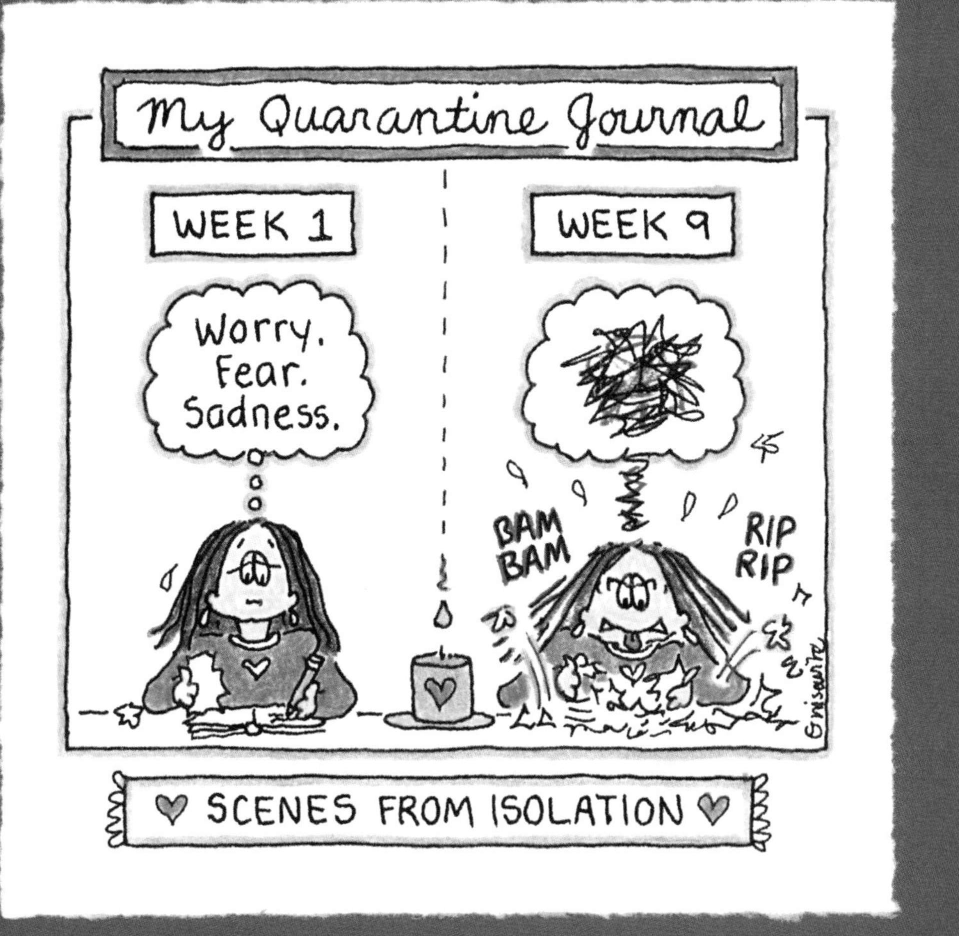
My Quarantine Journal
WEEK 1
WEEK 9
Worry.
Fear.
Sadness.
BAM
BAM
RIP
RIP
SCENES FROM ISOLATION

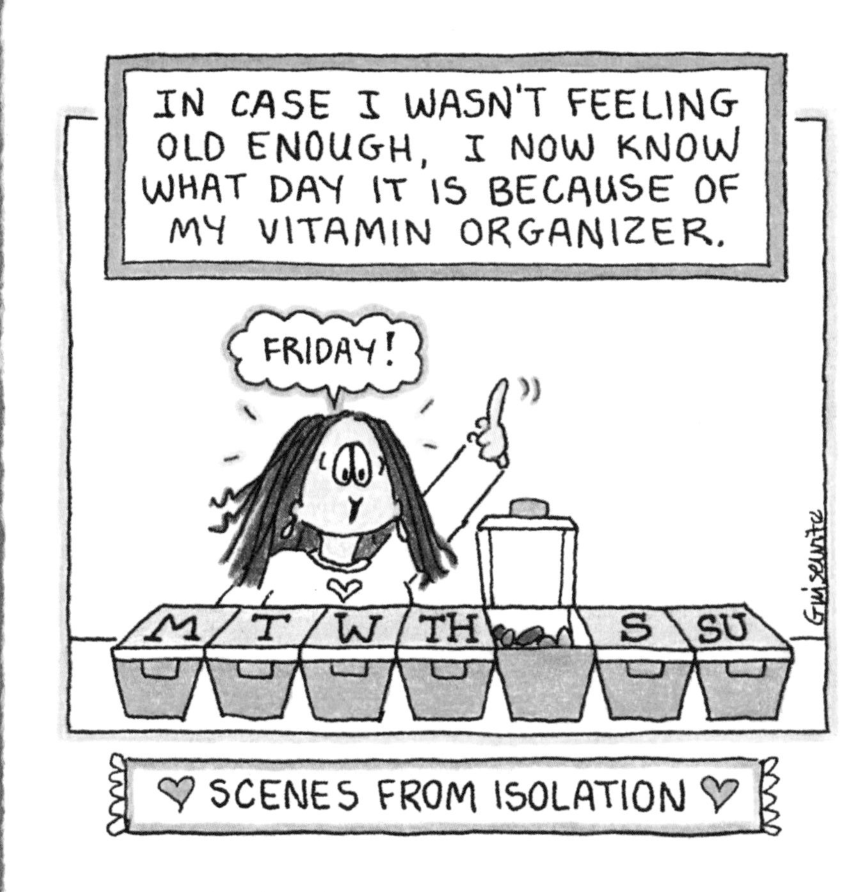
IN CASE I WASN'T FEELING OLD ENOUGH, I NOW KNOW WHAT DAY IT IS BECAUSE OF MY VITAMIN ORGANIZER.
FRIDAY!
M
T
W
TH
S
SU
Guisewite
SCENES FROM ISOLATION

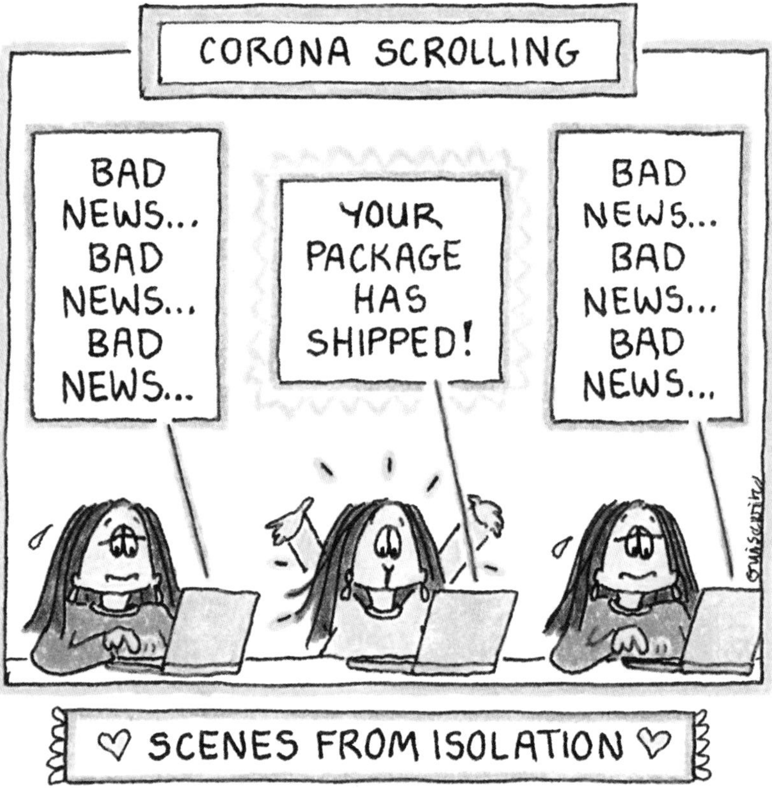
CORONA SCROLLING
BAD NEWS... BAD NEWS... BAD NEWS...
YOUR PACKAGE HAS SHIPPED!
BAD NEWS... BAD NEWS... BAD NEWS...
♡ SCENES FROM ISOLATION ♡

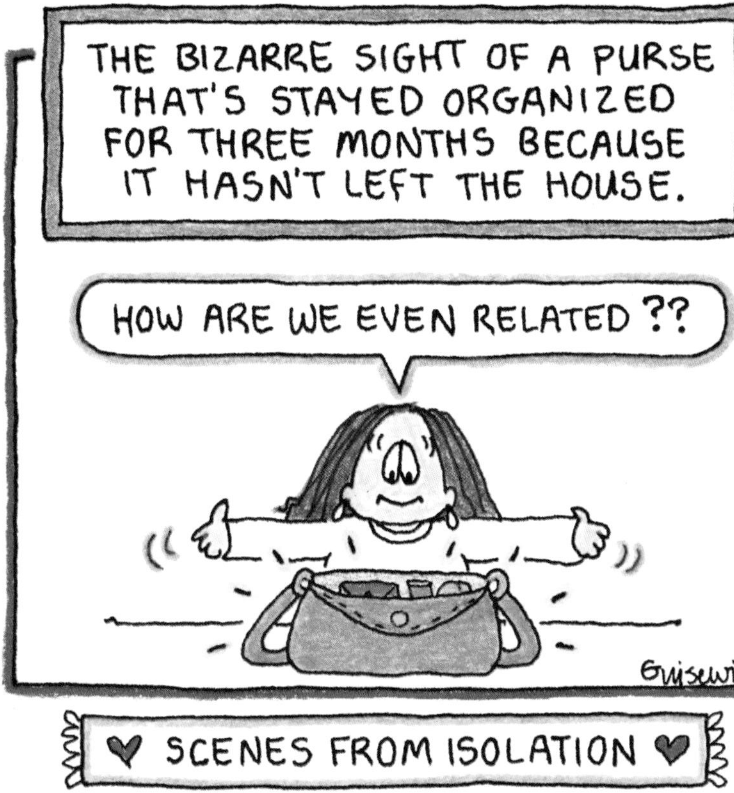
THE BIZARRE SIGHT OF A PURSE THAT'S STAYED ORGANIZED FOR THREE MONTHS BECAUSE IT HASN'T LEFT THE HOUSE.
HOW ARE WE EVEN RELATED??
Guisewite
SCENES FROM ISOLATION

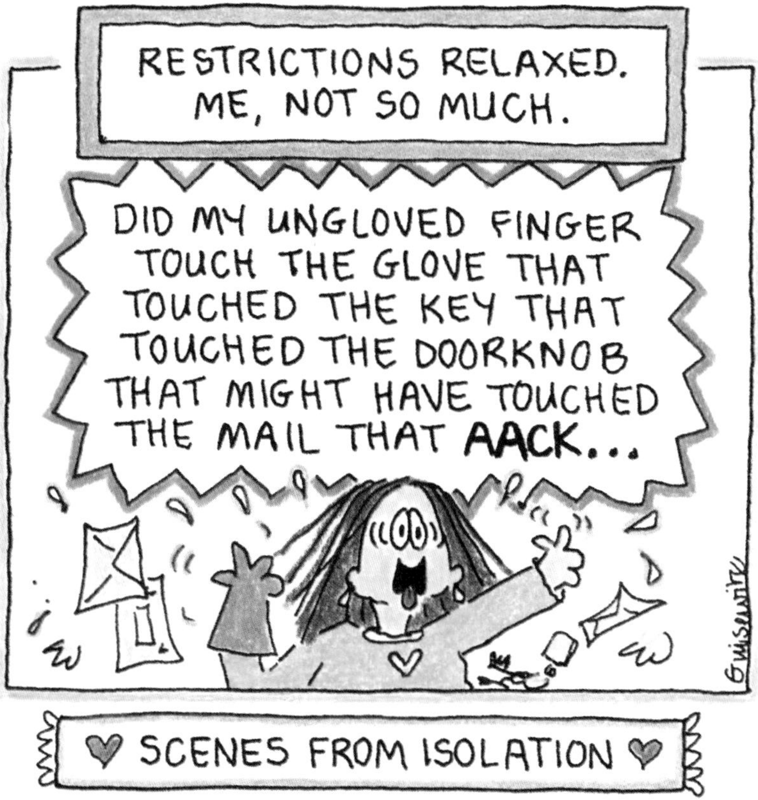
RESTRICTIONS RELAXED. ME, NOT SO MUCH.
DID MY UNGLOVED FINGER TOUCH THE GLOVE THAT TOUCHED THE KEY THAT TOUCHED THE DOORKNOB THAT MIGHT HAVE TOUCHED THE MAIL THAT AACK...
SCENES FROM ISOLATION

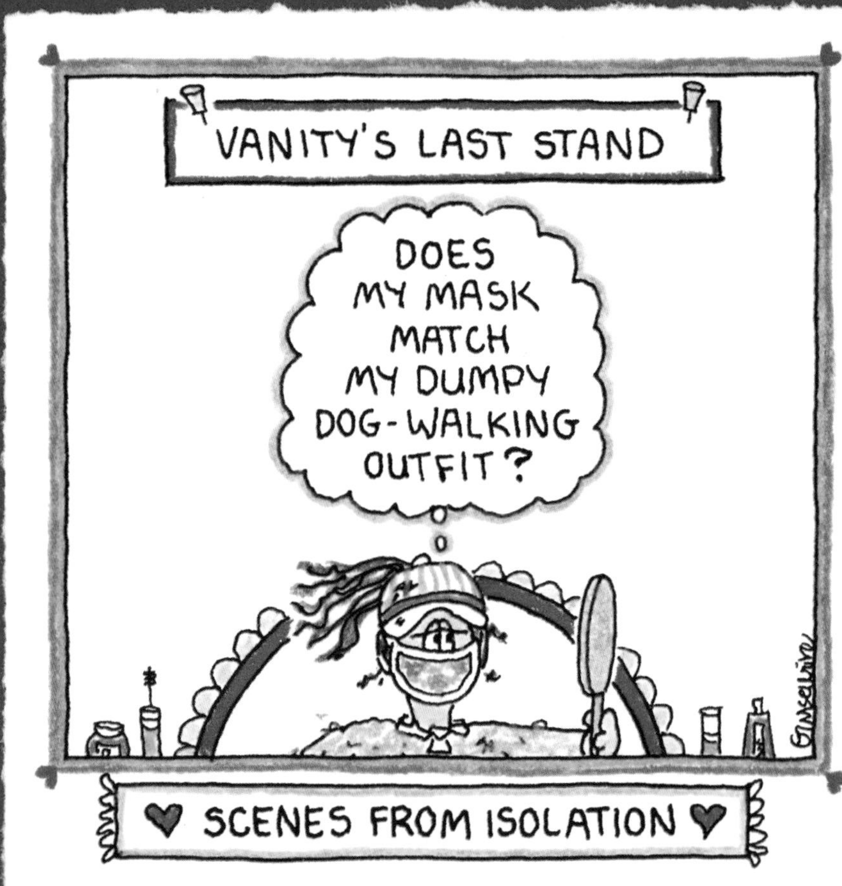
VANITY'S LAST STAND
DOES MY MASK MATCH MY DUMPY DOG-WALKING OUTFIT?
SCENES FROM ISOLATION

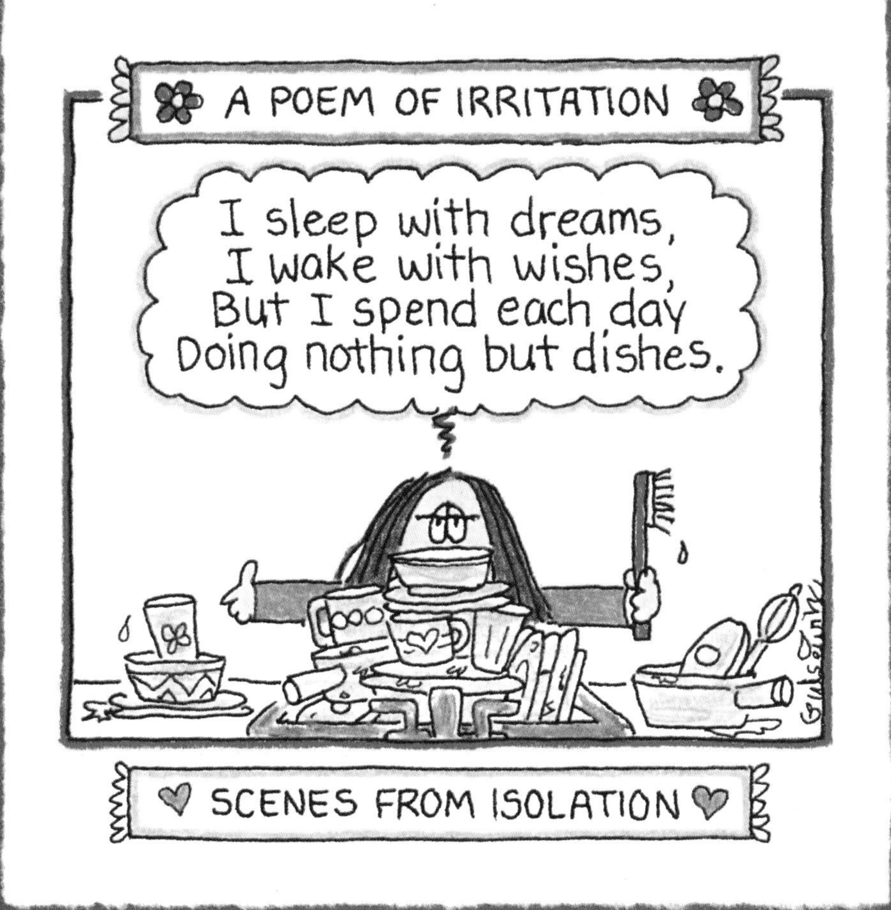
A POEM OF IRRITATION
I sleep with dreams,
I wake with wishes,
But I spend each day
Doing nothing but dishes.
SCENES FROM ISOLATION

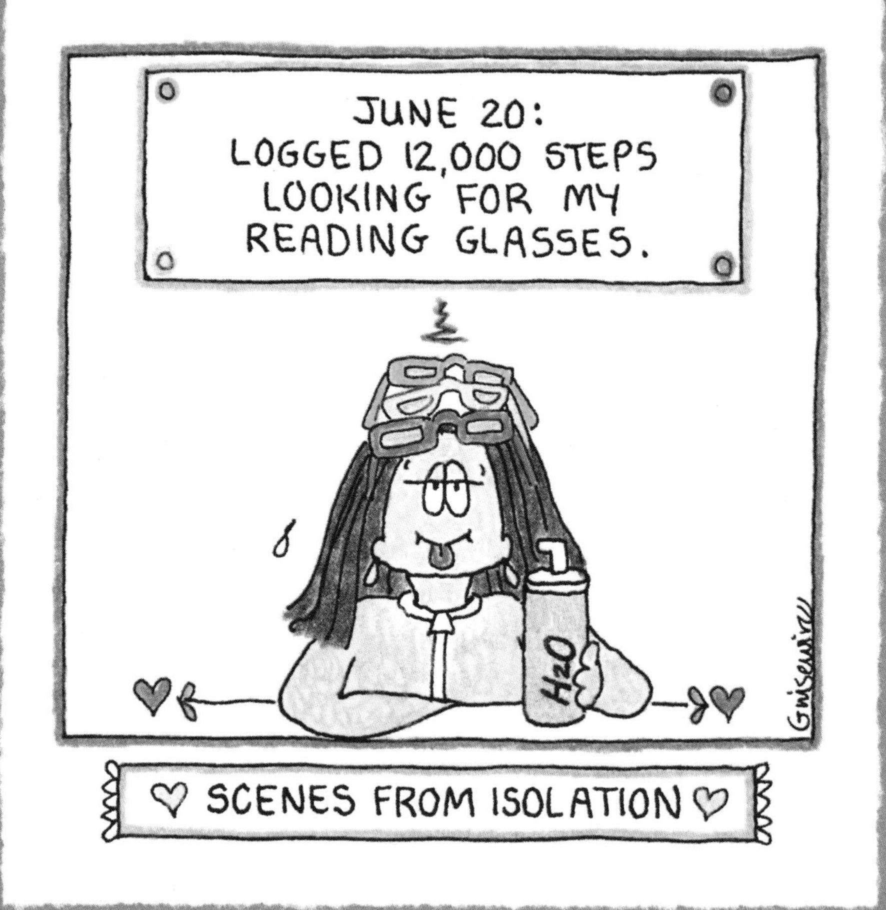
JUNE 20:
LOGGED 12,000 STEPS
LOOKING FOR MY
READING GLASSES.
H2O
Guisewite
SCENES FROM ISOLATION

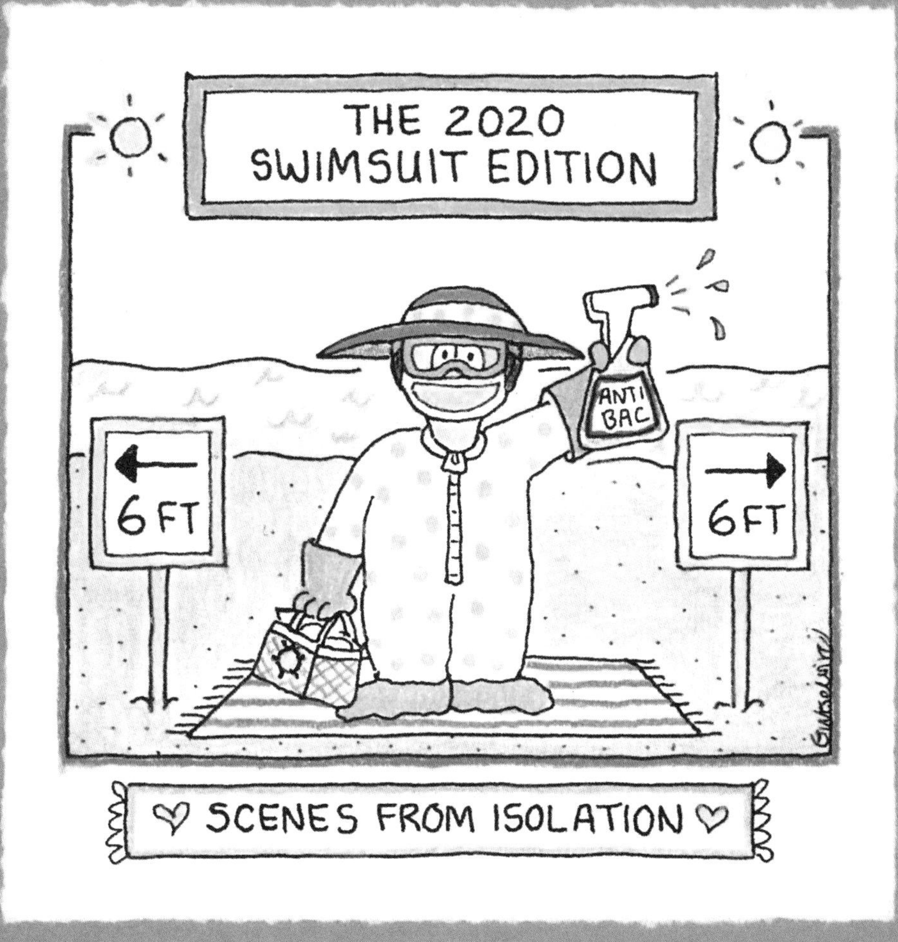
THE 2020
SWIMSUIT EDITION
ANTI
BAC
6 FT
6 FT
SCENES FROM ISOLATION

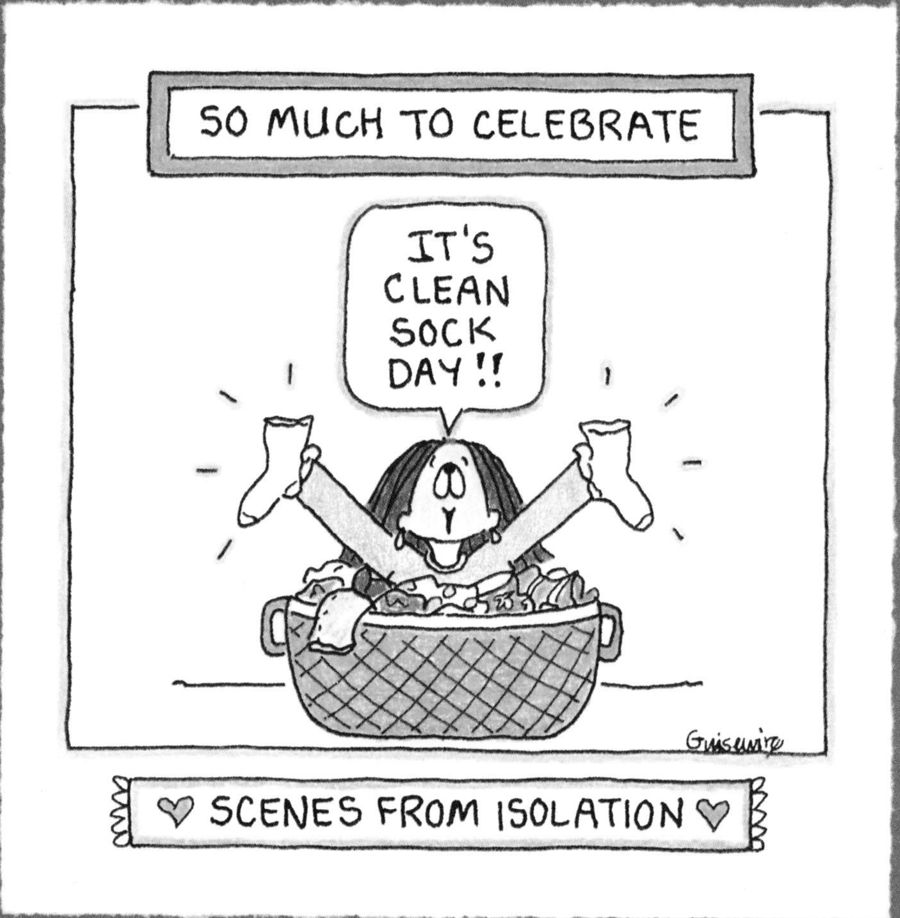
SO MUCH TO CELEBRATE
IT'S CLEAN SOCK DAY!!
SCENES FROM ISOLATION

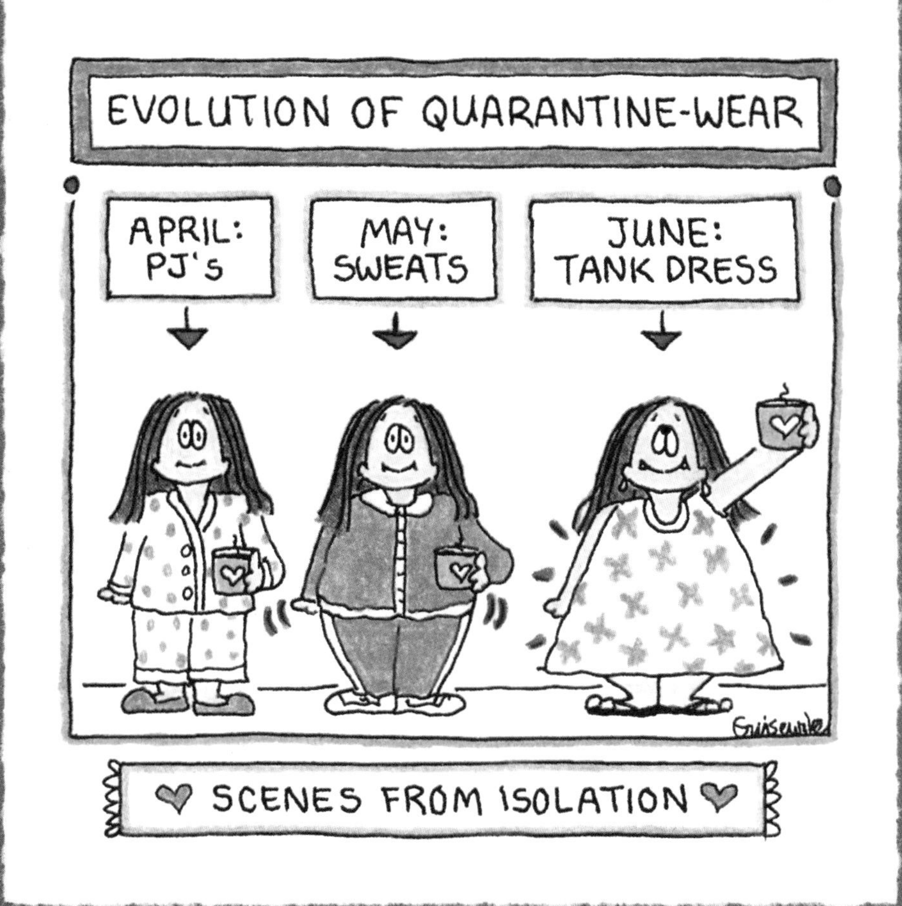
EVOLUTION OF QUARANTINE-WEAR
APRIL: PJ's
MAY: SWEATS
JUNE: TANK DRESS
SCENES FROM ISOLATION

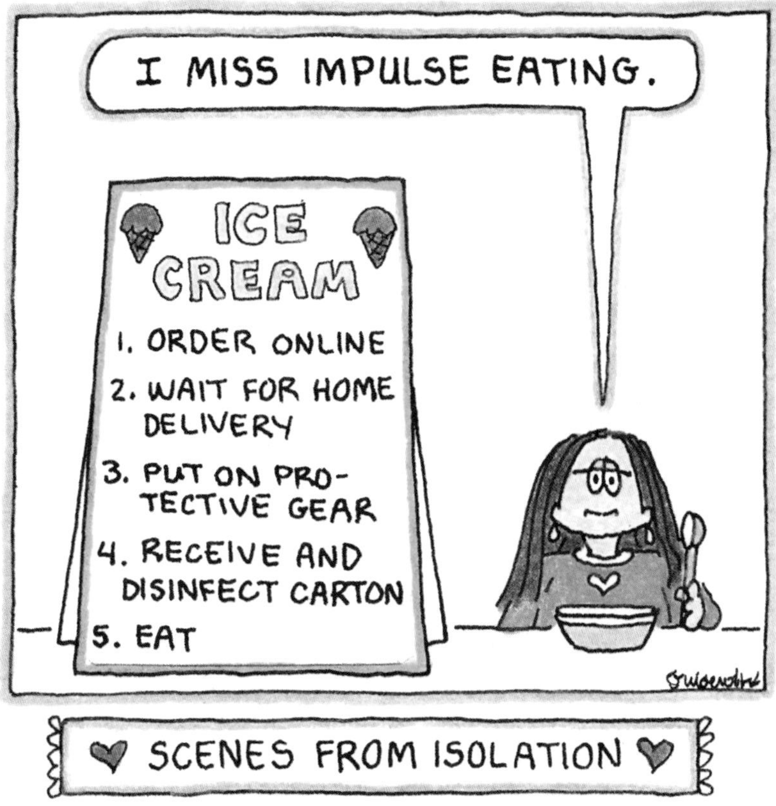
I MISS IMPULSE EATING.
ICE CREAM
1. ORDER ONLINE
2. WAIT FOR HOME DELIVERY
3. PUT ON PRO-TECTIVE GEAR
4. RECEIVE AND DISINFECT CARTON
5. EAT
SCENES FROM ISOLATION

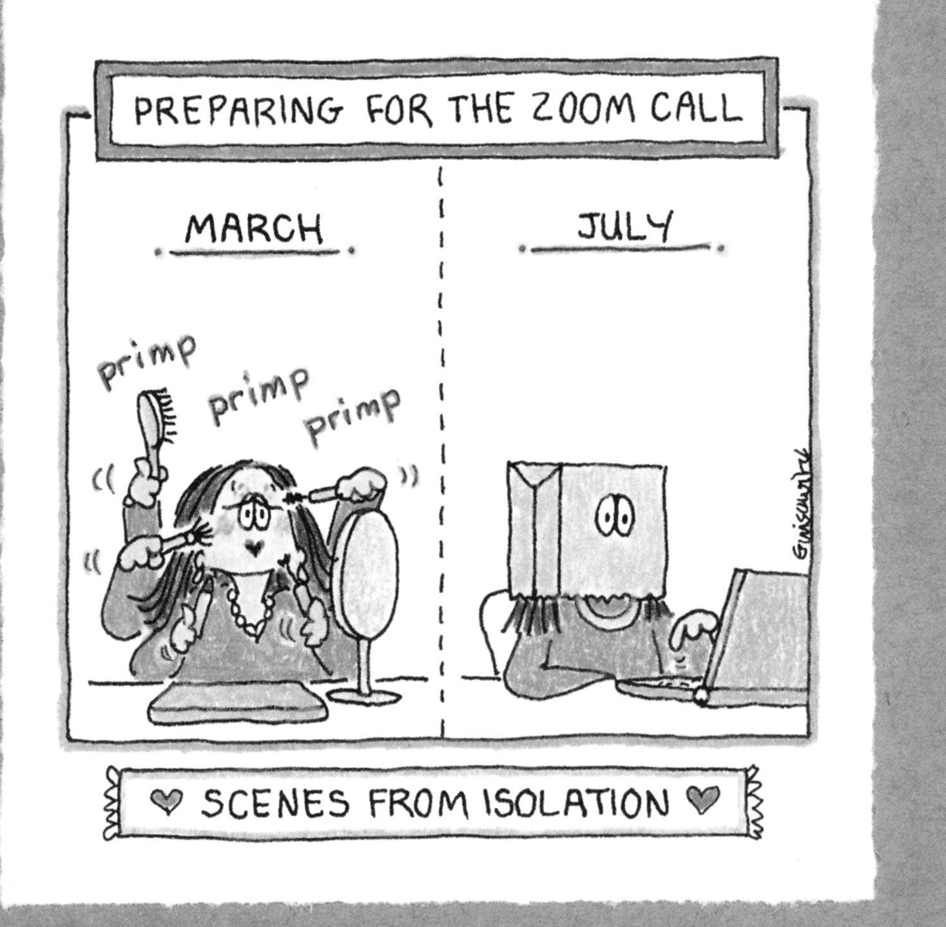
PREPARING FOR THE ZOOM CALL
MARCH
JULY
primp
primp
primp
♡ SCENES FROM ISOLATION ♡

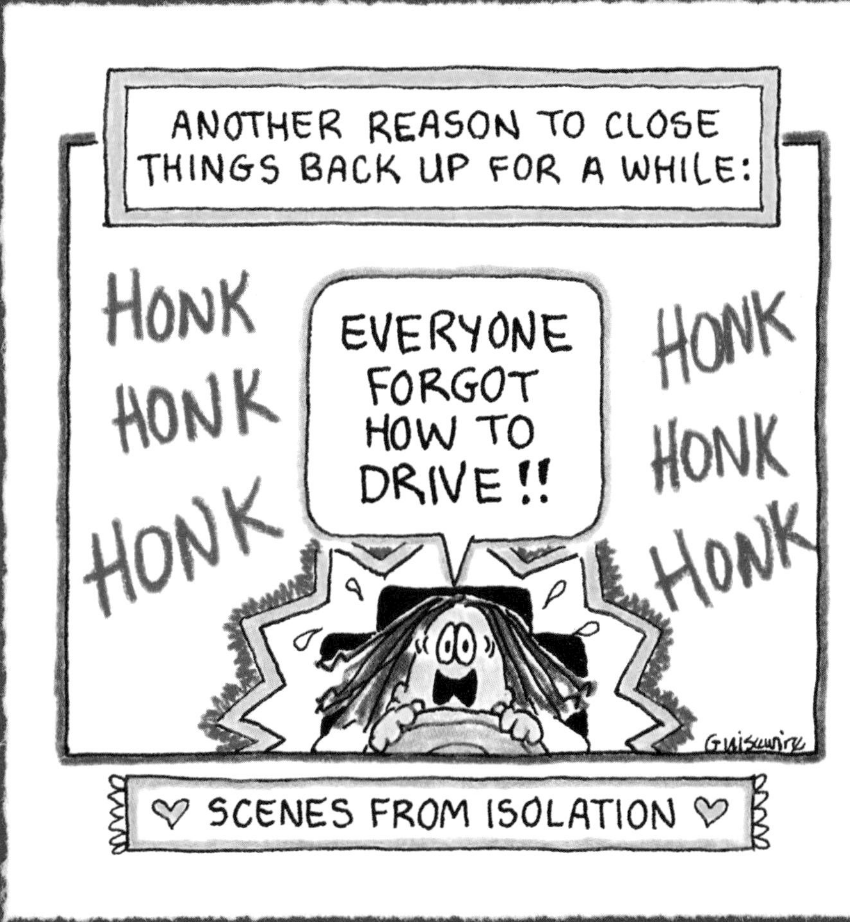
ANOTHER REASON TO CLOSE THINGS BACK UP FOR A WHILE:
HONK
HONK
HONK
EVERYONE FORGOT HOW TO DRIVE!!
HONK
HONK
HONK
SCENES FROM ISOLATION

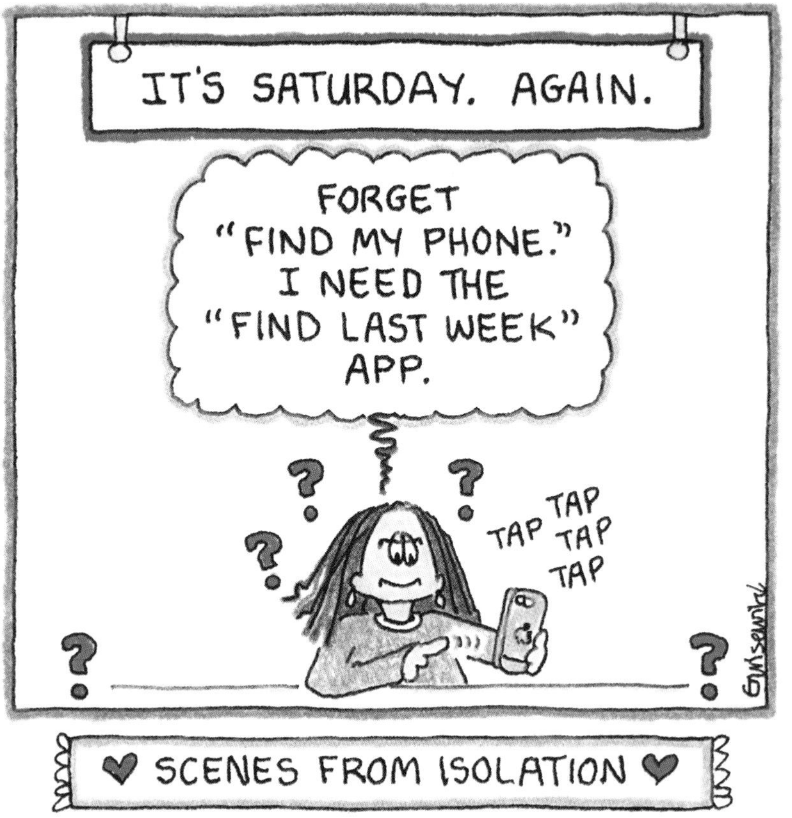
IT'S SATURDAY. AGAIN.
FORGET "FIND MY PHONE." I NEED THE "FIND LAST WEEK" APP.
TAP TAP TAP TAP
SCENES FROM ISOLATION

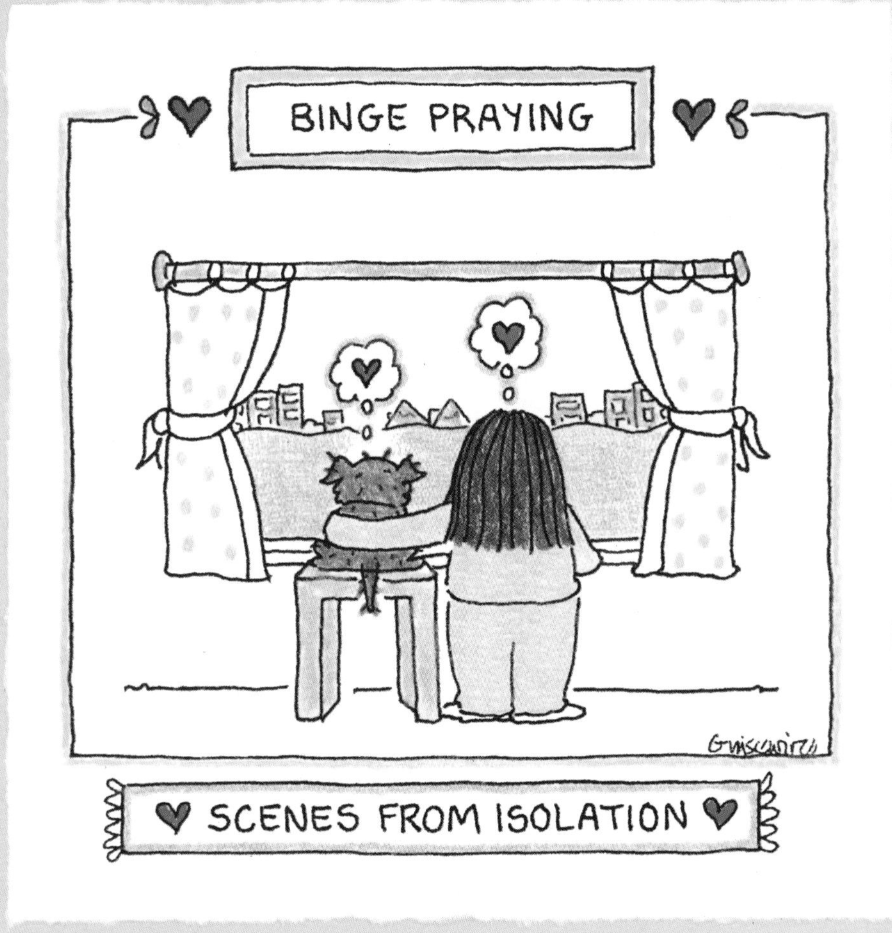
BINGE PRAYING
SCENES FROM ISOLATION

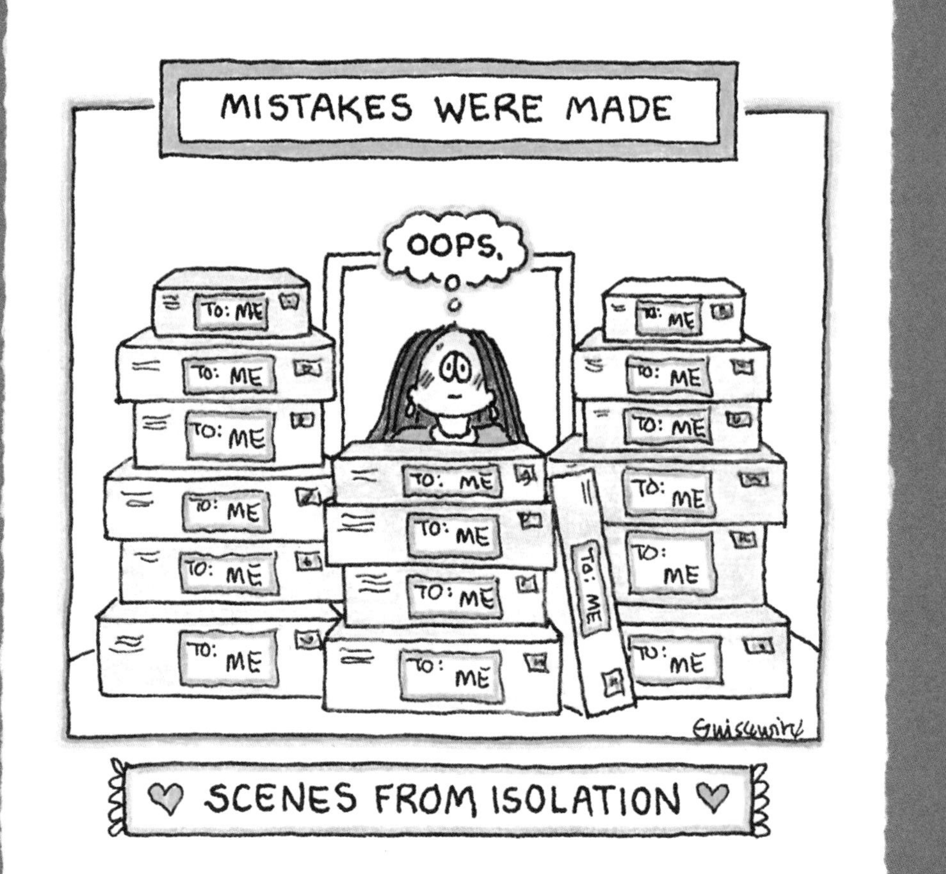
MISTAKES WERE MADE
OOPS.
TO: ME
TO: ME
TO: ME
TO: ME
TO: ME
TO: ME
TO: ME
TO: ME
TO: ME
TO: ME
TO: ME
TO: ME
TO: ME
TO: ME
TO: ME
TO: ME
TO: ME
SCENES FROM ISOLATION

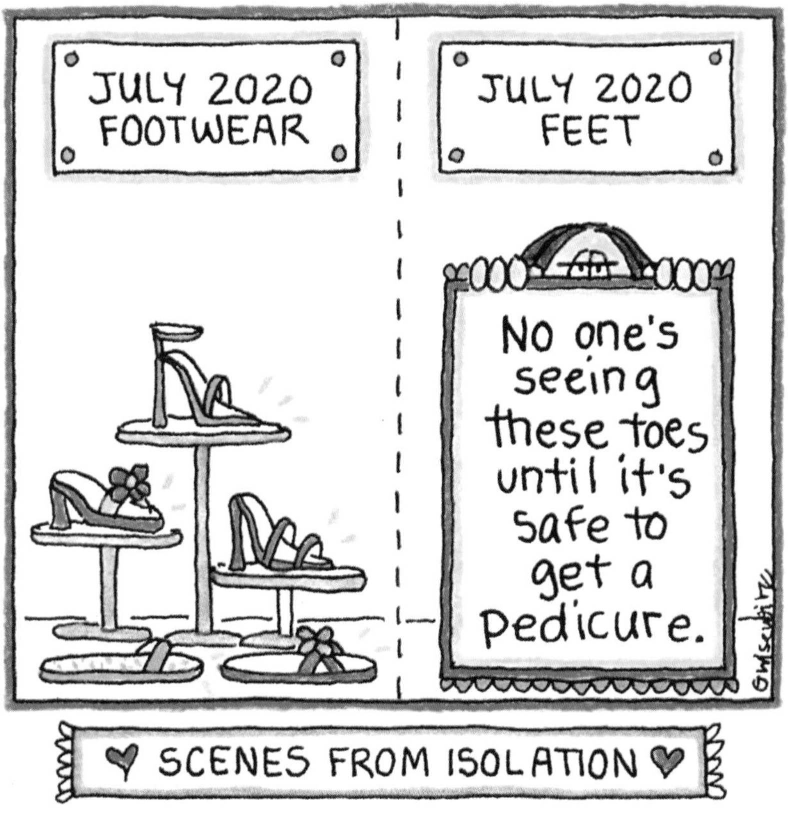
JULY 2020
FOOTWEAR
JULY 2020
FEET
No one's seeing these toes until it's safe to get a pedicure.
SCENES FROM ISOLATION

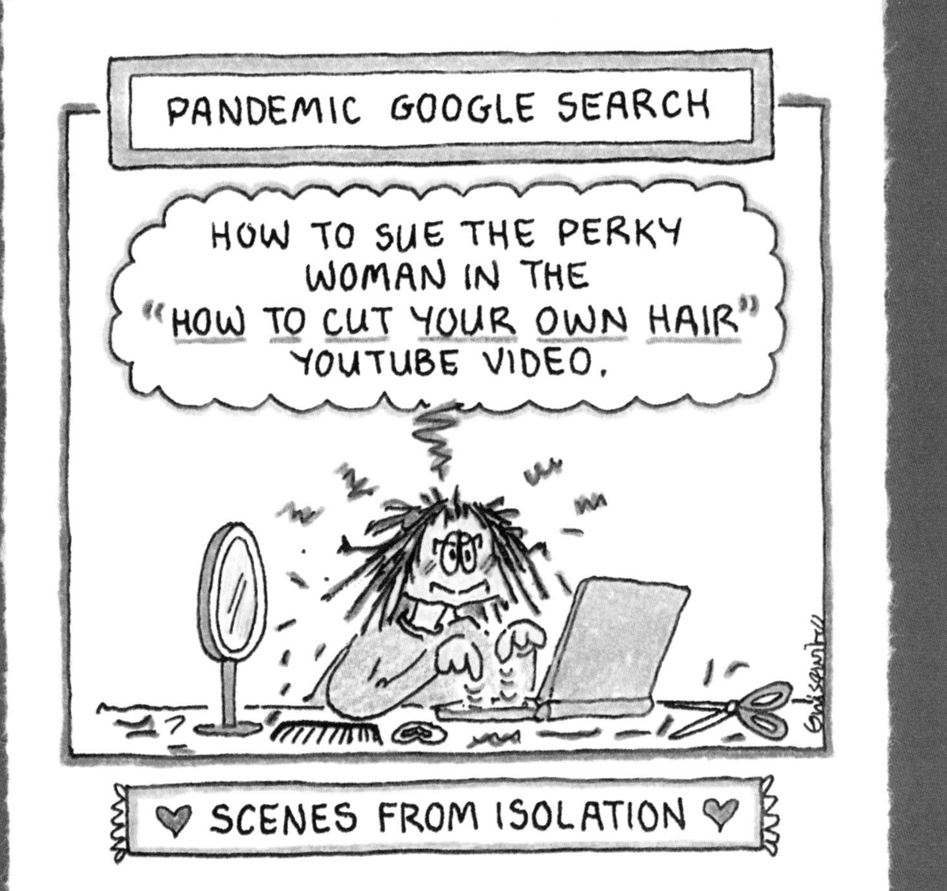
PANDEMIC GOOGLE SEARCH
HOW TO SUE THE PERKY WOMAN IN THE "HOW TO CUT YOUR OWN HAIR" YOUTUBE VIDEO.
SCENES FROM ISOLATION

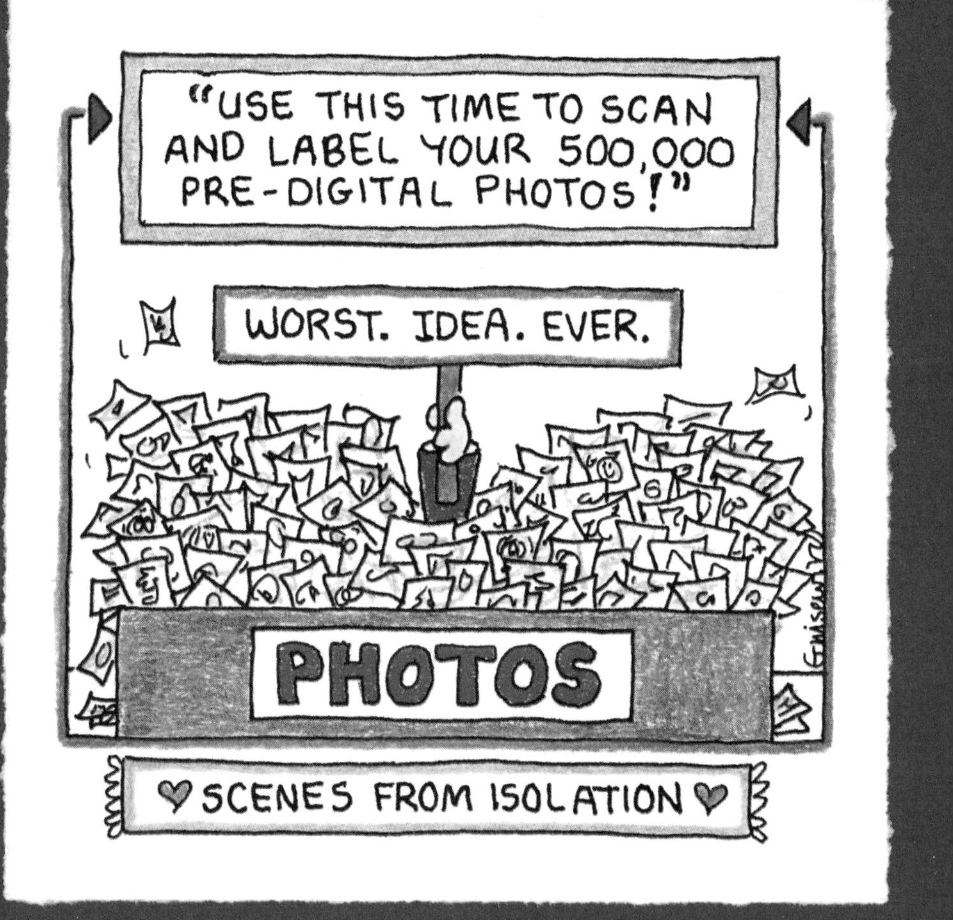
"USE THIS TIME TO SCAN AND LABEL YOUR 500,000 PRE-DIGITAL PHOTOS!"
WORST. IDEA. EVER.
PHOTOS
♥ SCENES FROM ISOLATION ♥
G. Wilson

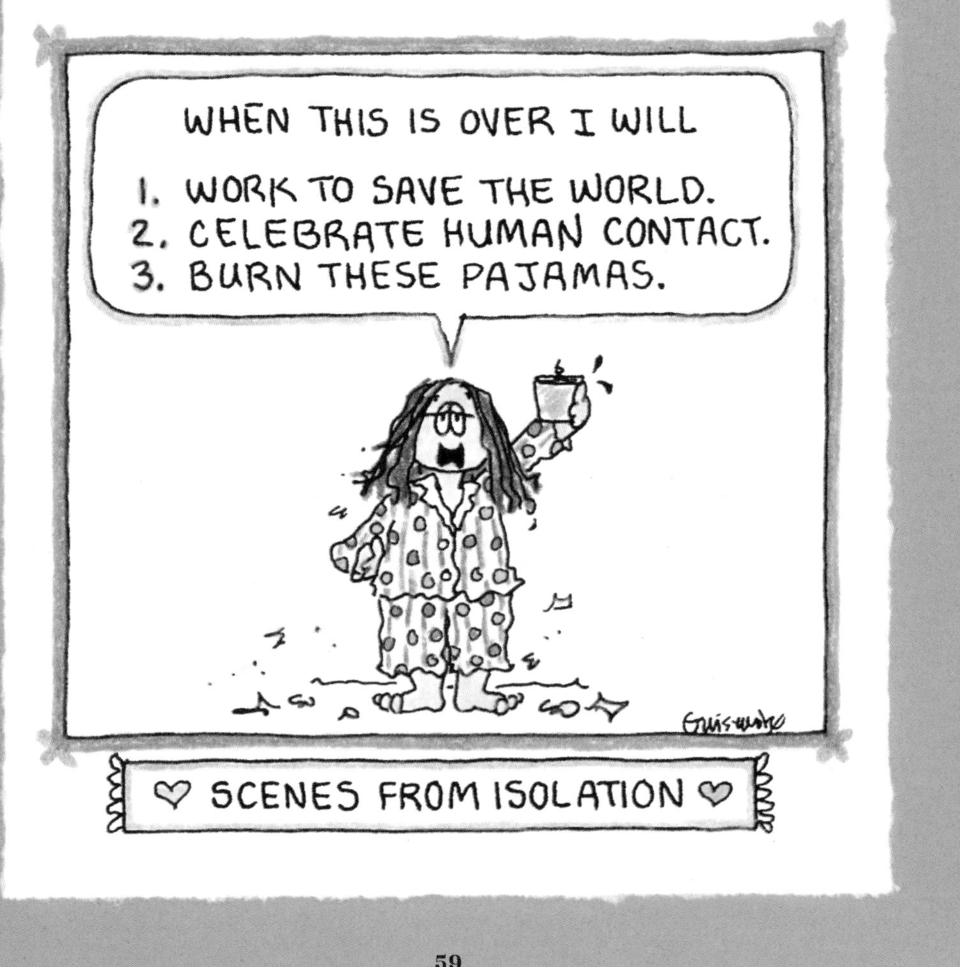
WHEN THIS IS OVER I WILL
1. WORK TO SAVE THE WORLD.
2. CELEBRATE HUMAN CONTACT.
3. BURN THESE PAJAMAS.
SCENES FROM ISOLATION

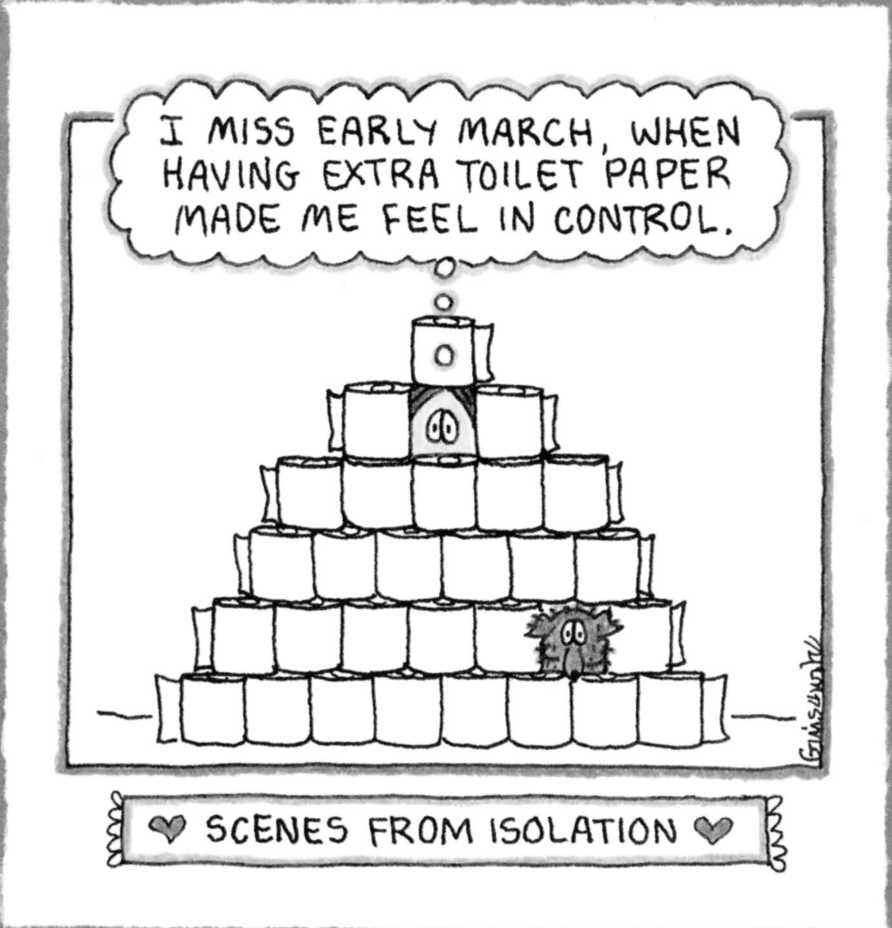
I MISS EARLY MARCH, WHEN HAVING EXTRA TOILET PAPER MADE ME FEEL IN CONTROL.
SCENES FROM ISOLATION

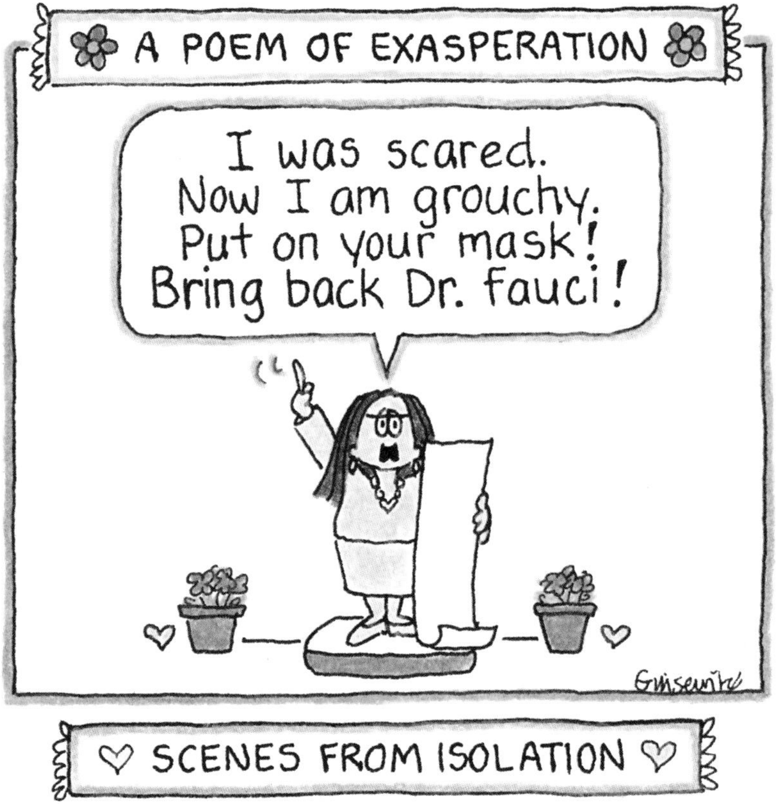
A POEM OF EXASPERATION
I was scared.
Now I am grouchy.
Put on your mask!
Bring back Dr. fauci!
Guisewite
SCENES FROM ISOLATION

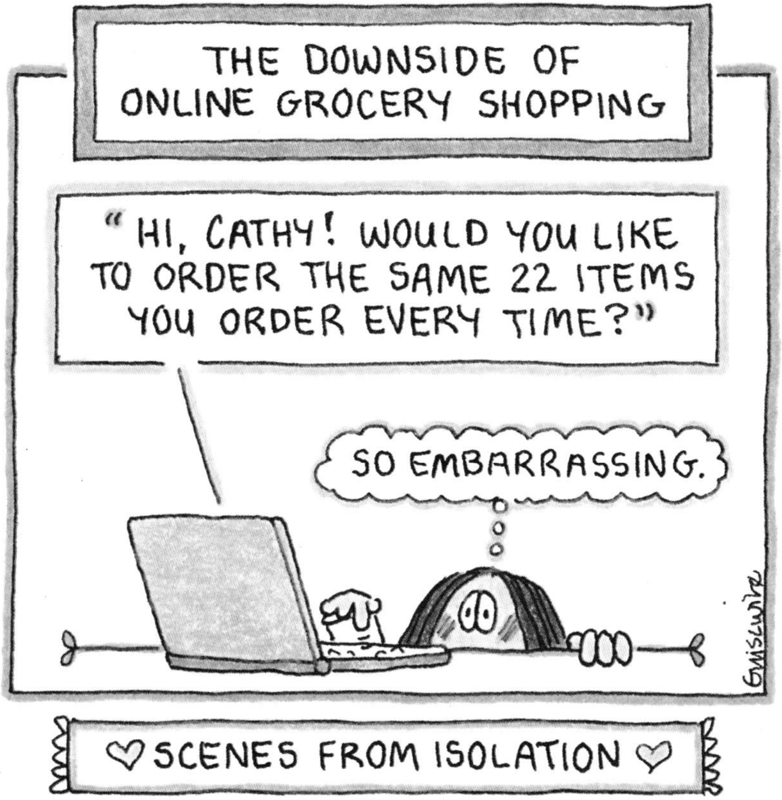
THE DOWNSIDE OF ONLINE GROCERY SHOPPING
"HI, CATHY! WOULD YOU LIKE TO ORDER THE SAME 22 ITEMS YOU ORDER EVERY TIME?"
SO EMBARRASSING.
GUISEWITE
SCENES FROM ISOLATION

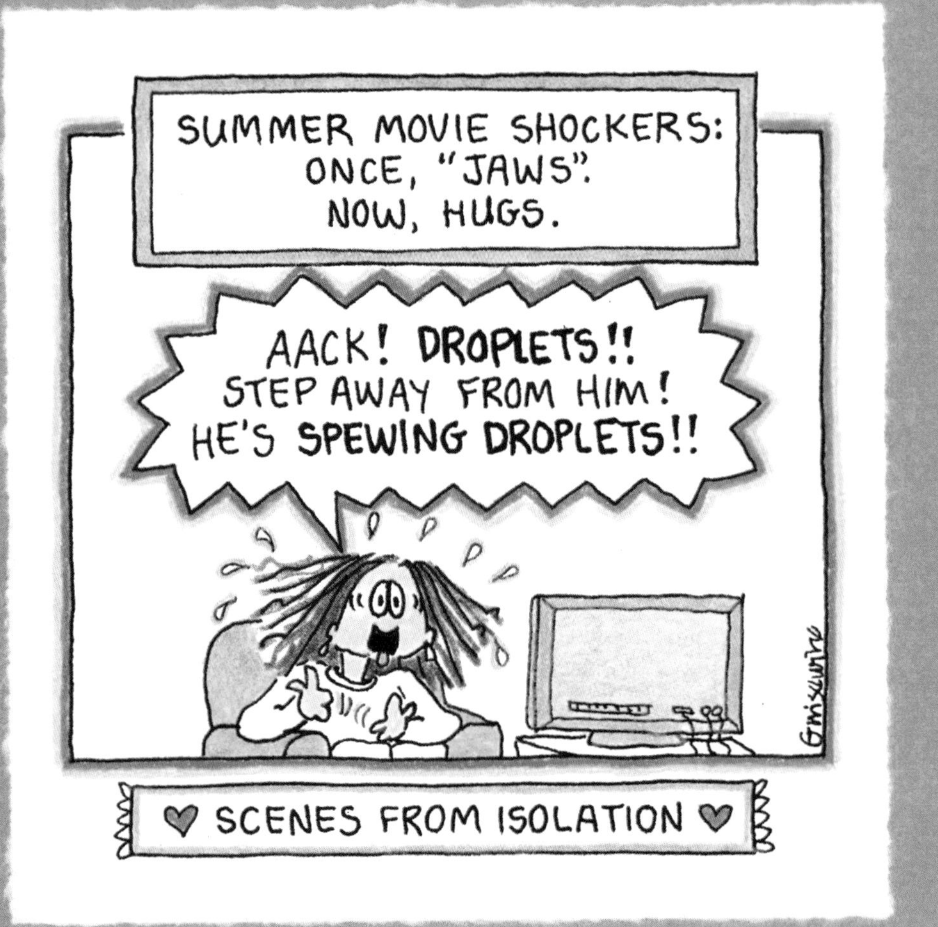
SUMMER MOVIE SHOCKERS: ONCE, "JAWS". NOW, HUGS.
AACK! DROPLETS!! STEP AWAY FROM HIM! HE'S SPEWING DROPLETS!!
Guisewite
♥ SCENES FROM ISOLATION ♥

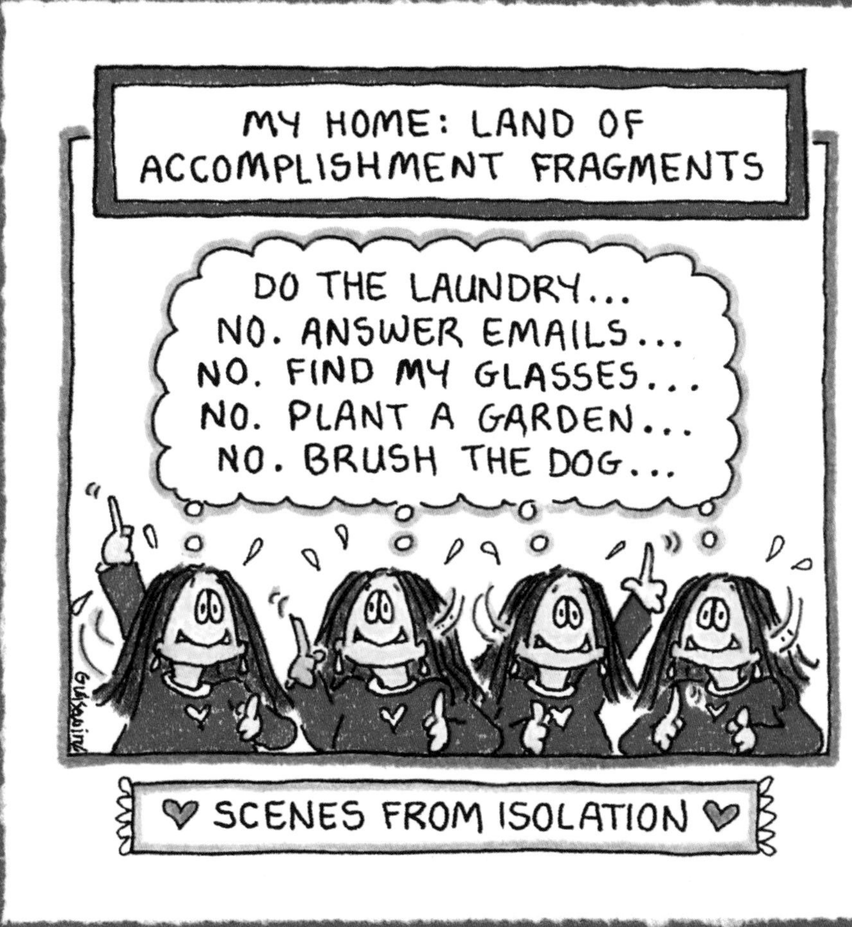
MY HOME: LAND OF ACCOMPLISHMENT FRAGMENTS
DO THE LAUNDRY... NO. ANSWER EMAILS... NO. FIND MY GLASSES... NO. PLANT A GARDEN... NO. BRUSH THE DOG...
SCENES FROM ISOLATION

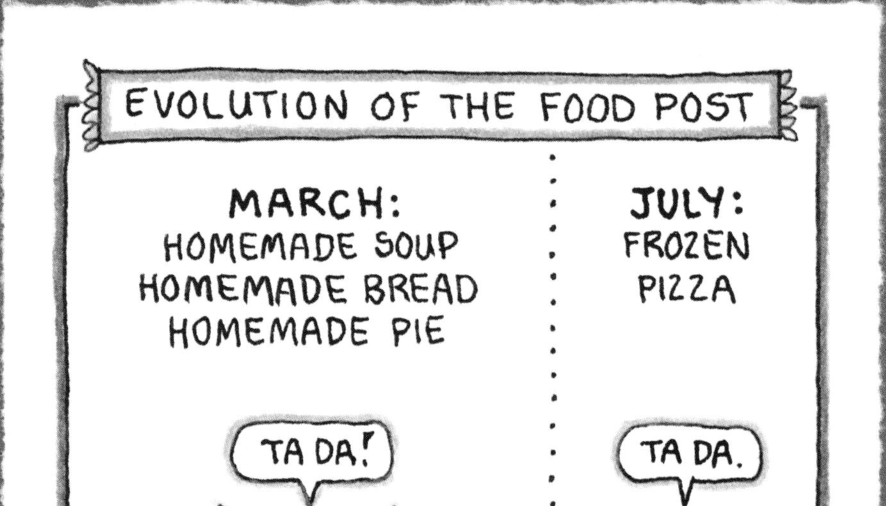
EVOLUTION OF THE FOOD POST
MARCH:
HOMEMADE SOUP
HOMEMADE BREAD
HOMEMADE PIE
TA DA!
JULY:
FROZEN
PIZZA
TA DA.
PIZZA
SCENES FROM ISOLATION

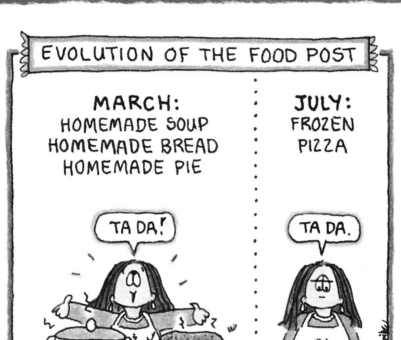

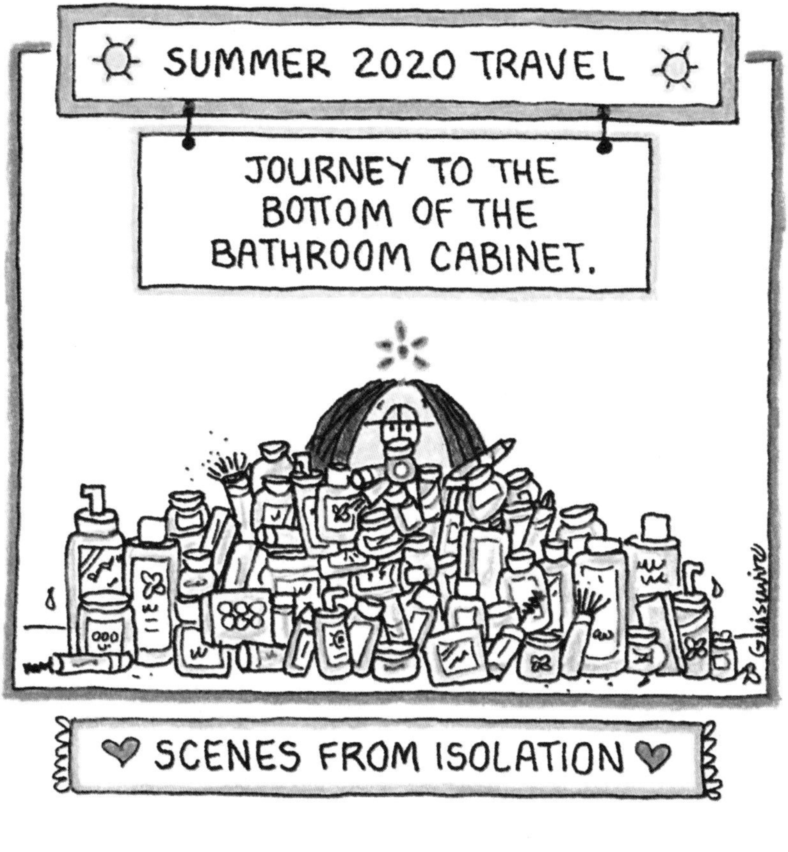
SUMMER 2020 TRAVEL
JOURNEY TO THE BOTTOM OF THE BATHROOM CABINET.
SCENES FROM ISOLATION

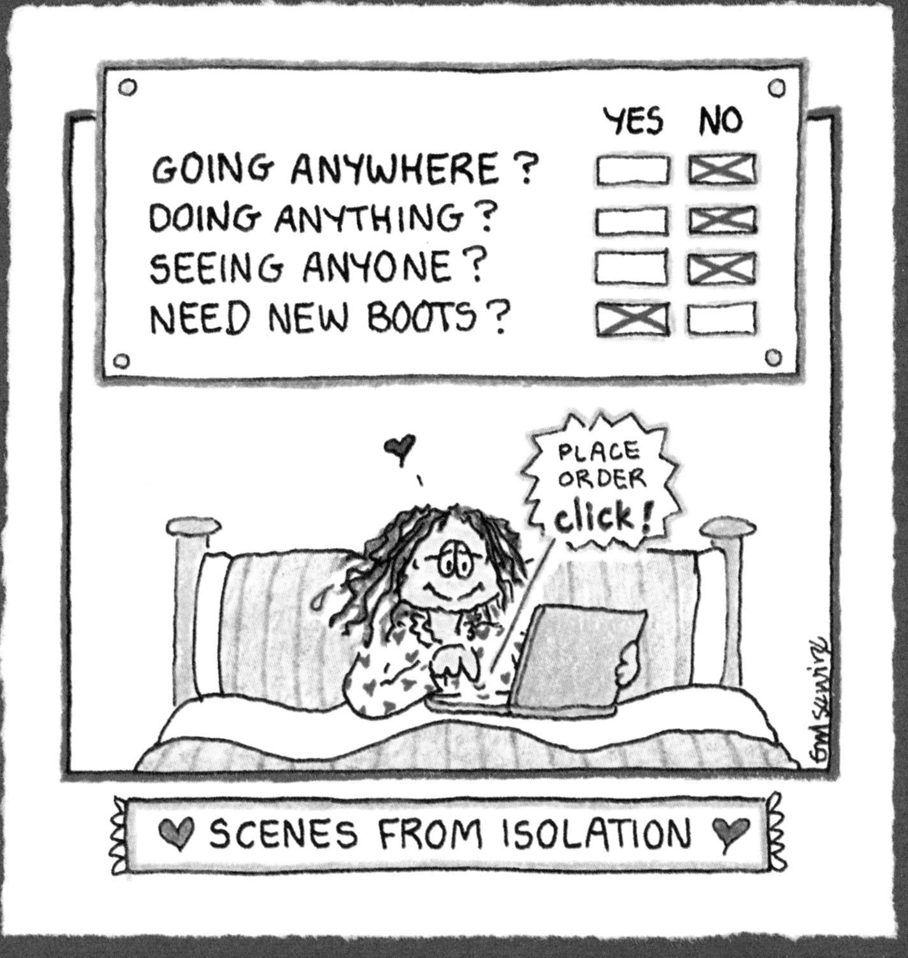
YES NO
GOING ANYWHERE?
DOING ANYTHING?
SEEING ANYONE?
NEED NEW BOOTS?
PLACE ORDER
click!
SCENES FROM ISOLATION

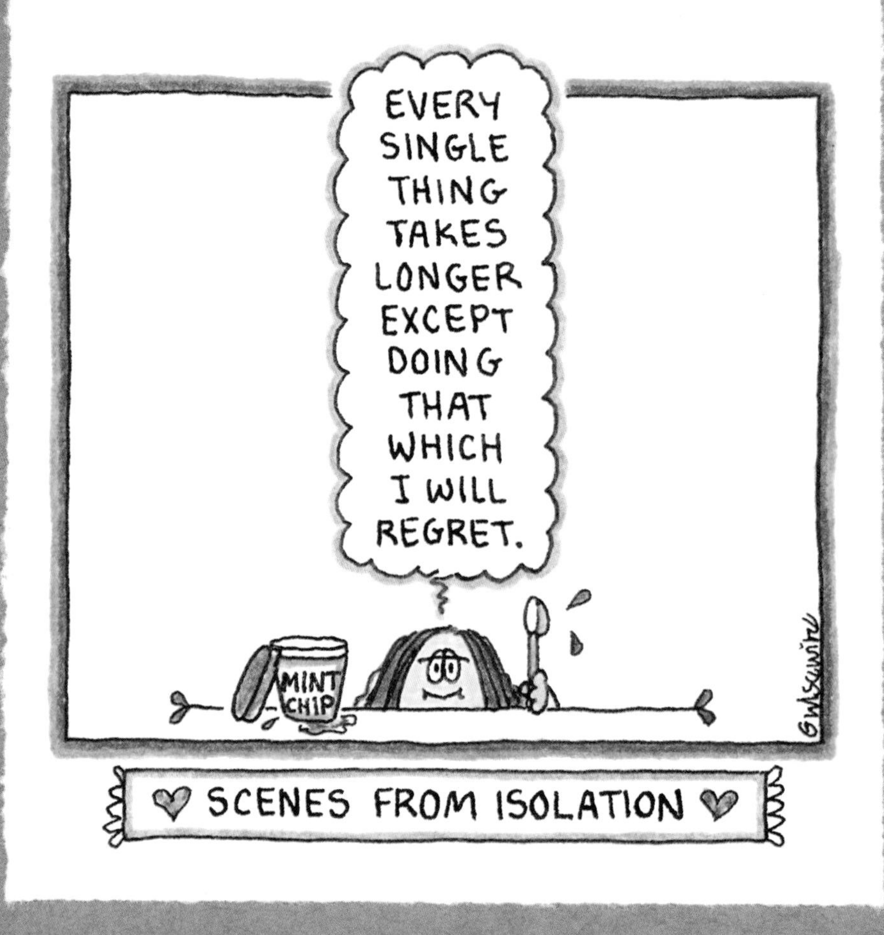
EVERY SINGLE THING TAKES LONGER EXCEPT DOING THAT WHICH I WILL REGRET.
MINT CHIP
SCENES FROM ISOLATION

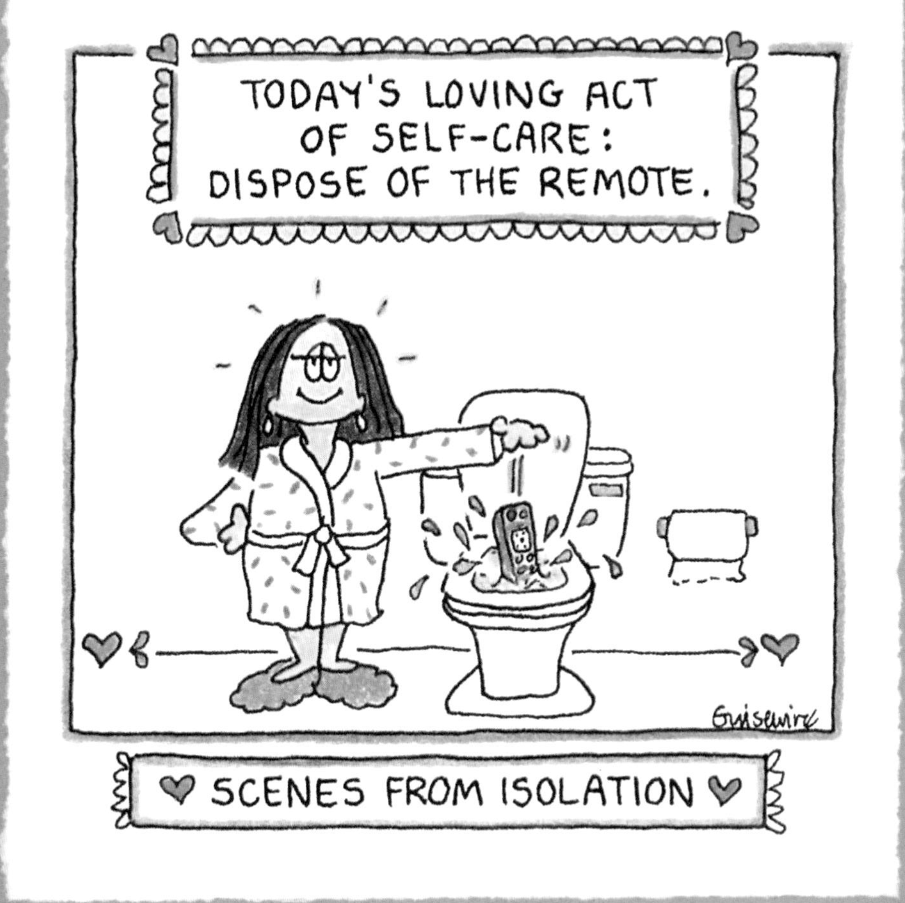
TODAY'S LOVING ACT OF SELF-CARE: DISPOSE OF THE REMOTE.
SCENES FROM ISOLATION

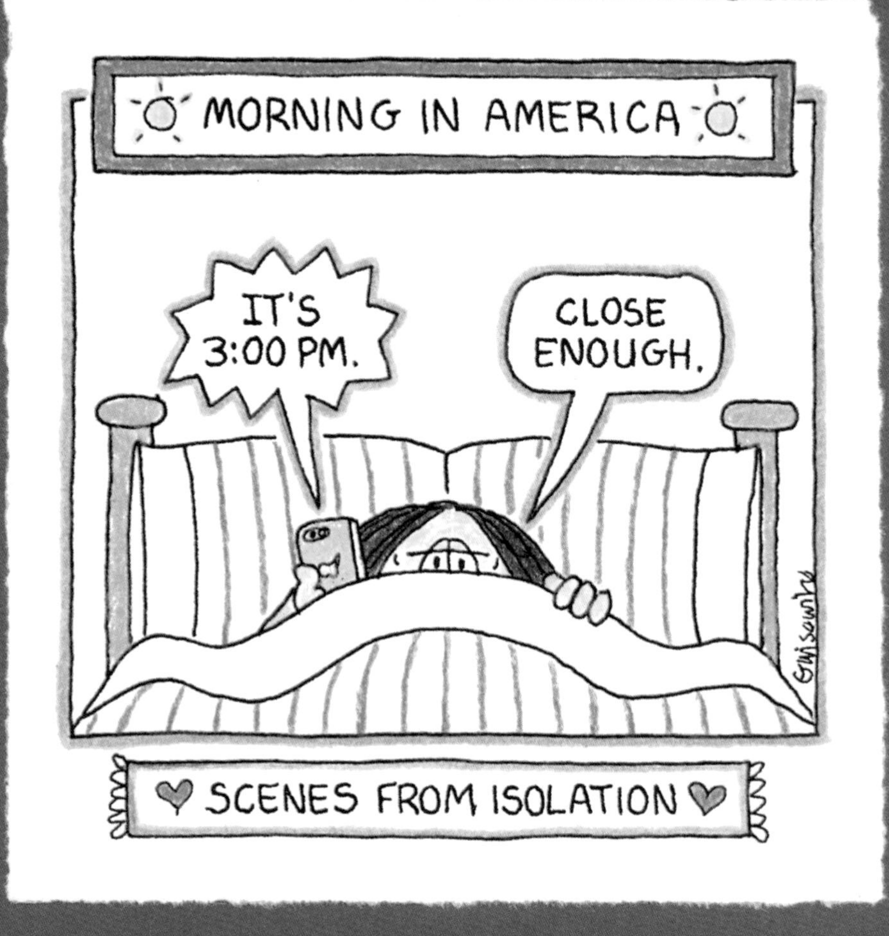
MORNING IN AMERICA
IT'S 3:00 PM.
CLOSE ENOUGH.
SCENES FROM ISOLATION

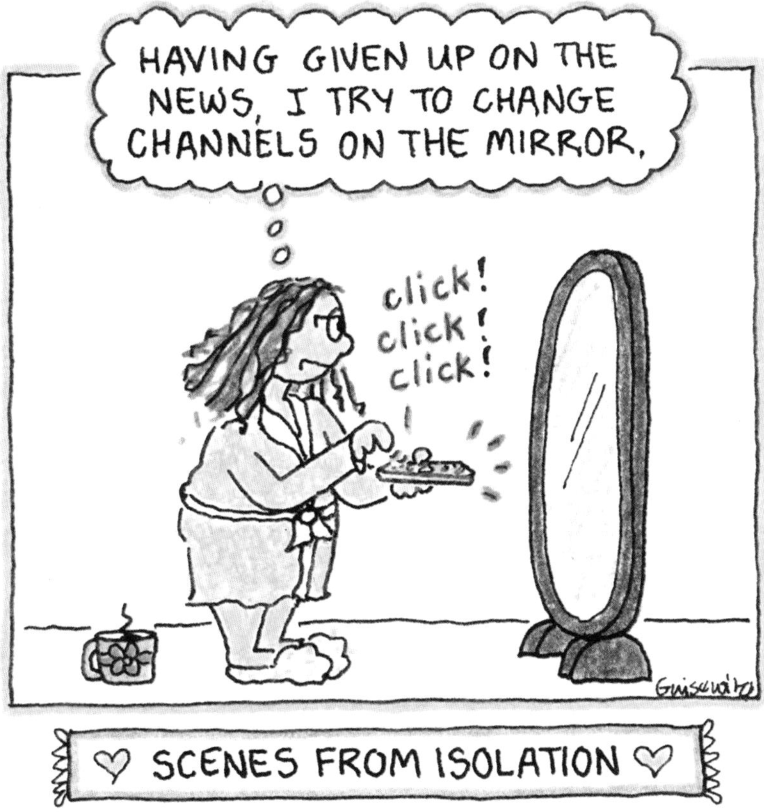
HAVING GIVEN UP ON THE NEWS, I TRY TO CHANGE CHANNELS ON THE MIRROR.
click! click! click!
♡ SCENES FROM ISOLATION ♡

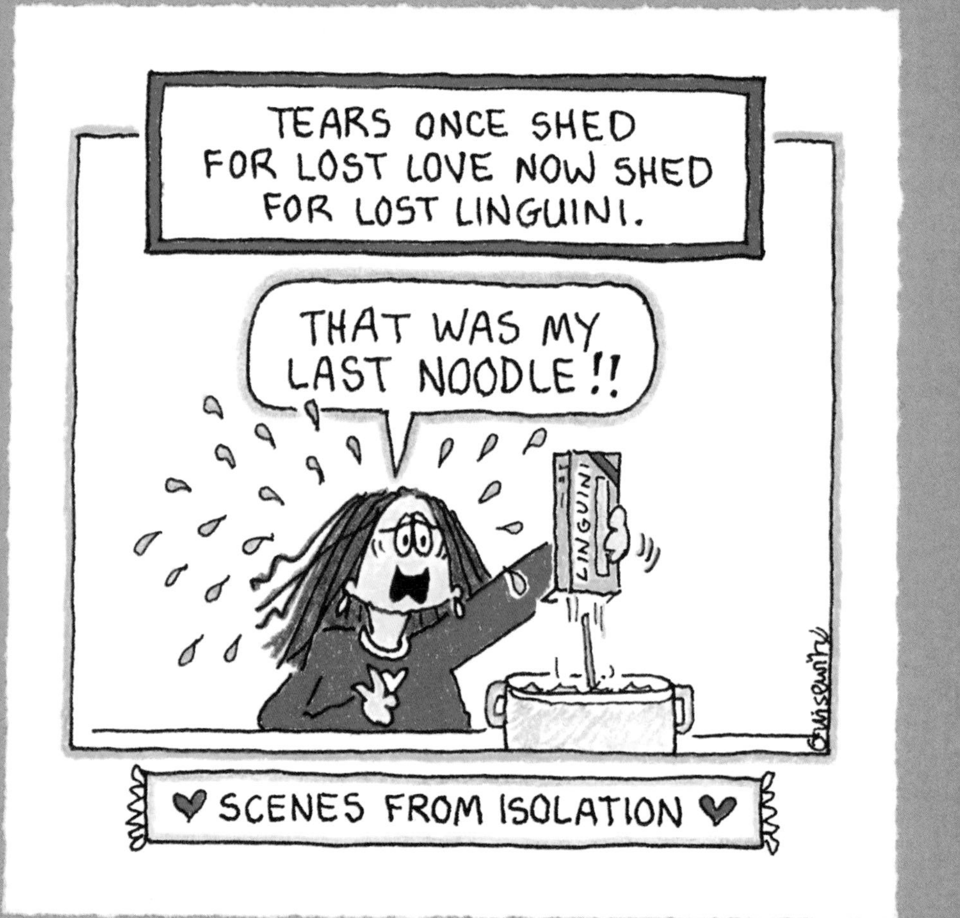
TEARS ONCE SHED
FOR LOST LOVE NOW SHED
FOR LOST LINGUINI.
THAT WAS MY
LAST NOODLE!!
LINGUINI
SCENES FROM ISOLATION

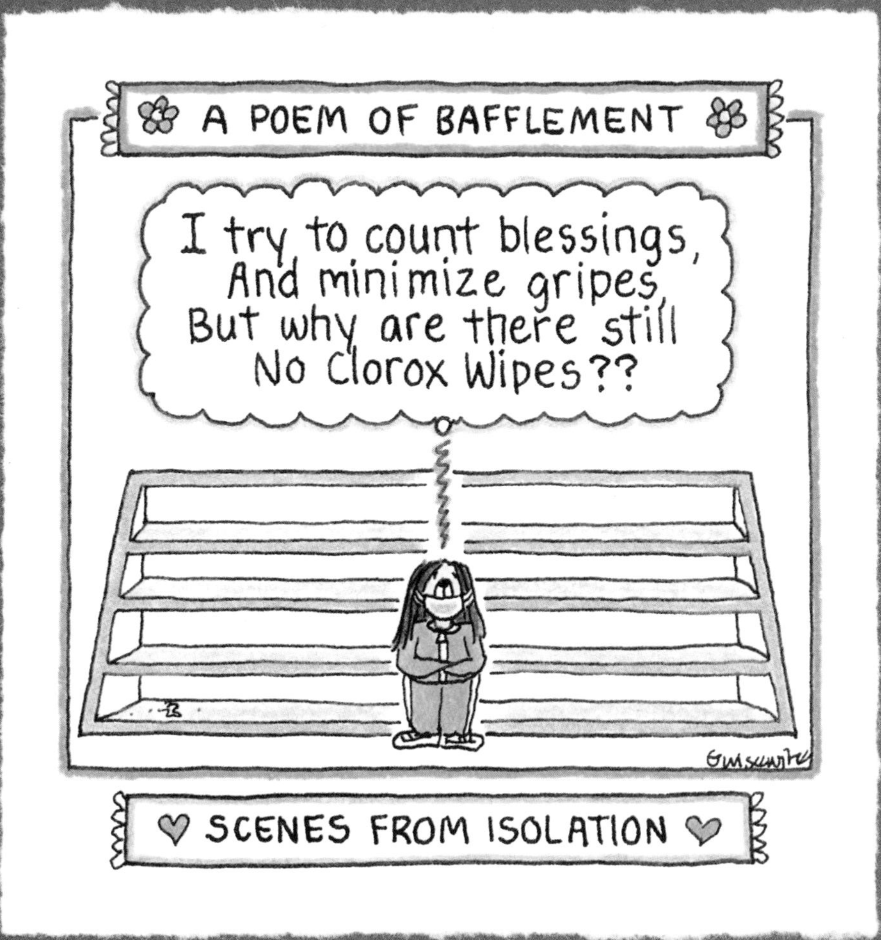
A POEM OF BAFFLEMENT
I try to count blessings,
And minimize gripes,
But why are there still
No Clorox Wipes??
SCENES FROM ISOLATION

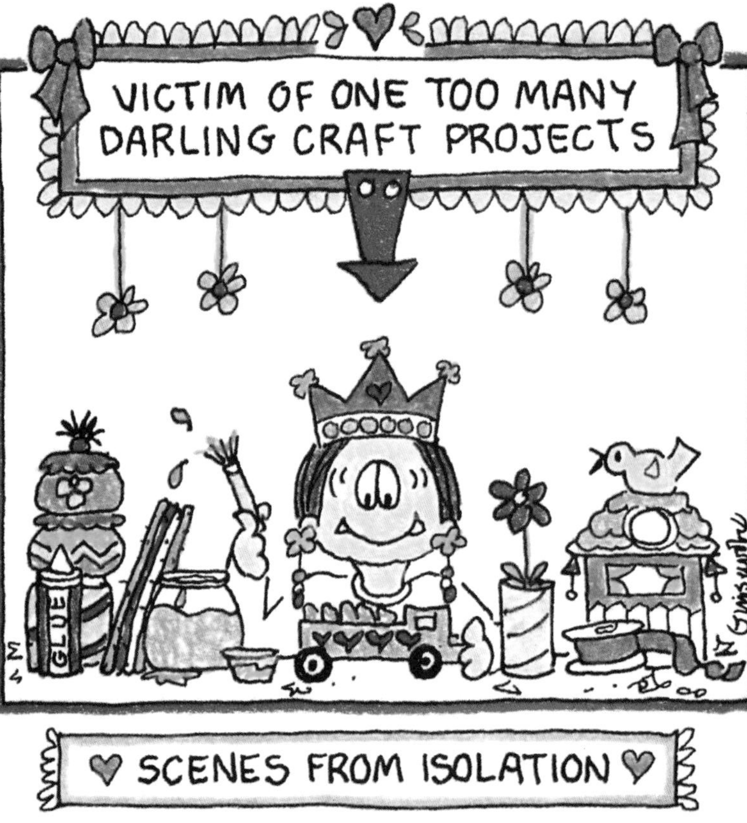
VICTIM OF ONE TOO MANY DARLING CRAFT PROJECTS
GLUE
SCENES FROM ISOLATION

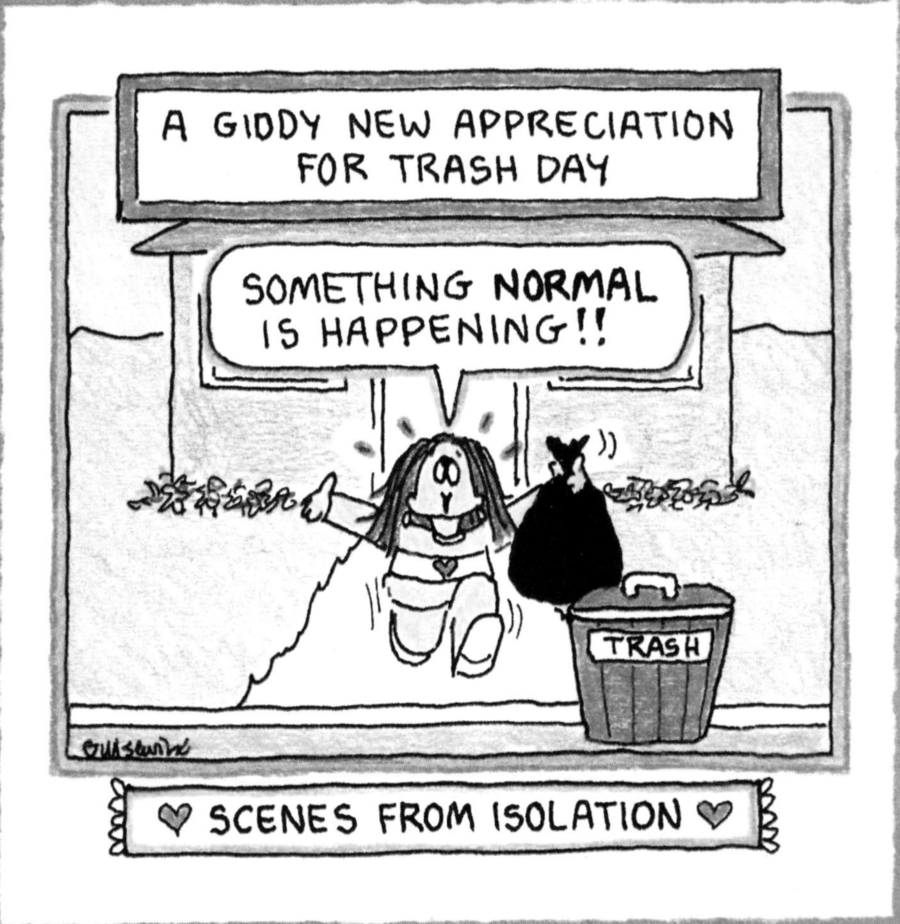
A GIDDY NEW APPRECIATION FOR TRASH DAY
SOMETHING NORMAL IS HAPPENING!!
TRASH
SCENES FROM ISOLATION

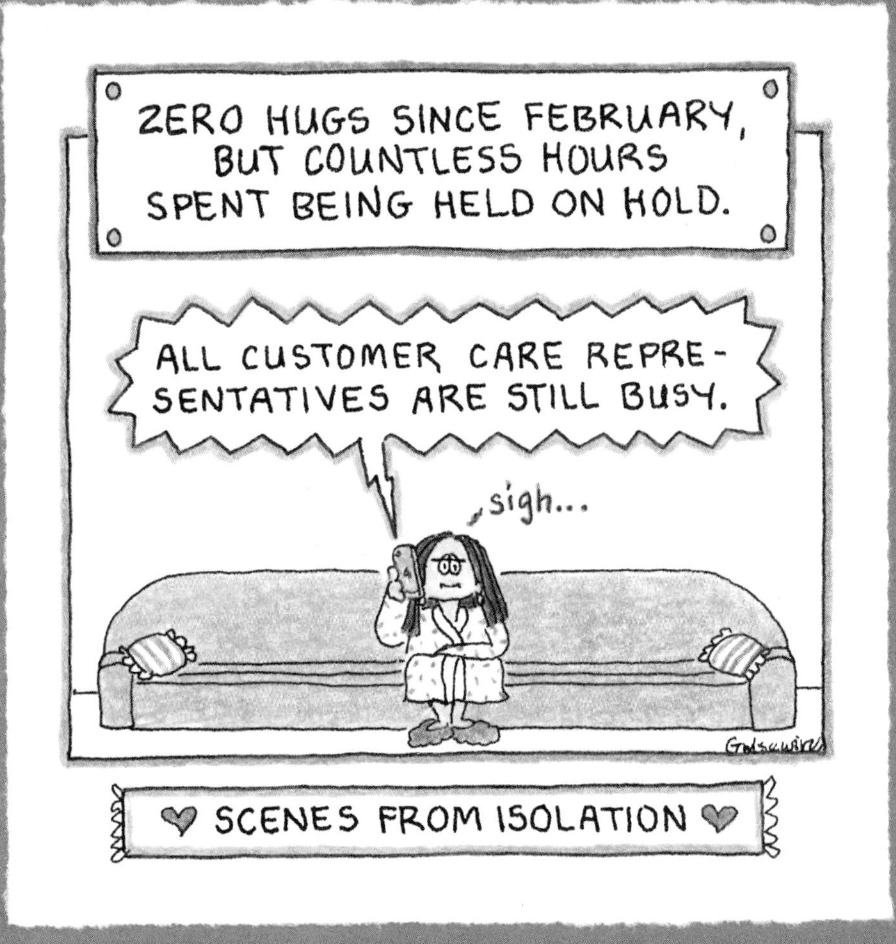
ZERO HUGS SINCE FEBRUARY, BUT COUNTLESS HOURS SPENT BEING HELD ON HOLD.
ALL CUSTOMER CARE REPRESENTATIVES ARE STILL BUSY.
sigh...
SCENES FROM ISOLATION

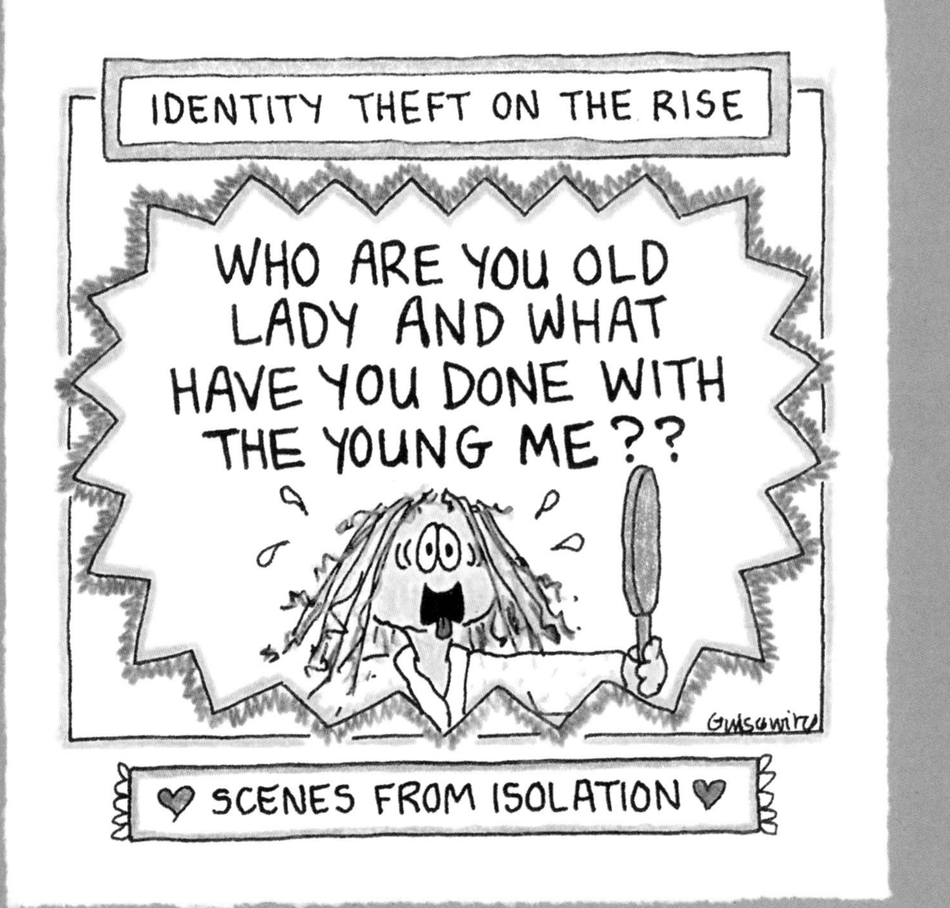
IDENTITY THEFT ON THE RISE
WHO ARE YOU OLD LADY AND WHAT HAVE YOU DONE WITH THE YOUNG ME??
Gulsowitz
SCENES FROM ISOLATION

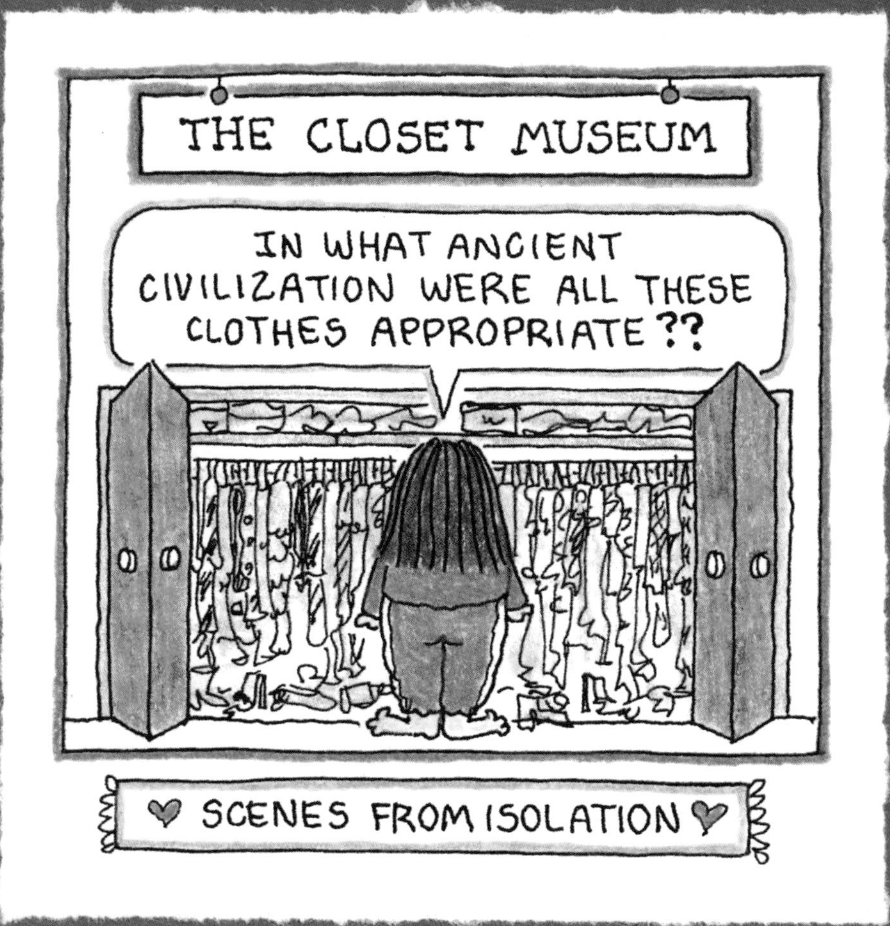
THE CLOSET MUSEUM
IN WHAT ANCIENT CIVILIZATION WERE ALL THESE CLOTHES APPROPRIATE??
SCENES FROM ISOLATION

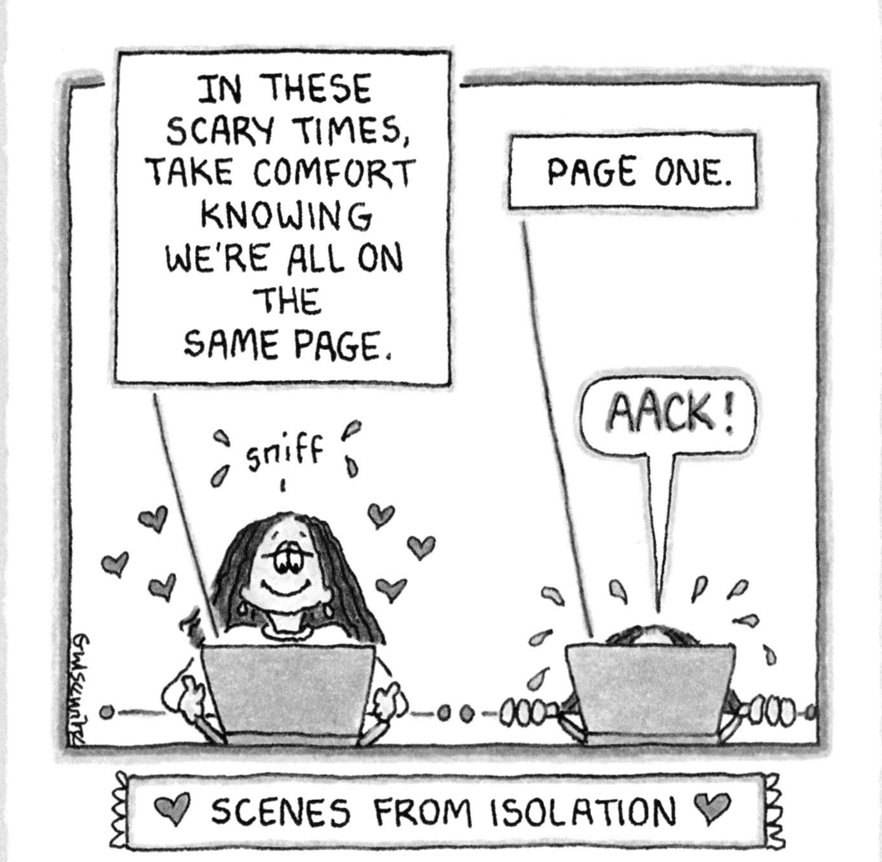
IN THESE SCARY TIMES, TAKE COMFORT KNOWING WE'RE ALL ON THE SAME PAGE.
sniff
PAGE ONE.
AACK!
SCENES FROM ISOLATION

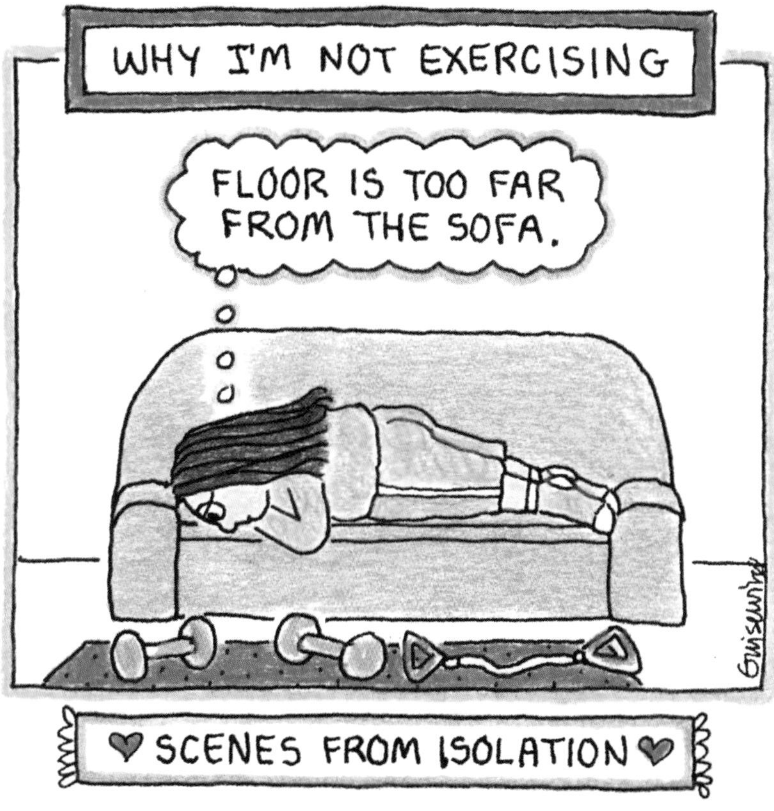
WHY I'M NOT EXERCISING
FLOOR IS TOO FAR FROM THE SOFA.
SCENES FROM ISOLATION

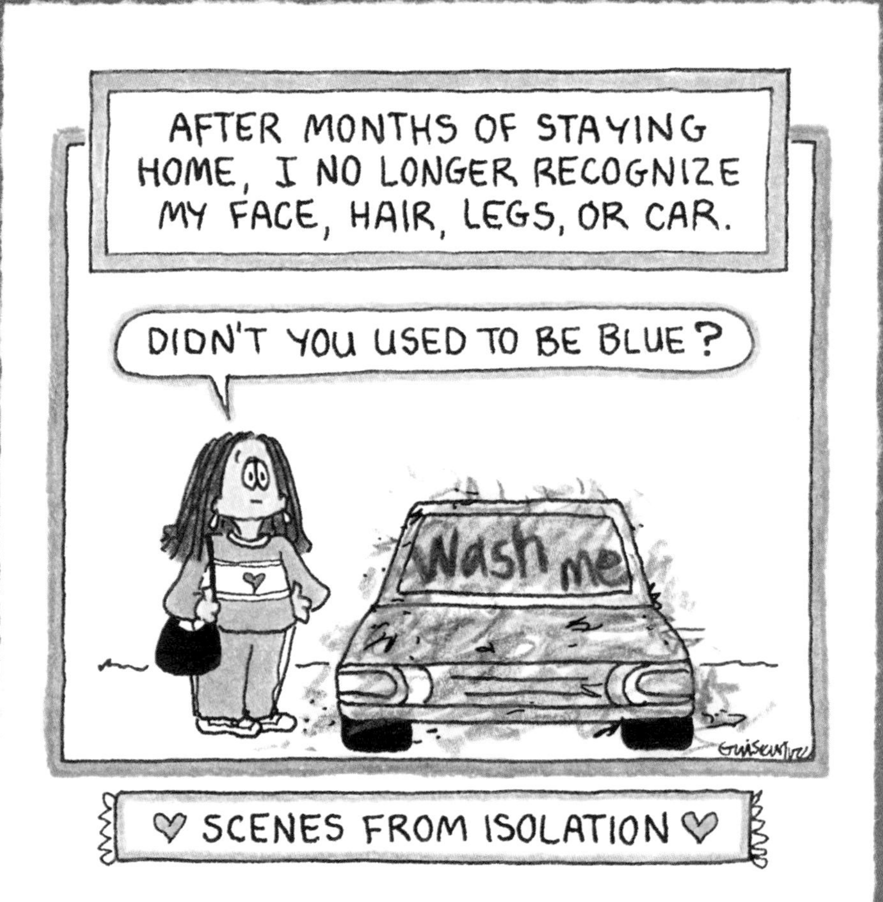
AFTER MONTHS OF STAYING HOME, I NO LONGER RECOGNIZE MY FACE, HAIR, LEGS, OR CAR.
DIDN'T YOU USED TO BE BLUE?
Wash me
GUISEWITE
SCENES FROM ISOLATION

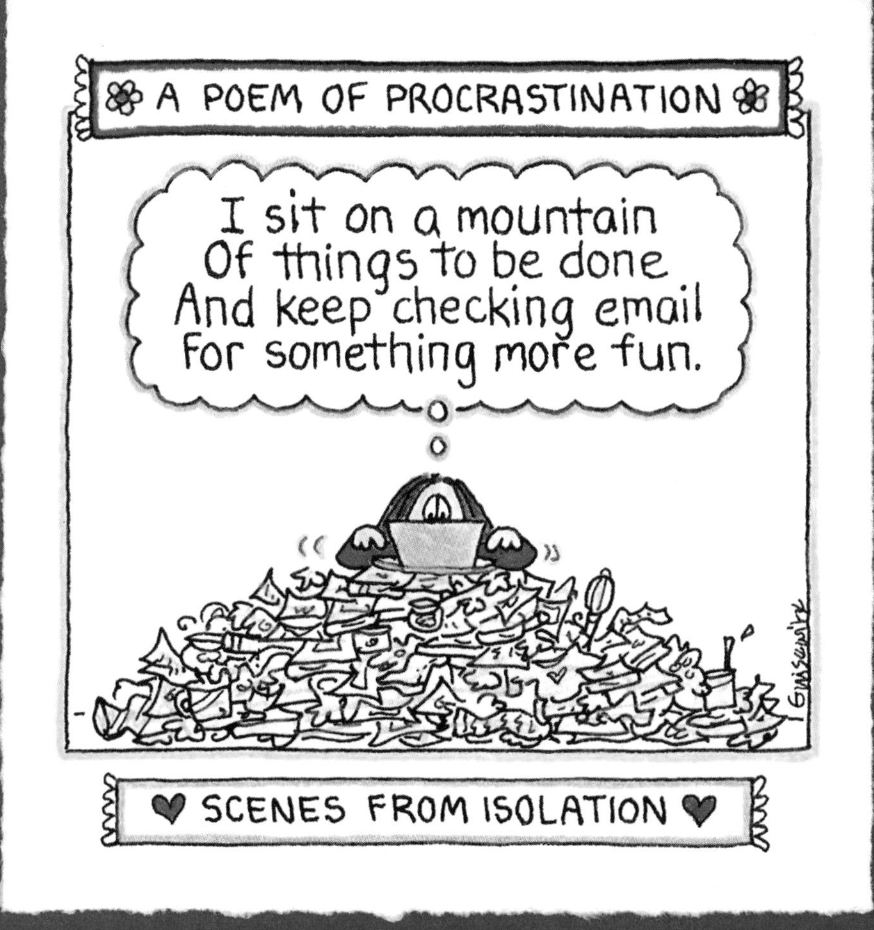
A POEM OF PROCRASTINATION
I sit on a mountain
Of things to be done
And keep checking email
For something more fun.
SCENES FROM ISOLATION

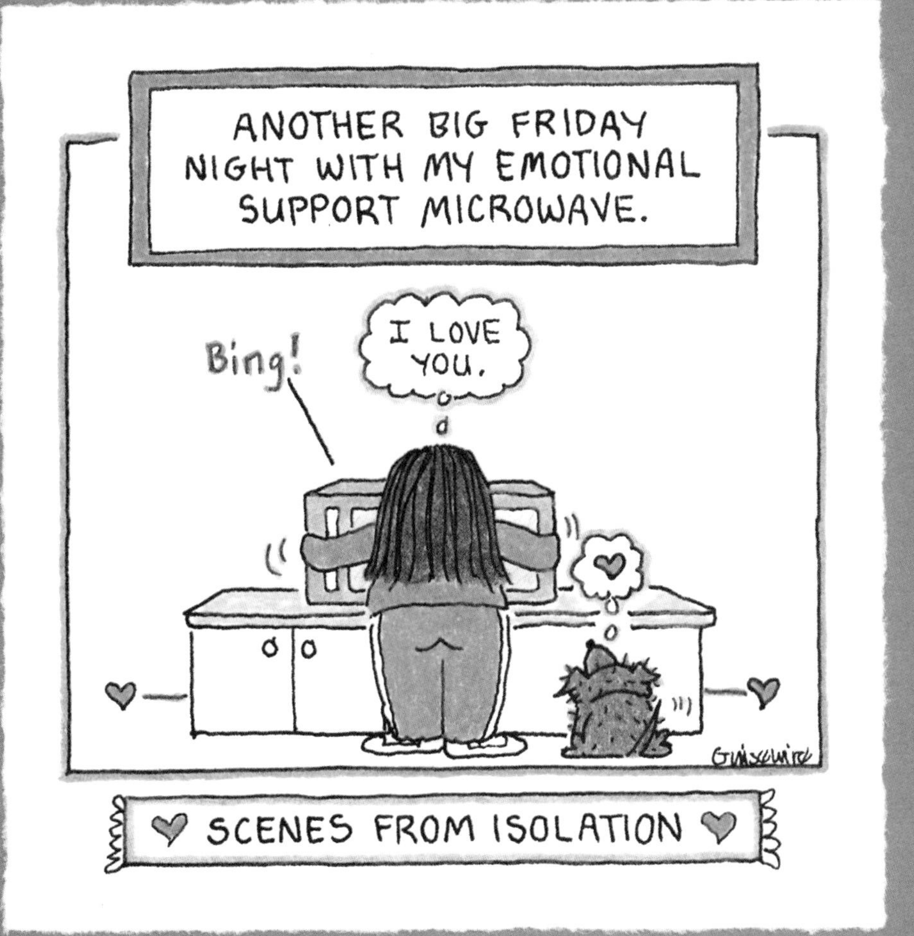
ANOTHER BIG FRIDAY NIGHT WITH MY EMOTIONAL SUPPORT MICROWAVE.
Bing!
I LOVE YOU.
SCENES FROM ISOLATION

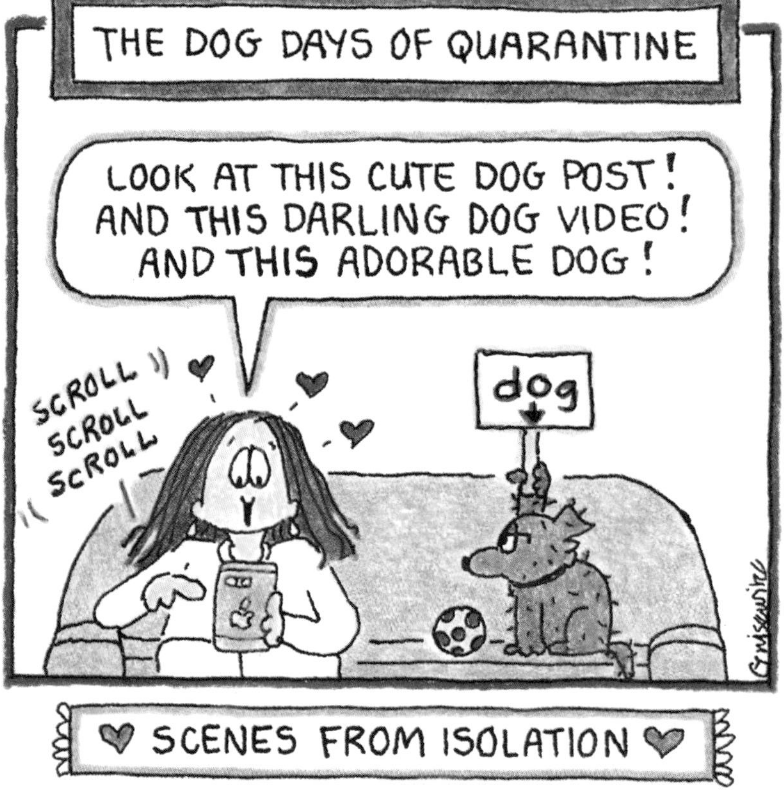
THE DOG DAYS OF QUARANTINE
LOOK AT THIS CUTE DOG POST! AND THIS DARLING DOG VIDEO! AND THIS ADORABLE DOG!
SCROLL SCROLL SCROLL
dog
SCENES FROM ISOLATION

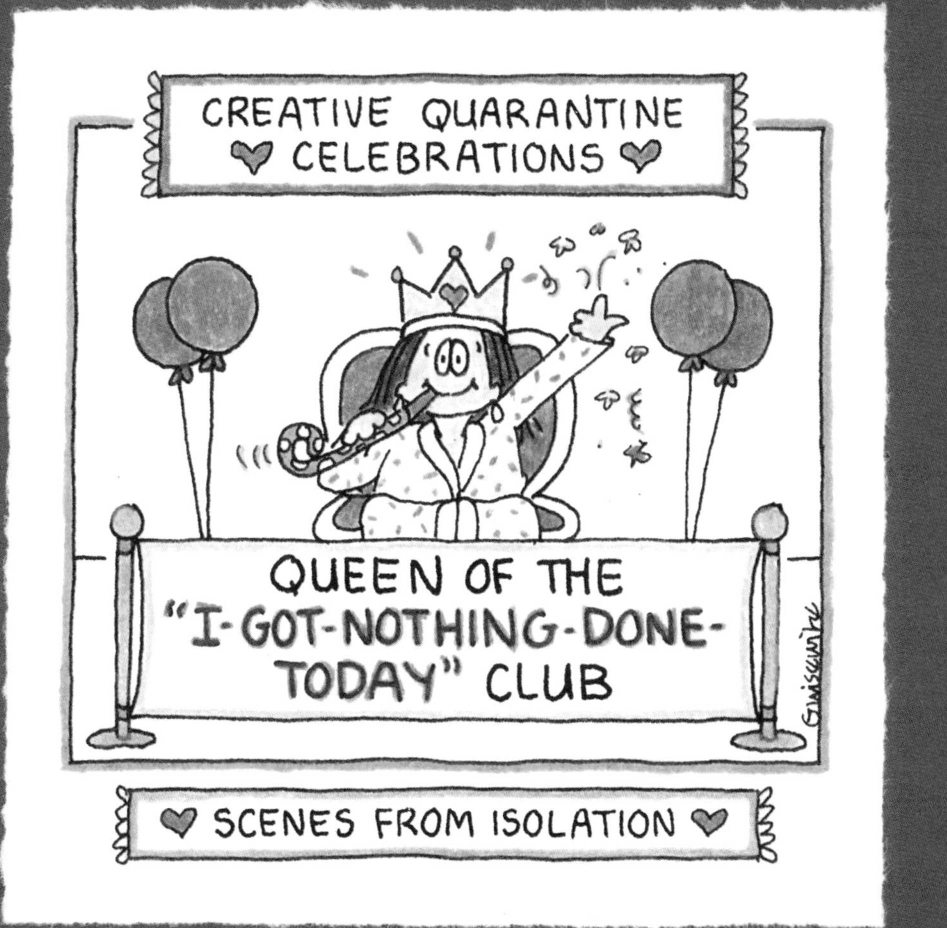
CREATIVE QUARANTINE
CELEBRATIONS
QUEEN OF THE
"I-GOT-NOTHING-DONE-
TODAY" CLUB
SCENES FROM ISOLATION

DRESSING THE BOTTOM HALF OF THE FACE FOR A ZOOM CALL:
1. BRUSH & FLOSS TEETH
2. WHITEN TEETH
3. FILL WRINKLES
4. FOUNDATION & POWDER
5. LIPLINER, LIPSTICK, GLOSS
CAN'T I JUST WEAR MY MASK??
Guisewite
SCENES FROM ISOLATION

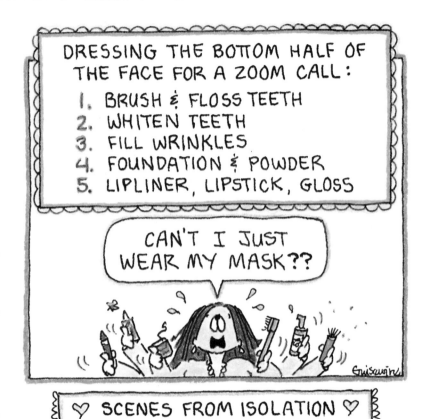

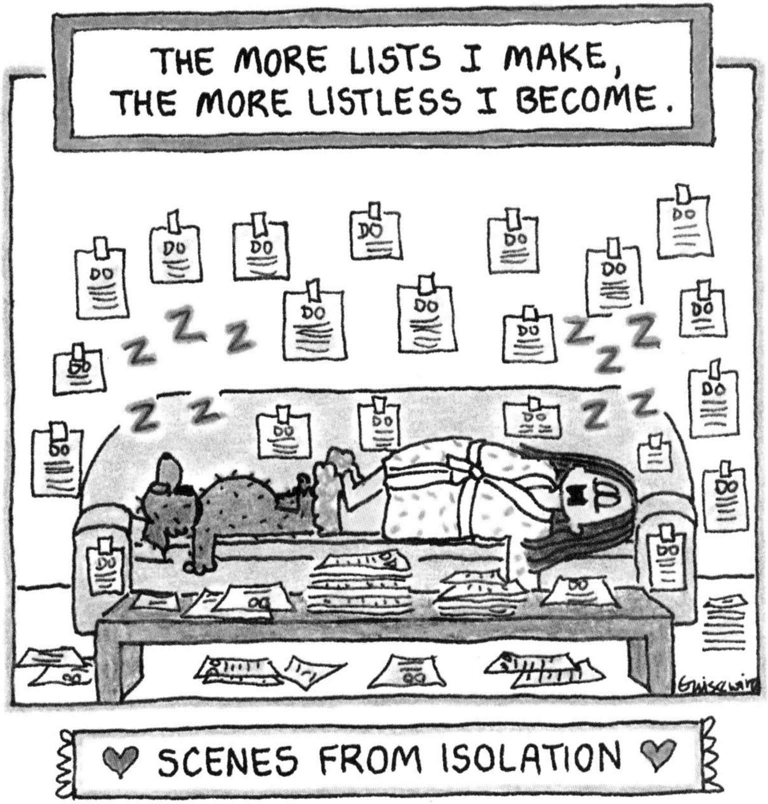
THE MORE LISTS I MAKE,
THE MORE LISTLESS I BECOME.
SCENES FROM ISOLATION

THE DANGER OF HOUSECLEANING
I DUSTED ONE SHELF. A TRINKET ON THE SHELF REMINDED ME OF A TRIP WHICH REMINDED ME OF A FRIEND WHICH REMINDED ME OF A PHOTO WHICH I AM NOW OBSESSED WITH FINDING AND FRAMING SO IT CAN GO ON THE DUSTED SHELF!
SCENES FROM ISOLATION

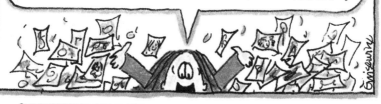

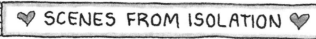

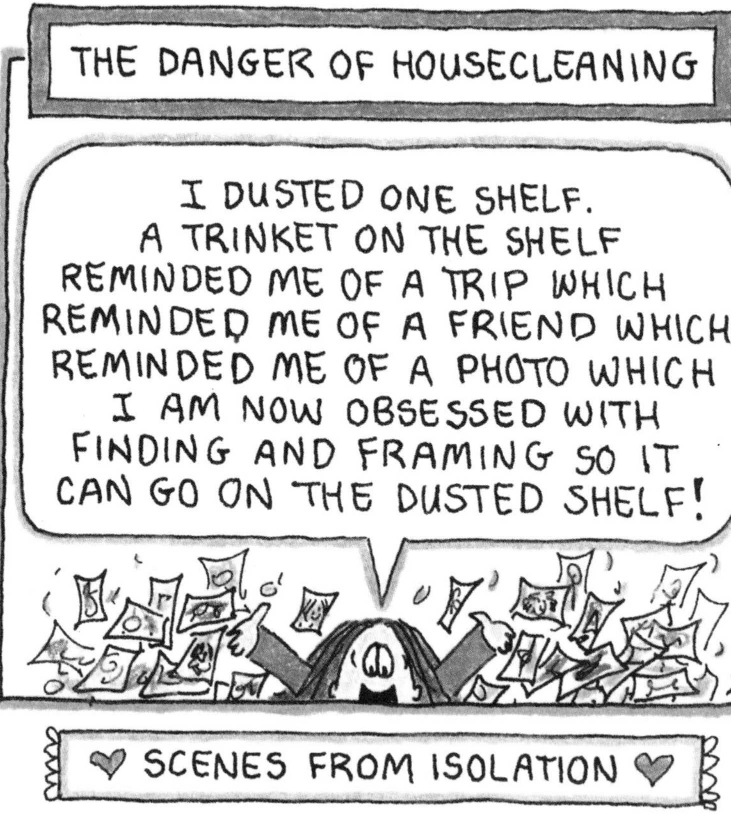

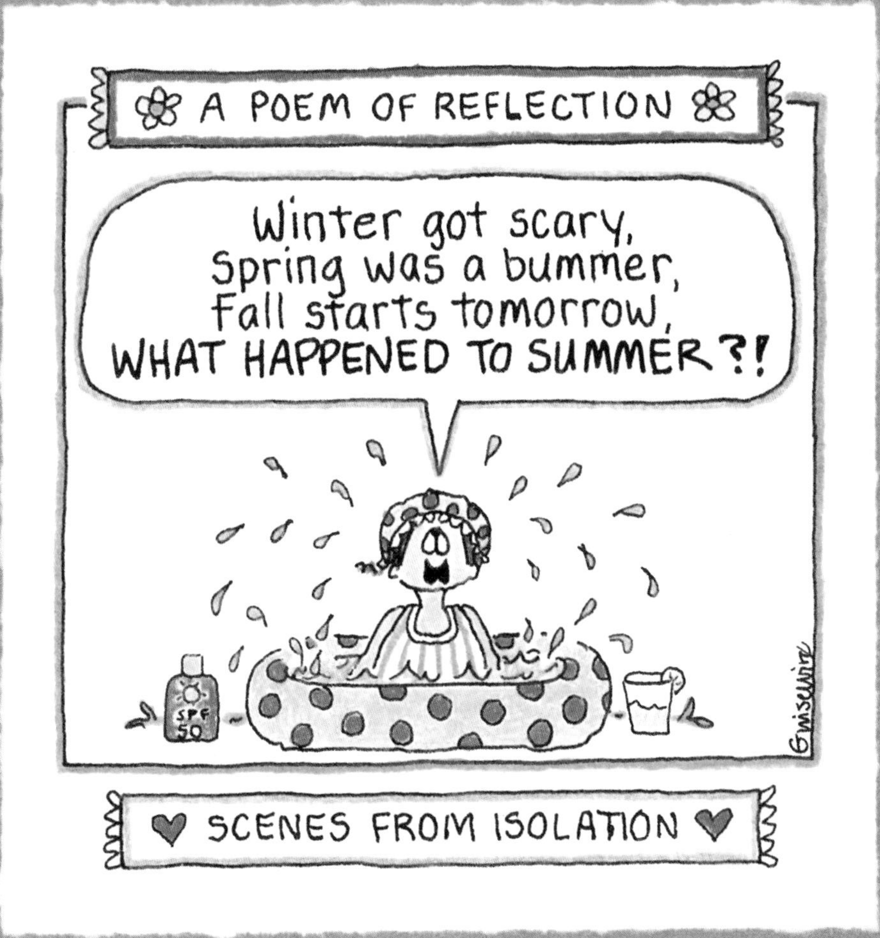
A POEM OF REFLECTION
Winter got scary,
Spring was a bummer,
Fall starts tomorrow,
WHAT HAPPENED TO SUMMER?!
SPF 50
Guisewite
SCENES FROM ISOLATION

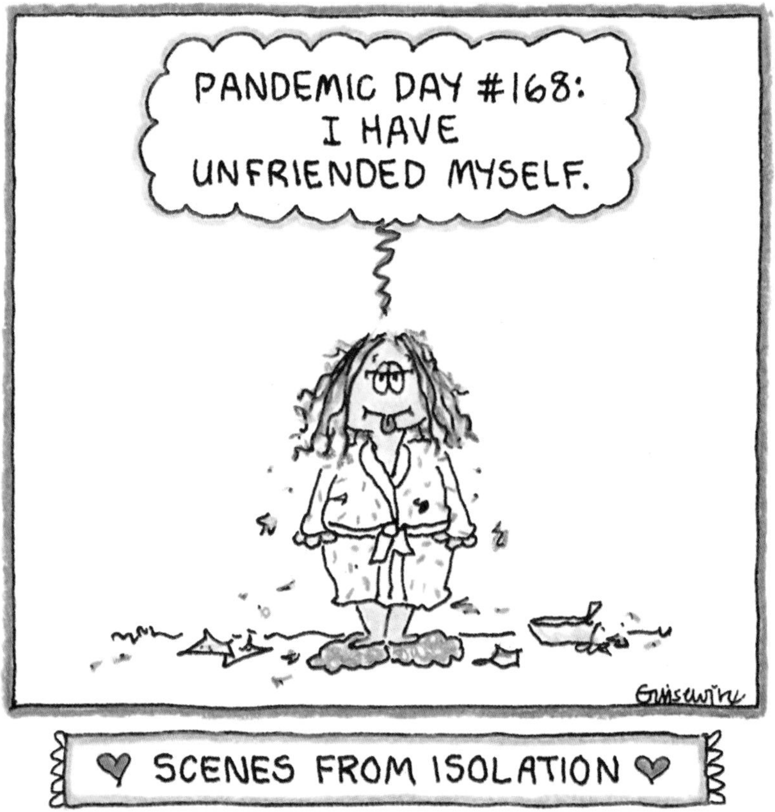
PANDEMIC DAY #168: I HAVE UNFRIENDED MYSELF.
SCENES FROM ISOLATION

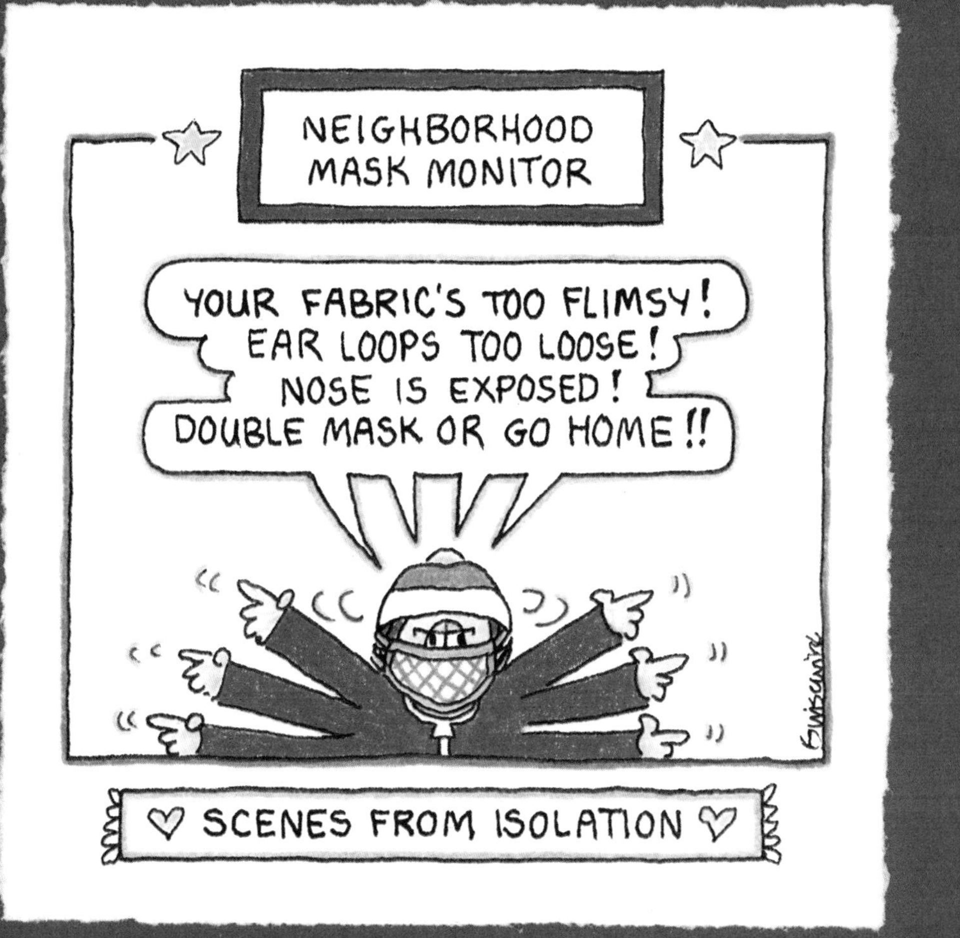
NEIGHBORHOOD MASK MONITOR
YOUR FABRIC'S TOO FLIMSY! EAR LOOPS TOO LOOSE! NOSE IS EXPOSED! DOUBLE MASK OR GO HOME!!
SCENES FROM ISOLATION

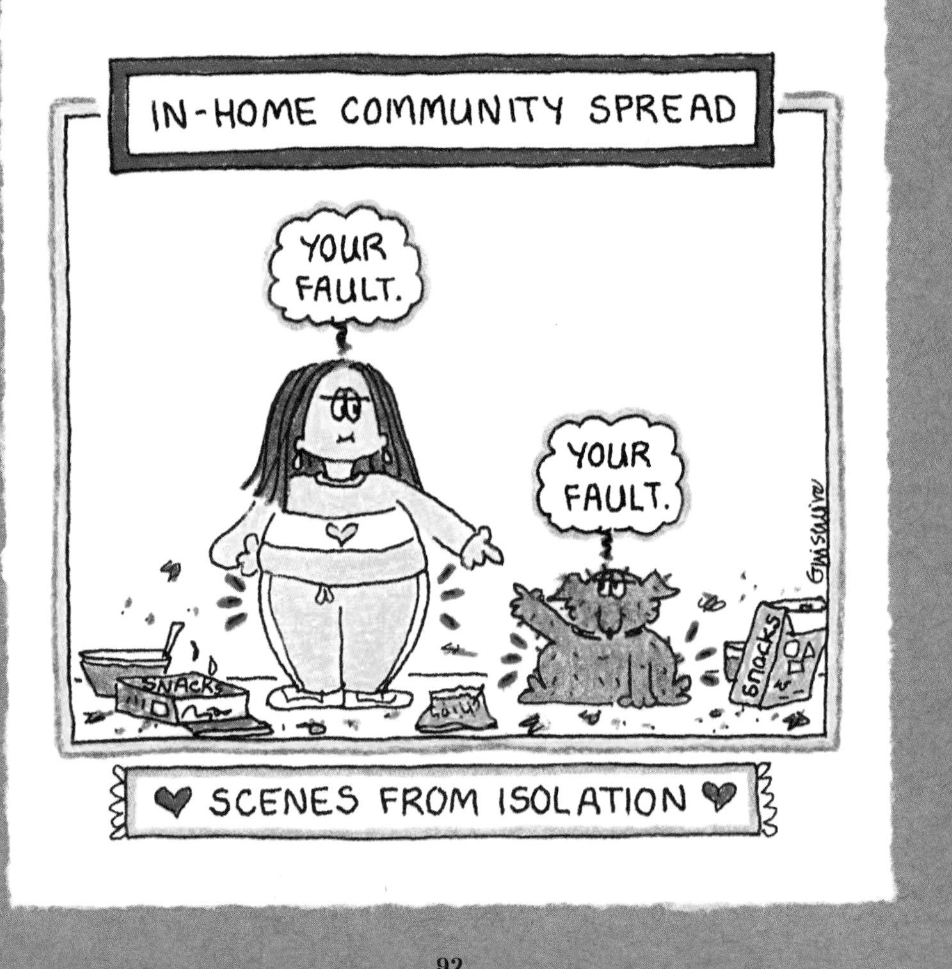
IN-HOME COMMUNITY SPREAD
YOUR FAULT.
YOUR FAULT.
SNACKS
SNACKS
SCENES FROM ISOLATION

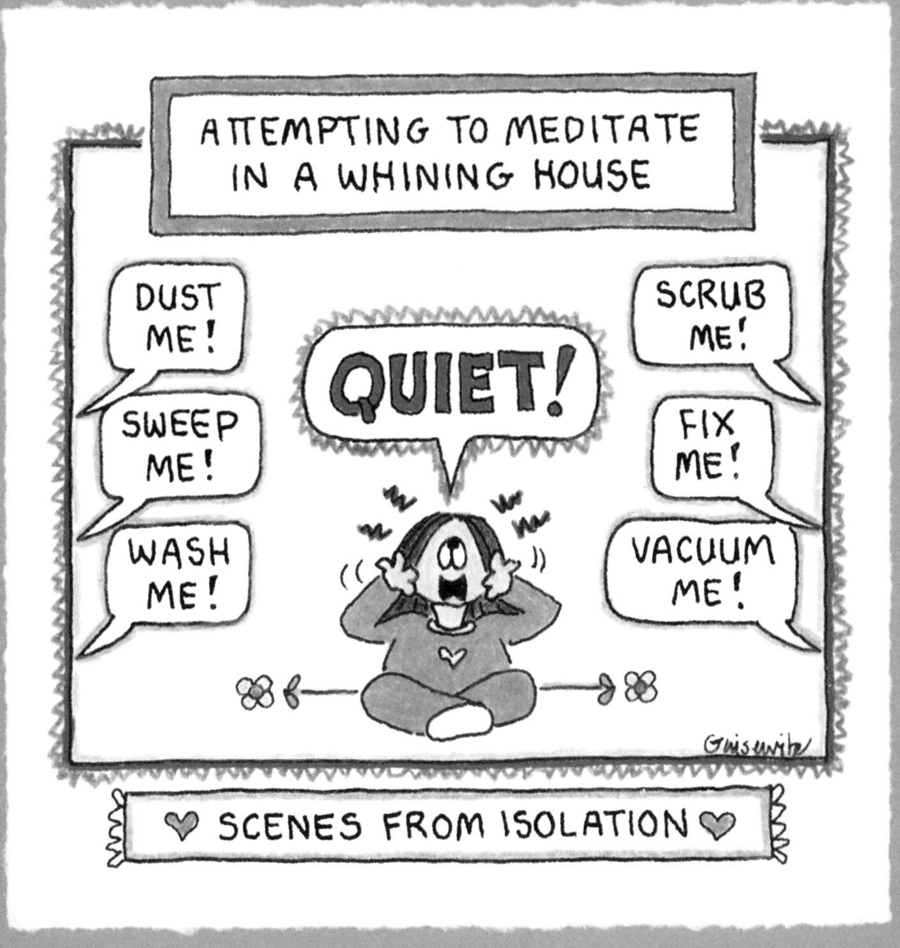
ATTEMPTING TO MEDITATE IN A WHINING HOUSE
DUST ME!
SWEEP ME!
WASH ME!
QUIET!
SCRUB ME!
FIX ME!
VACUUM ME!
SCENES FROM ISOLATION

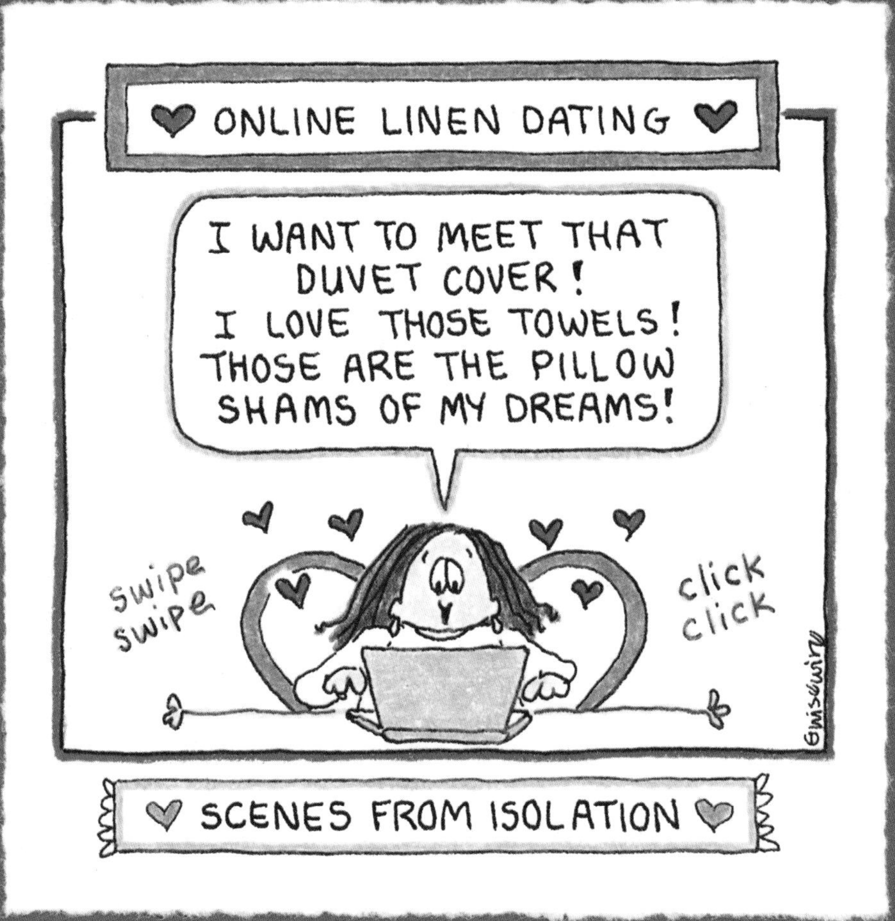
ONLINE LINEN DATING
I WANT TO MEET THAT DUVET COVER! I LOVE THOSE TOWELS! THOSE ARE THE PILLOW SHAMS OF MY DREAMS!
swipe swipe
click click
SCENES FROM ISOLATION

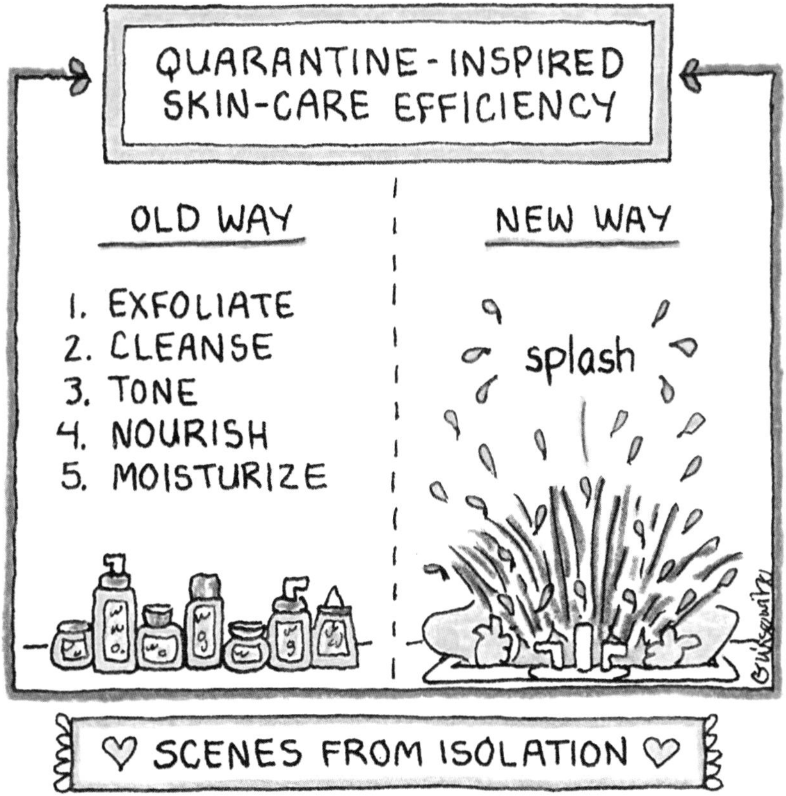
QUARANTINE-INSPIRED SKIN-CARE EFFICIENCY
OLD WAY
1. EXFOLIATE
2. CLEANSE
3. TONE
4. NOURISH
5. MOISTURIZE
NEW WAY
splash
♡ SCENES FROM ISOLATION ♡

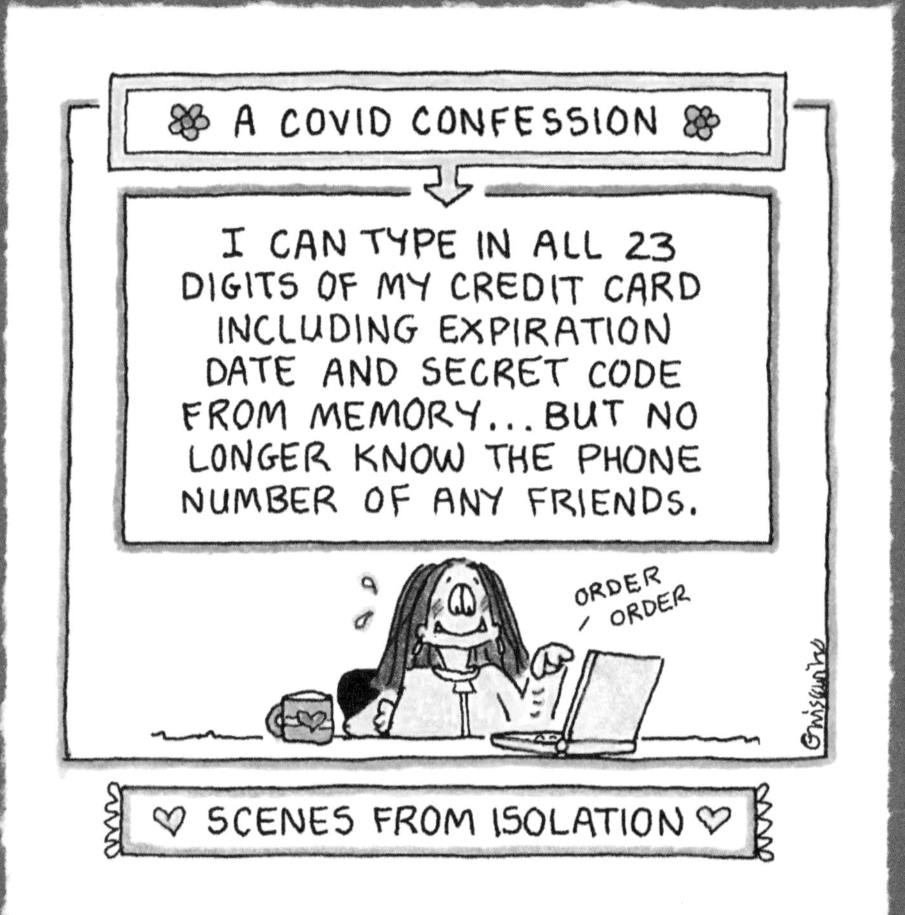
A COVID CONFESSION
I CAN TYPE IN ALL 23 DIGITS OF MY CREDIT CARD INCLUDING EXPIRATION DATE AND SECRET CODE FROM MEMORY... BUT NO LONGER KNOW THE PHONE NUMBER OF ANY FRIENDS.
ORDER ORDER
©Guisewite
SCENES FROM ISOLATION

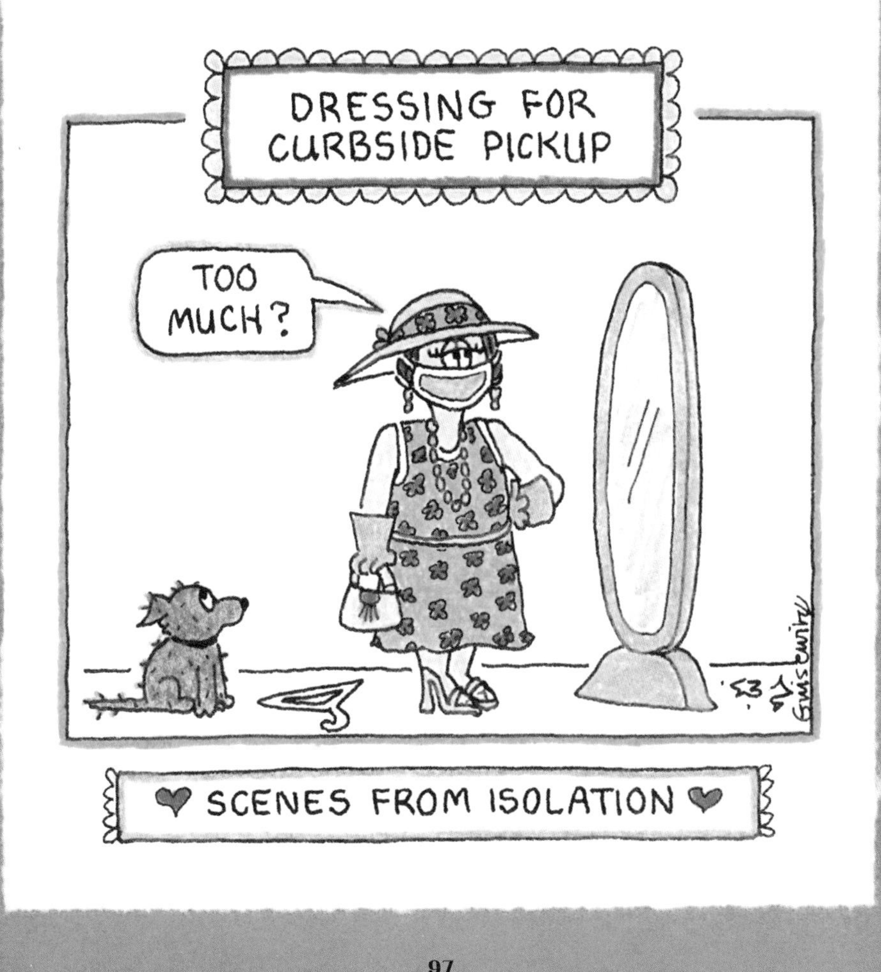
DRESSING FOR CURBSIDE PICKUP
TOO MUCH?
SCENES FROM ISOLATION

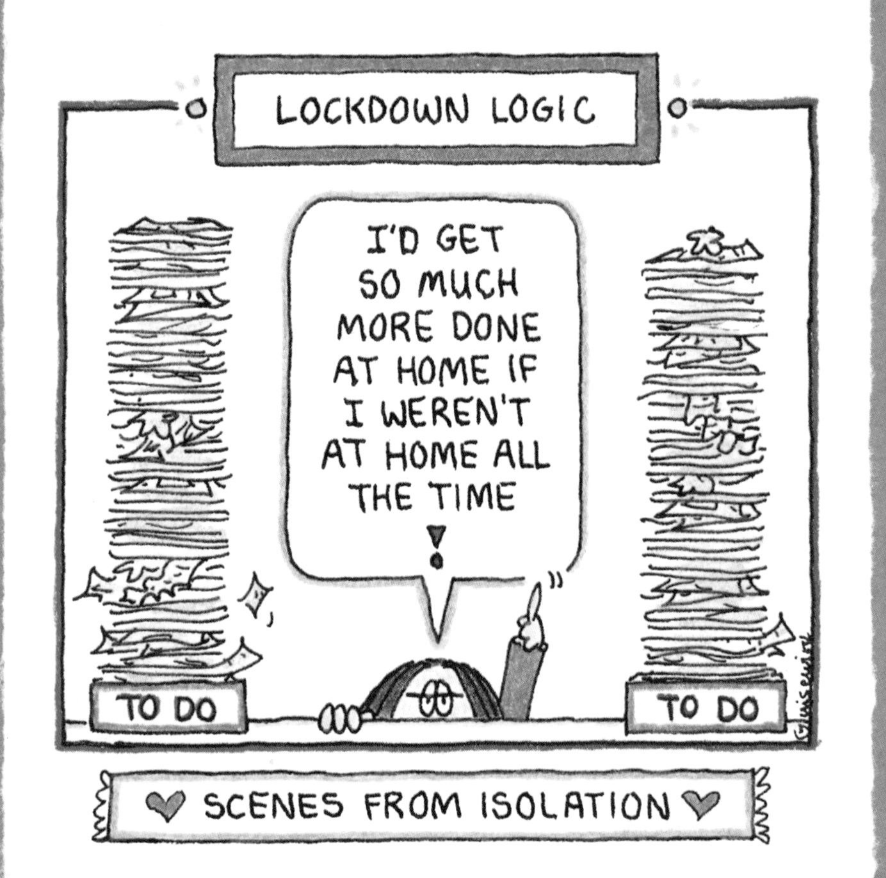
LOCKDOWN LOGIC
I'D GET SO MUCH MORE DONE AT HOME IF I WEREN'T AT HOME ALL THE TIME
TO DO
TO DO
SCENES FROM ISOLATION

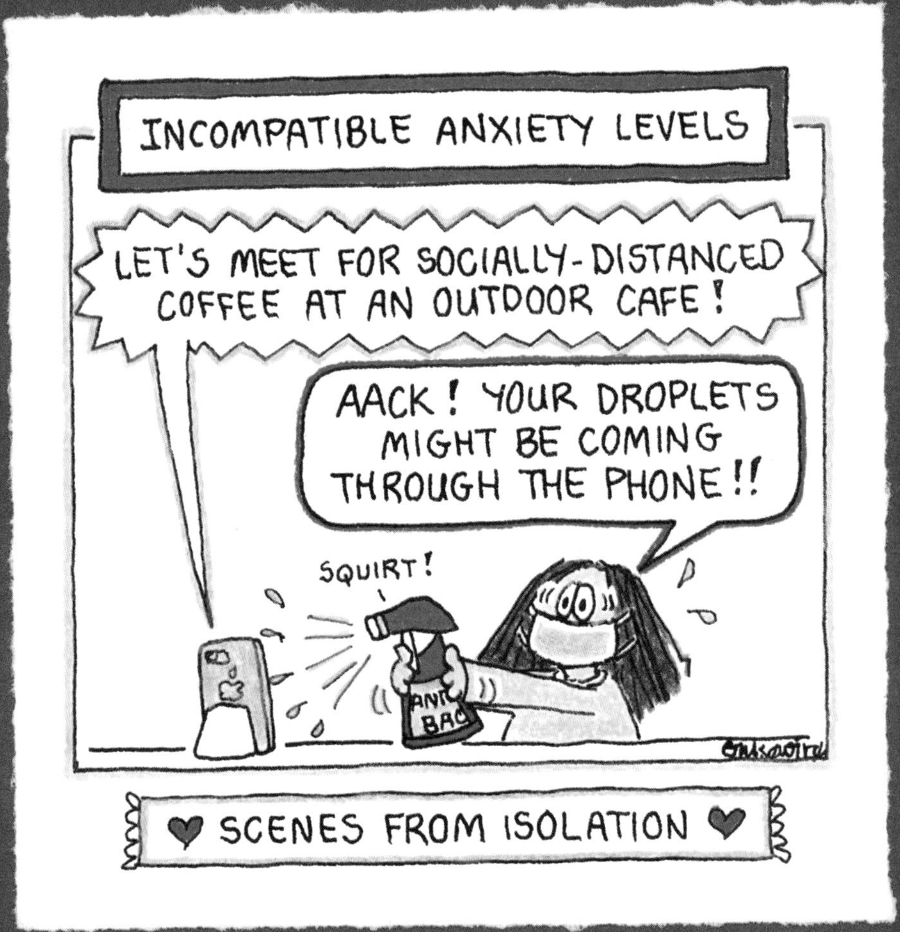
INCOMPATIBLE ANXIETY LEVELS
LET'S MEET FOR SOCIALLY-DISTANCED COFFEE AT AN OUTDOOR CAFE!
AACK! YOUR DROPLETS MIGHT BE COMING THROUGH THE PHONE!!
SQUIRT!
ANTI BAC
♥ SCENES FROM ISOLATION ♥

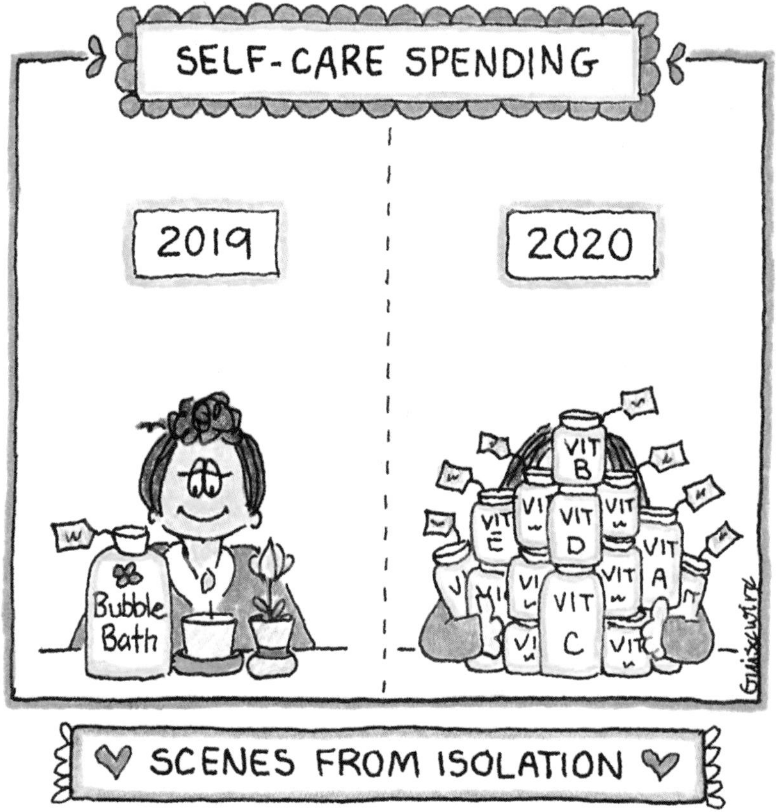
SELF-CARE SPENDING
2019
2020
Bubble Bath
VIT B
VIT D
VIT E
VIT A
VIT C
SCENES FROM ISOLATION

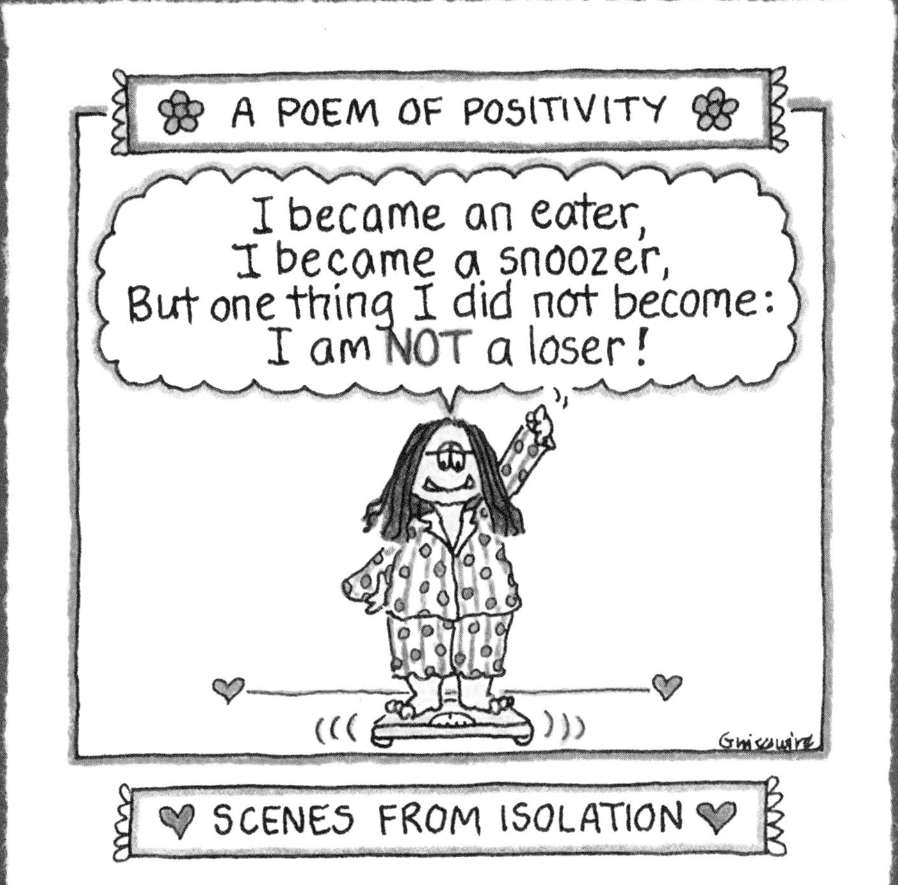
A POEM OF POSITIVITY
I became an eater,
I became a snoozer,
But one thing I did not become:
I am NOT a loser!
SCENES FROM ISOLATION

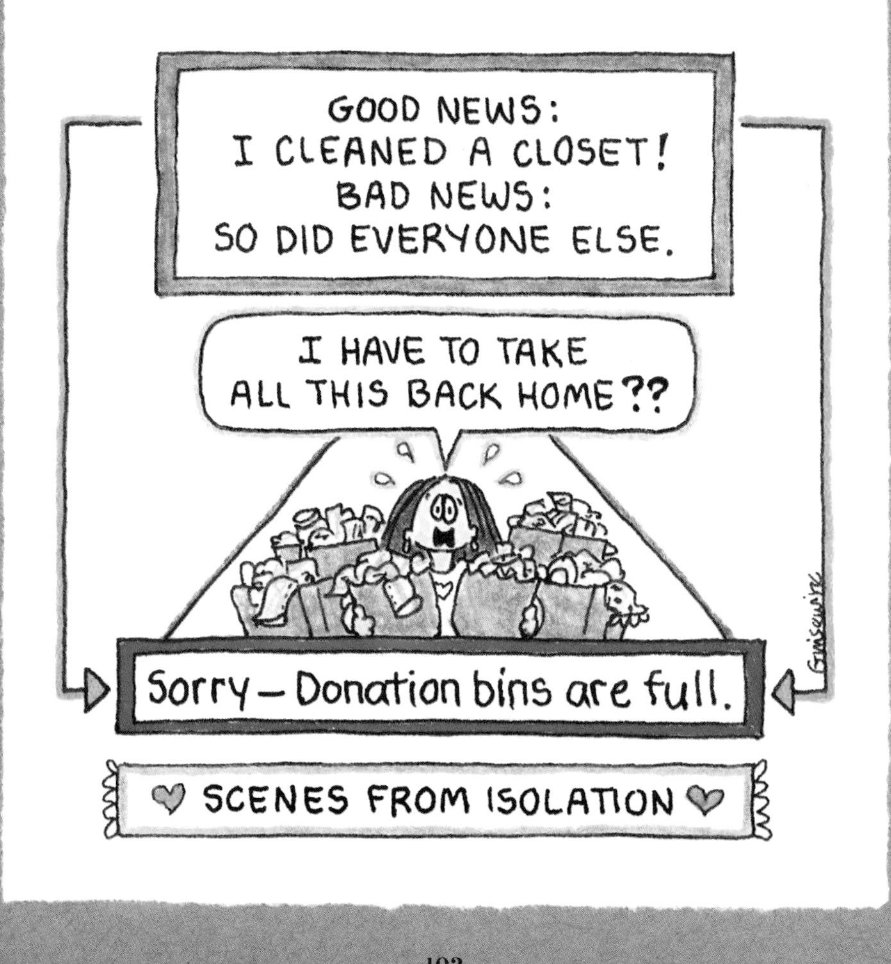
GOOD NEWS:
I CLEANED A CLOSET!
BAD NEWS:
SO DID EVERYONE ELSE.
I HAVE TO TAKE
ALL THIS BACK HOME??
Sorry — Donation bins are full.
SCENES FROM ISOLATION

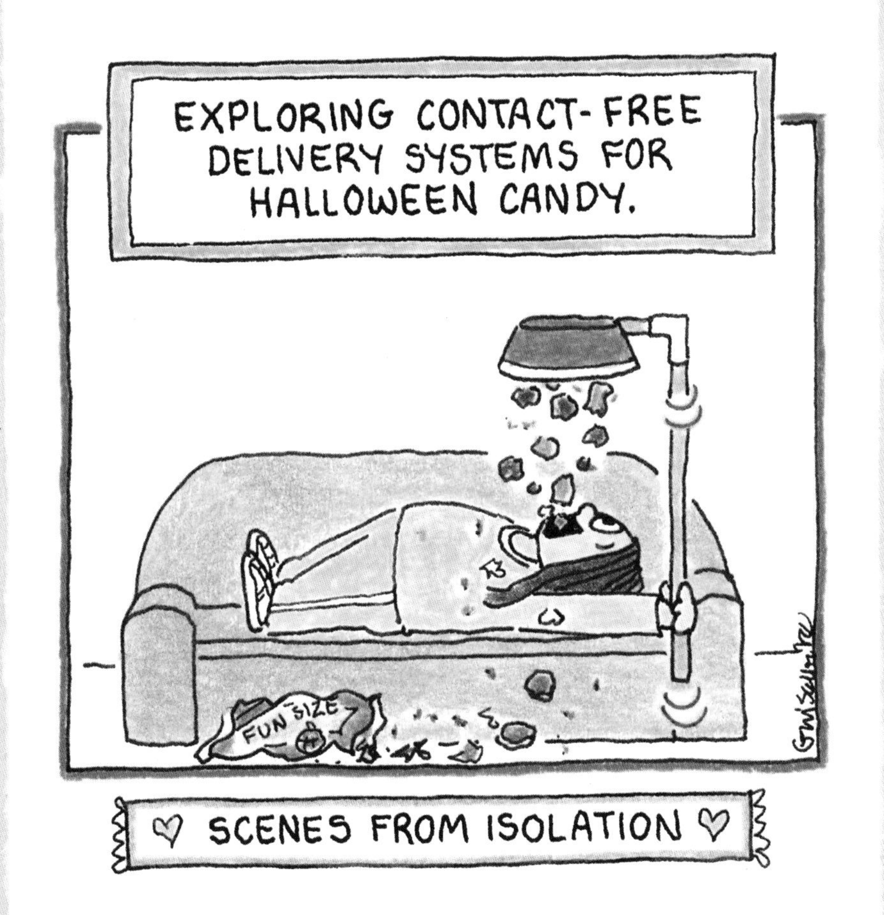
EXPLORING CONTACT-FREE DELIVERY SYSTEMS FOR HALLOWEEN CANDY.
FUN SIZE
SCENES FROM ISOLATION

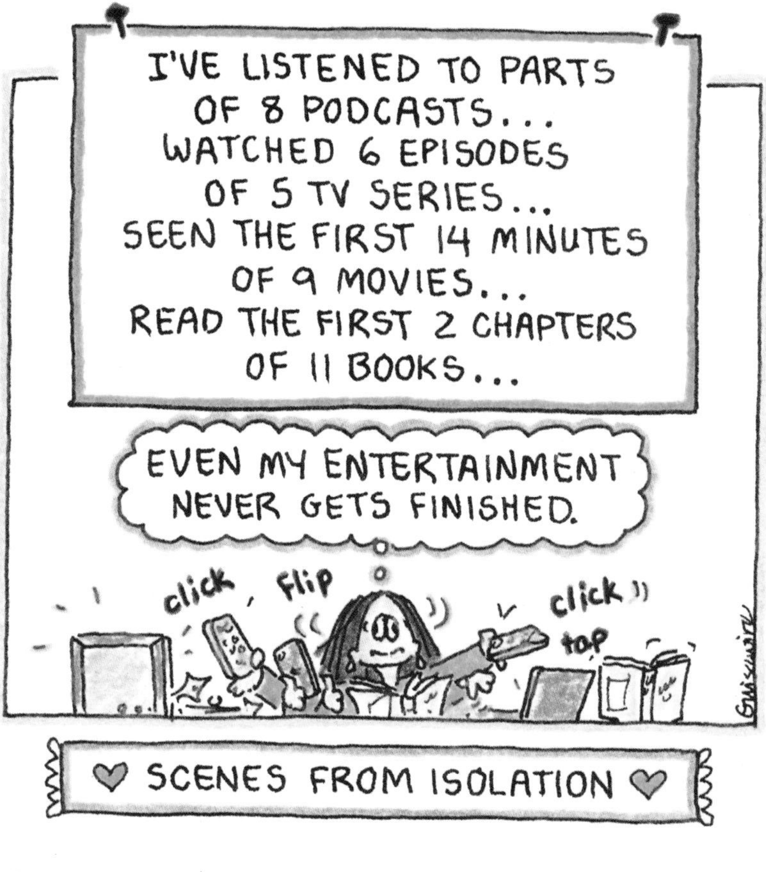
I'VE LISTENED TO PARTS OF 8 PODCASTS... WATCHED 6 EPISODES OF 5 TV SERIES... SEEN THE FIRST 14 MINUTES OF 9 MOVIES... READ THE FIRST 2 CHAPTERS OF 11 BOOKS...
EVEN MY ENTERTAINMENT NEVER GETS FINISHED.
click
flip
click
tap
SCENES FROM ISOLATION

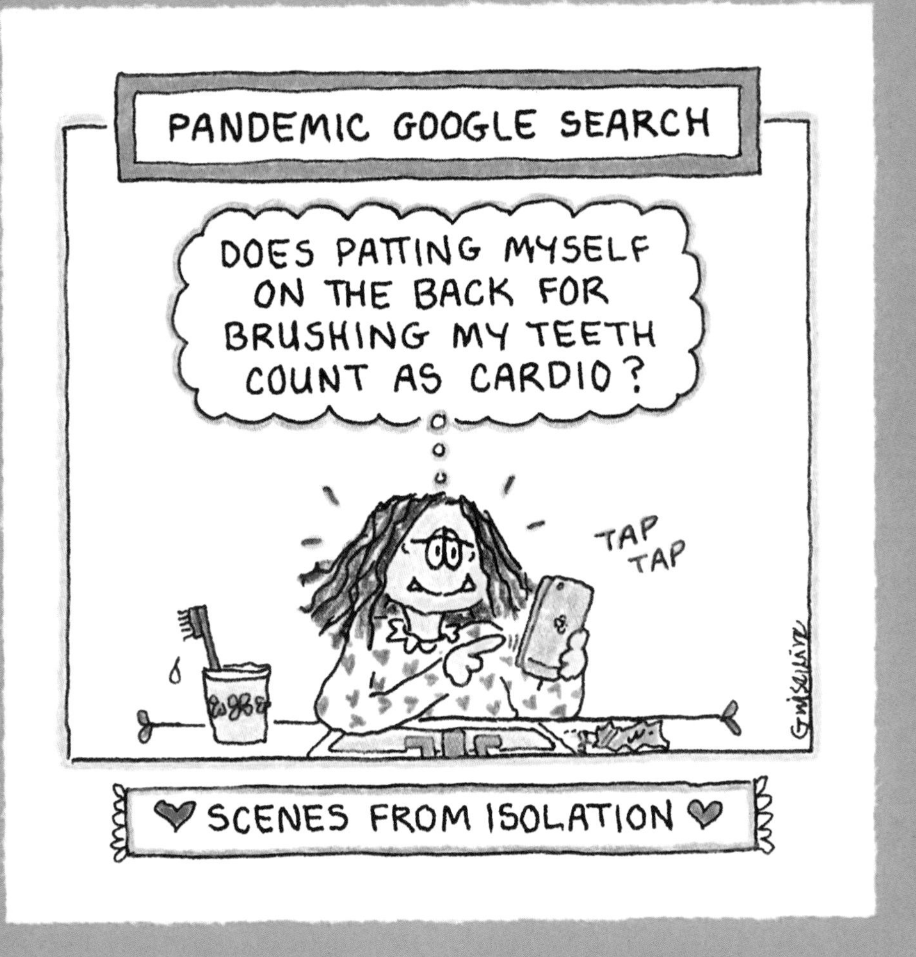
PANDEMIC GOOGLE SEARCH
DOES PATTING MYSELF ON THE BACK FOR BRUSHING MY TEETH COUNT AS CARDIO?
TAP TAP
SCENES FROM ISOLATION

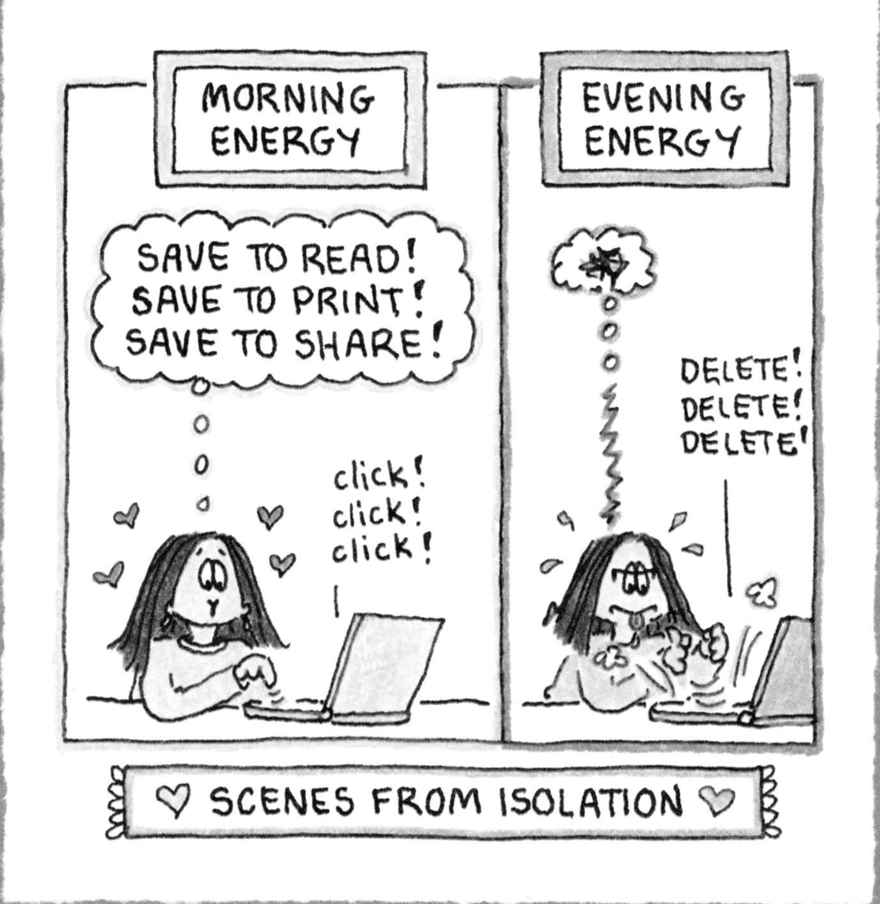
MORNING ENERGY
SAVE TO READ! SAVE TO PRINT! SAVE TO SHARE!
click! click! click!
EVENING ENERGY
DELETE! DELETE! DELETE!
SCENES FROM ISOLATION

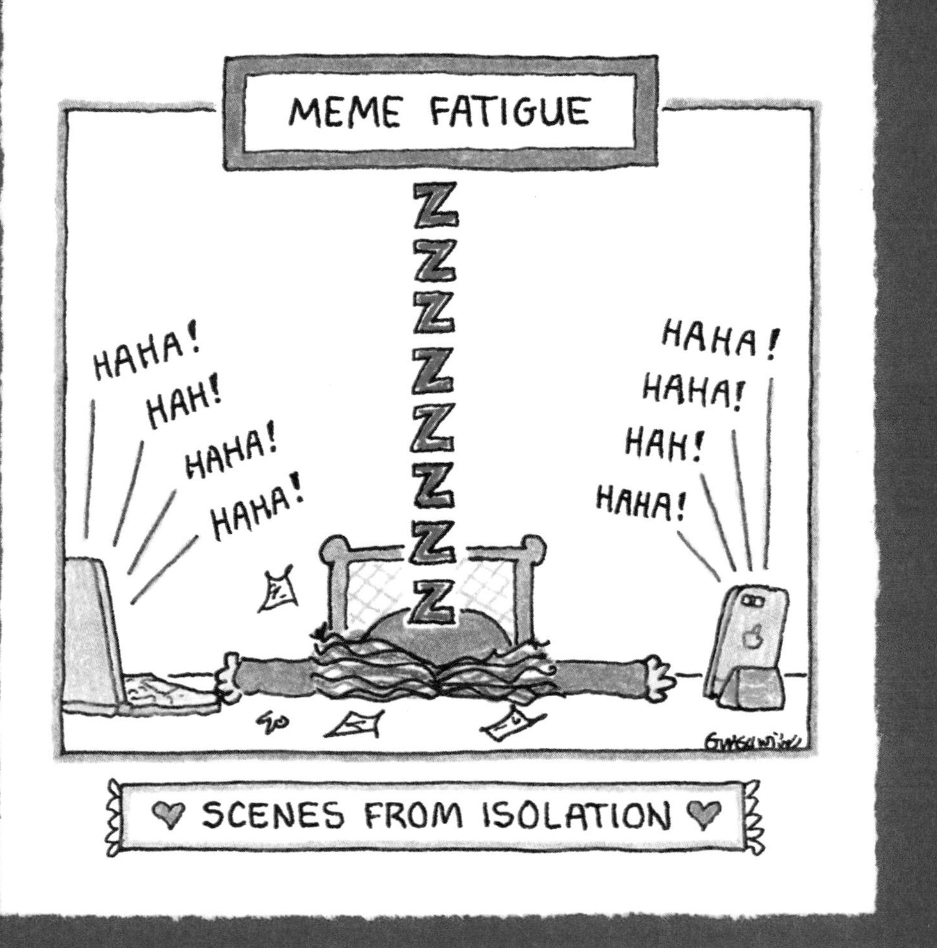
MEME FATIGUE
ZZZZZZZZ
HAHA!
HAH!
HAHA!
HAHA!
HAHA!
HAHA!
HAH!
HAHA!
SCENES FROM ISOLATION

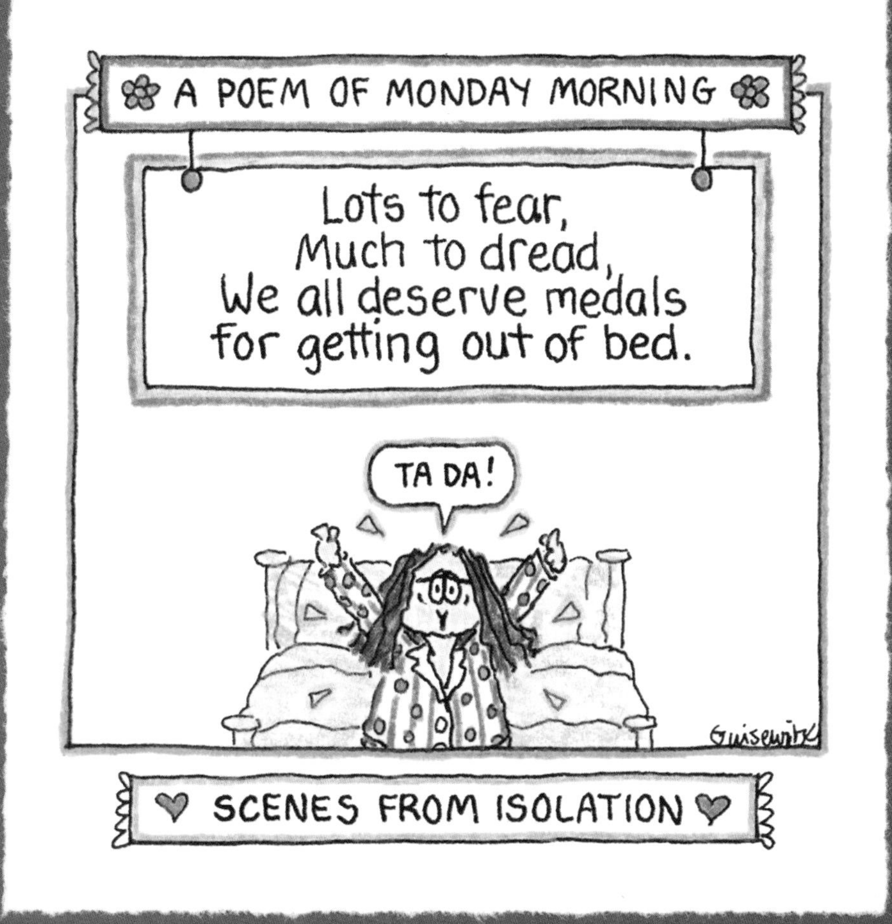
A POEM OF MONDAY MORNING
Lots to fear,
Much to dread,
We all deserve medals
for getting out of bed.
TA DA!
Guisewite
SCENES FROM ISOLATION

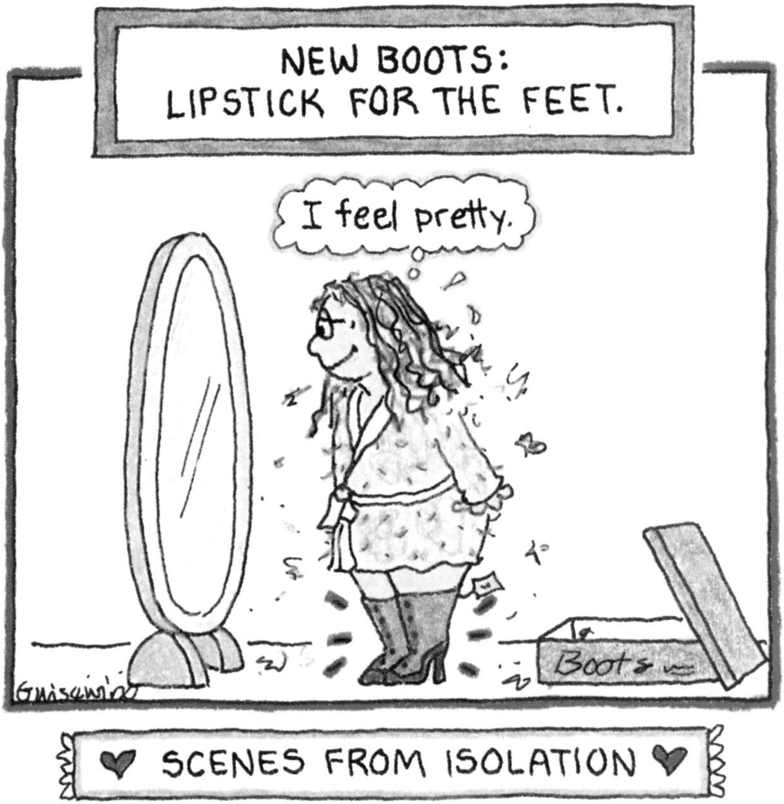
NEW BOOTS:
LIPSTICK FOR THE FEET.
I feel pretty.
Boots
SCENES FROM ISOLATION

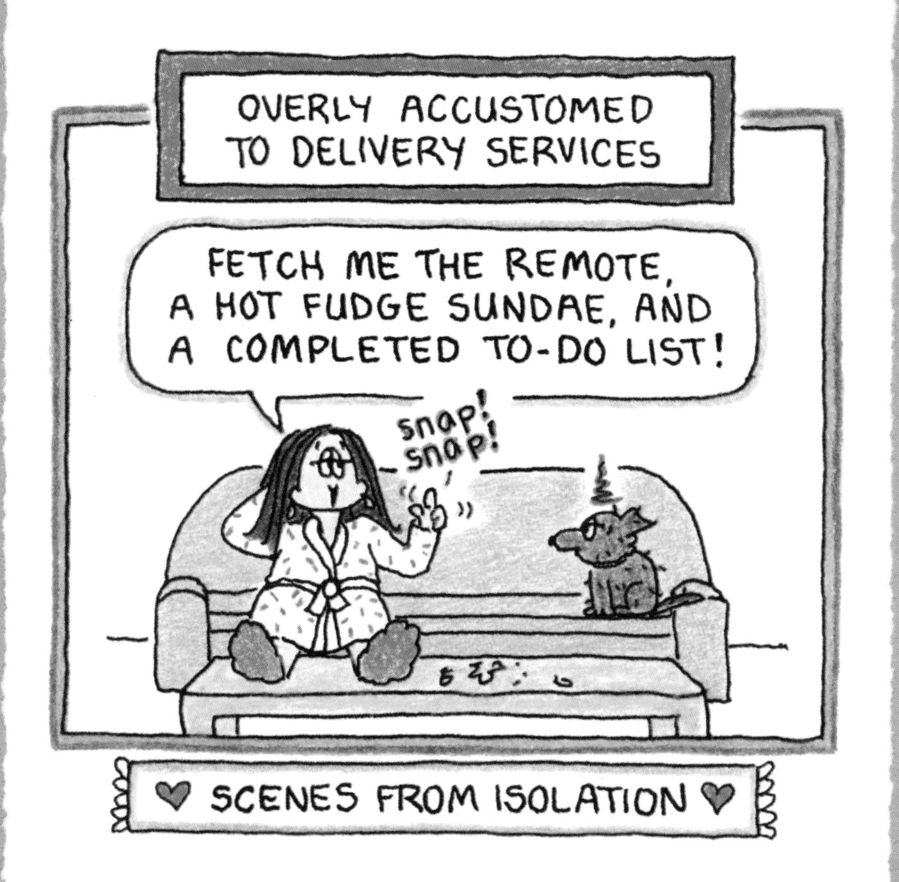
OVERLY ACCUSTOMED TO DELIVERY SERVICES
FETCH ME THE REMOTE, A HOT FUDGE SUNDAE, AND A COMPLETED TO-DO LIST!
snap! snap!
SCENES FROM ISOLATION

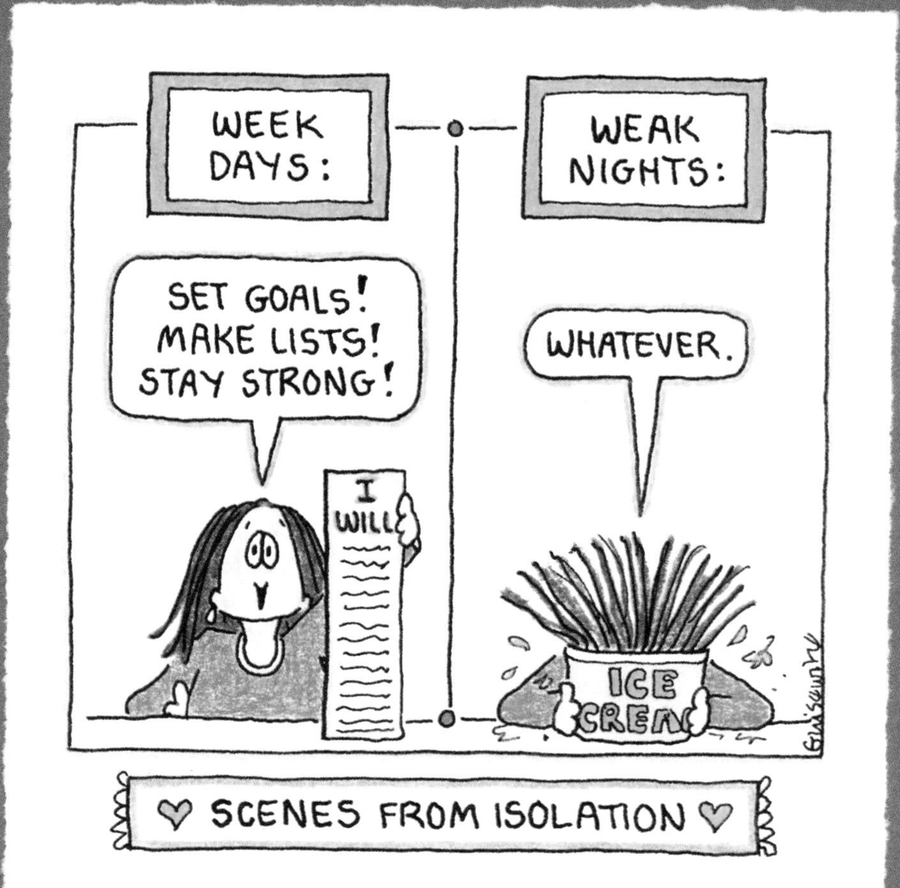
WEEK DAYS:
WEAK NIGHTS:
SET GOALS! MAKE LISTS! STAY STRONG!
I WILL
WHATEVER.
ICE CREA
SCENES FROM ISOLATION

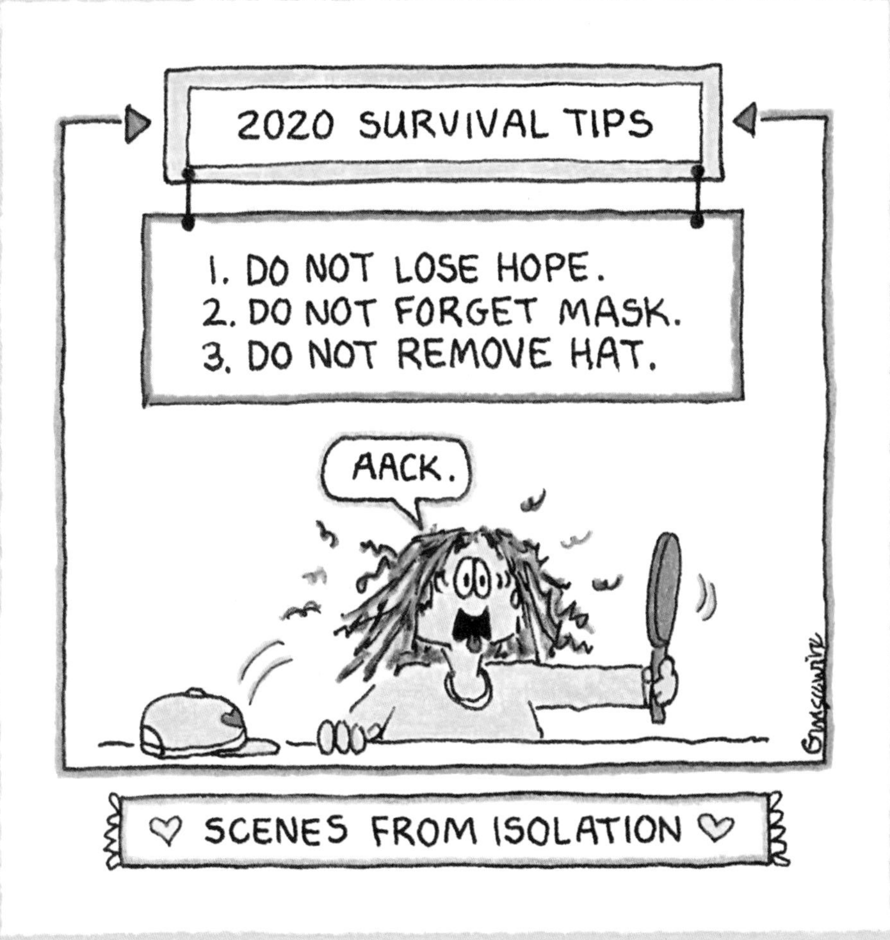
2020 SURVIVAL TIPS
1. DO NOT LOSE HOPE.
2. DO NOT FORGET MASK.
3. DO NOT REMOVE HAT.
AACK.
♡ SCENES FROM ISOLATION ♡

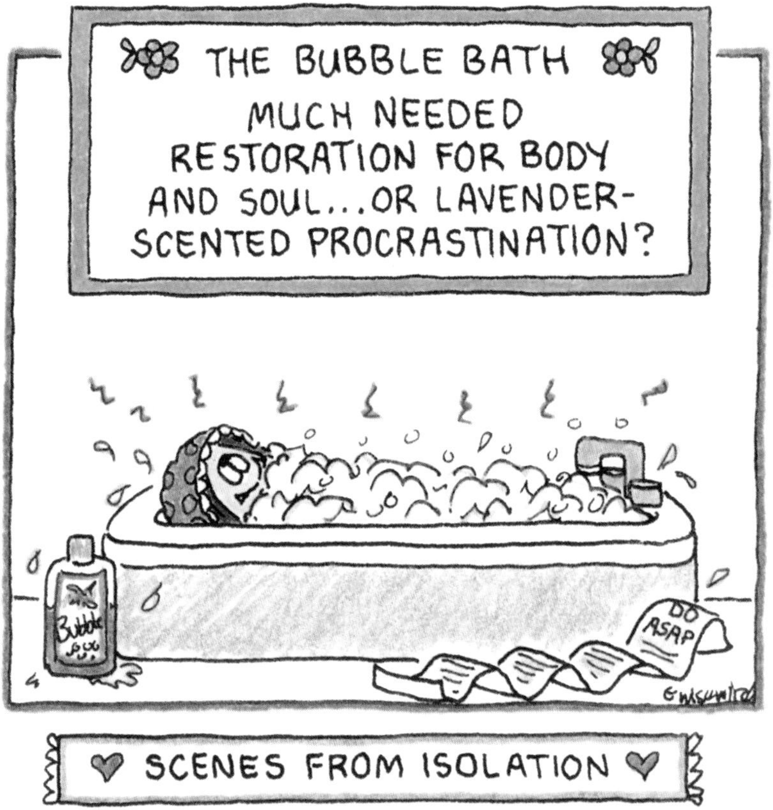
THE BUBBLE BATH
MUCH NEEDED RESTORATION FOR BODY AND SOUL...OR LAVENDER-SCENTED PROCRASTINATION?
Bubble
DO ASAP
SCENES FROM ISOLATION

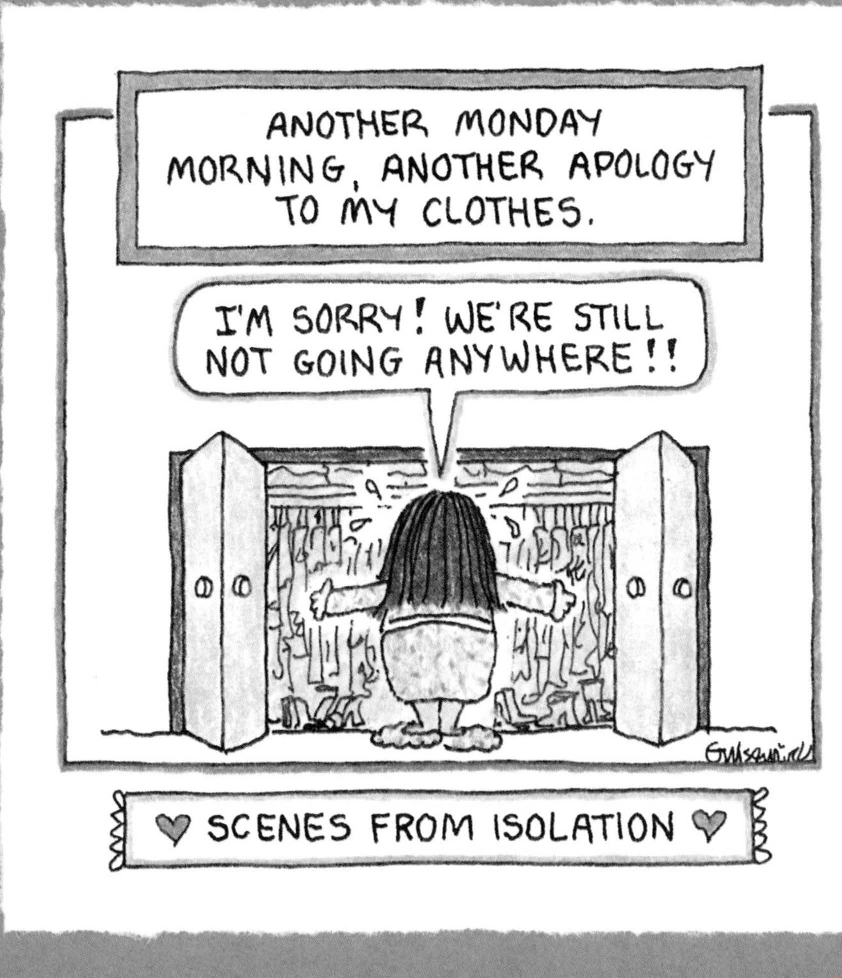
ANOTHER MONDAY MORNING, ANOTHER APOLOGY TO MY CLOTHES.
I'M SORRY! WE'RE STILL NOT GOING ANYWHERE!!
SCENES FROM ISOLATION

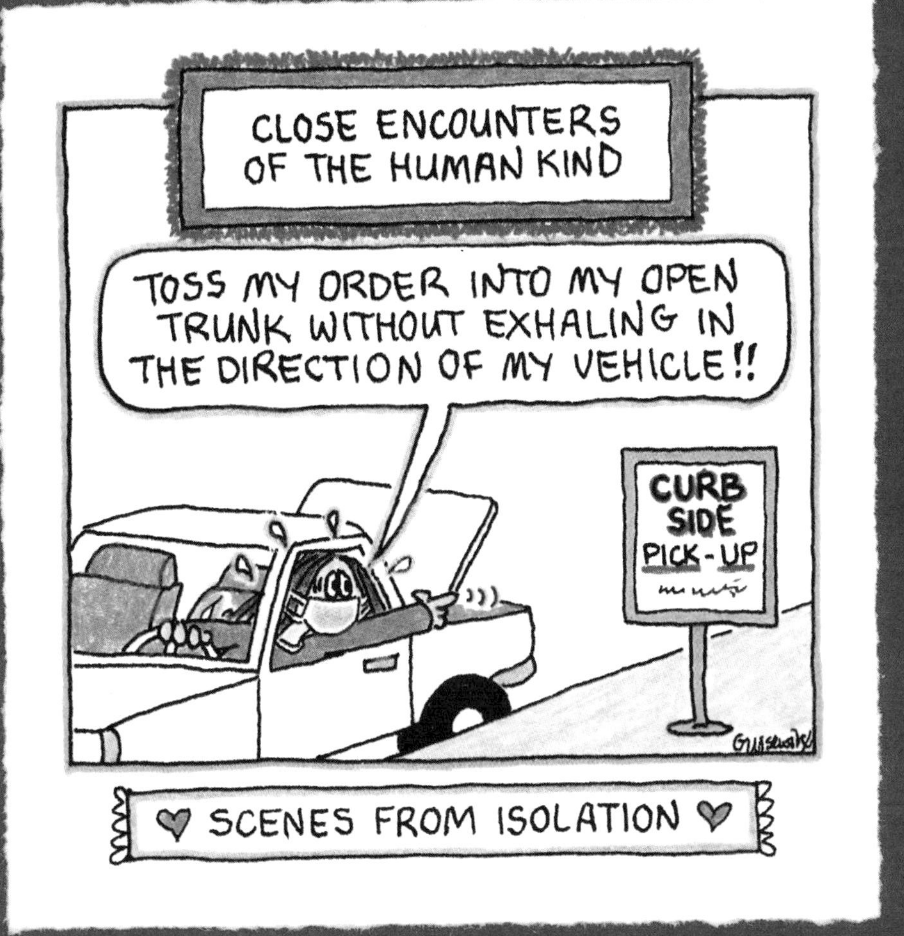
CLOSE ENCOUNTERS OF THE HUMAN KIND
TOSS MY ORDER INTO MY OPEN TRUNK WITHOUT EXHALING IN THE DIRECTION OF MY VEHICLE!!
CURB SIDE PICK-UP
SCENES FROM ISOLATION

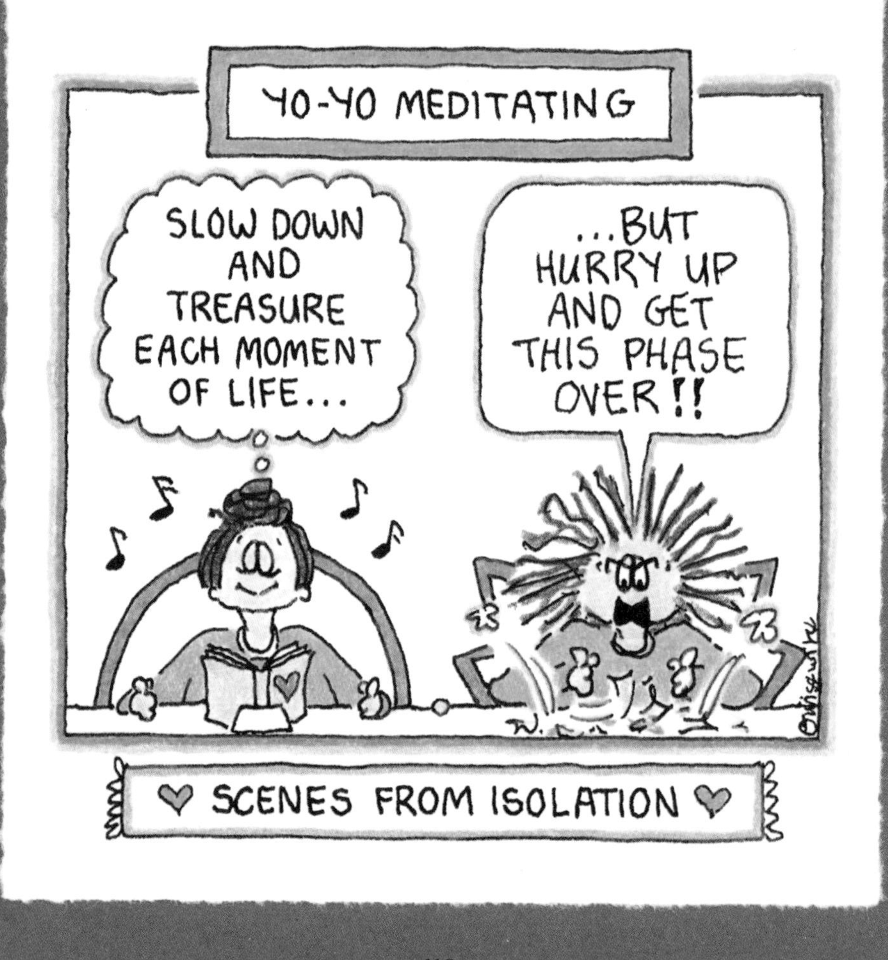
YO-YO MEDITATING
SLOW DOWN AND TREASURE EACH MOMENT OF LIFE...
...BUT HURRY UP AND GET THIS PHASE OVER!!
SCENES FROM ISOLATION

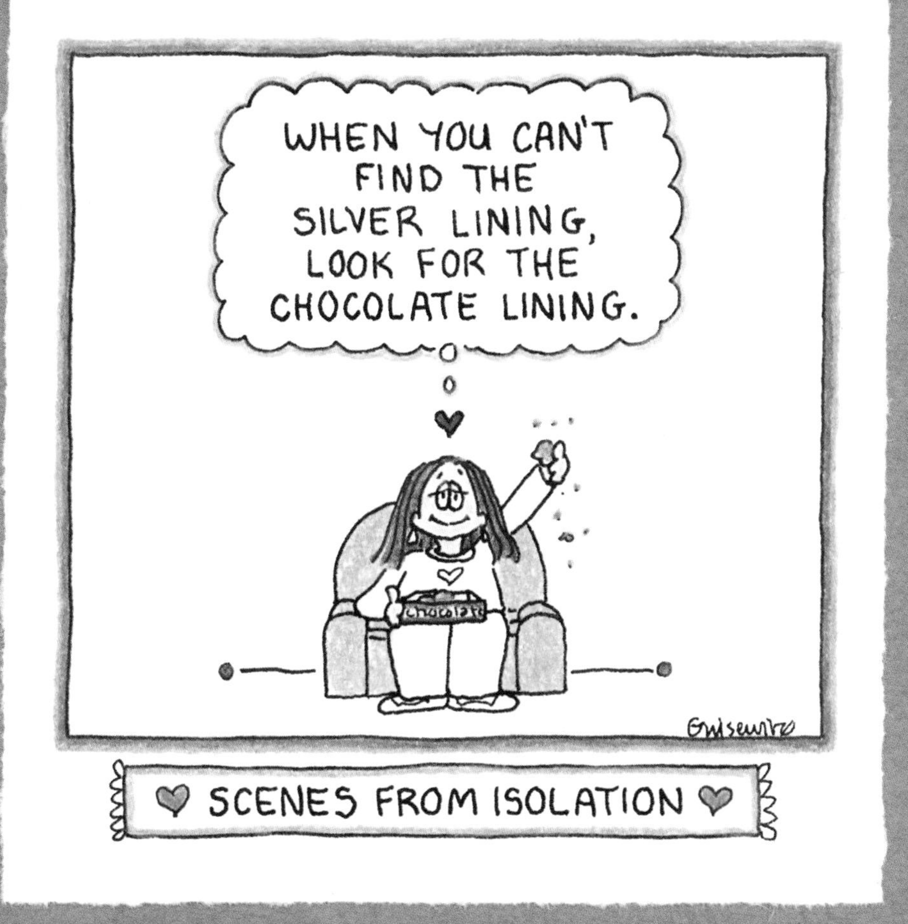
WHEN YOU CAN'T FIND THE SILVER LINING, LOOK FOR THE CHOCOLATE LINING.
CHOCOLATE
SCENES FROM ISOLATION

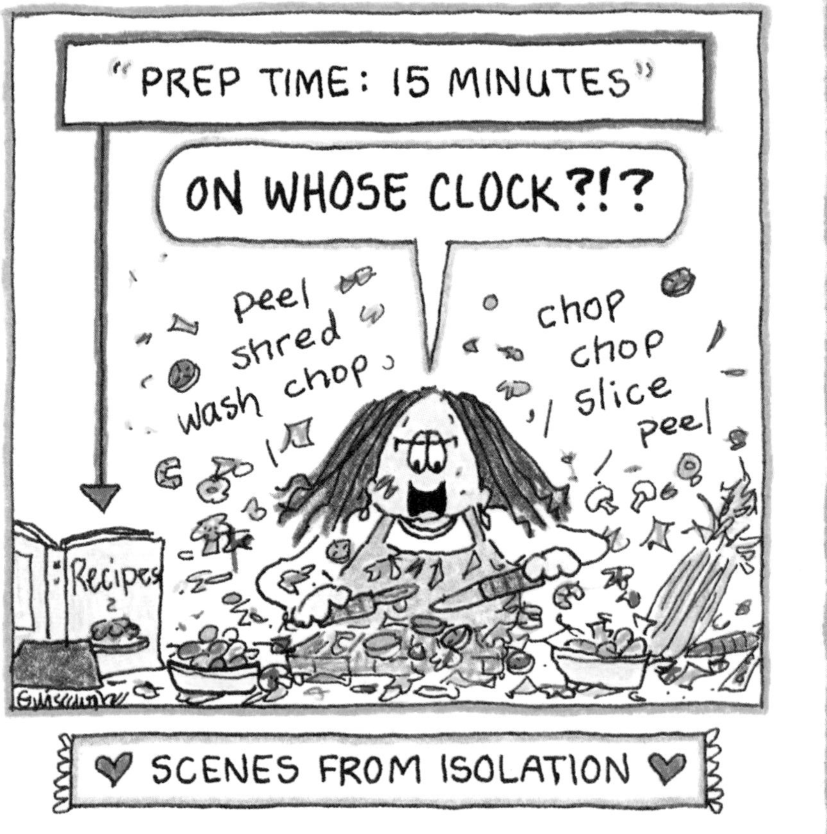
"PREP TIME: 15 MINUTES"
ON WHOSE CLOCK?!?
peel
shred
wash chop
chop
chop
slice
peel
Recipes
SCENES FROM ISOLATION

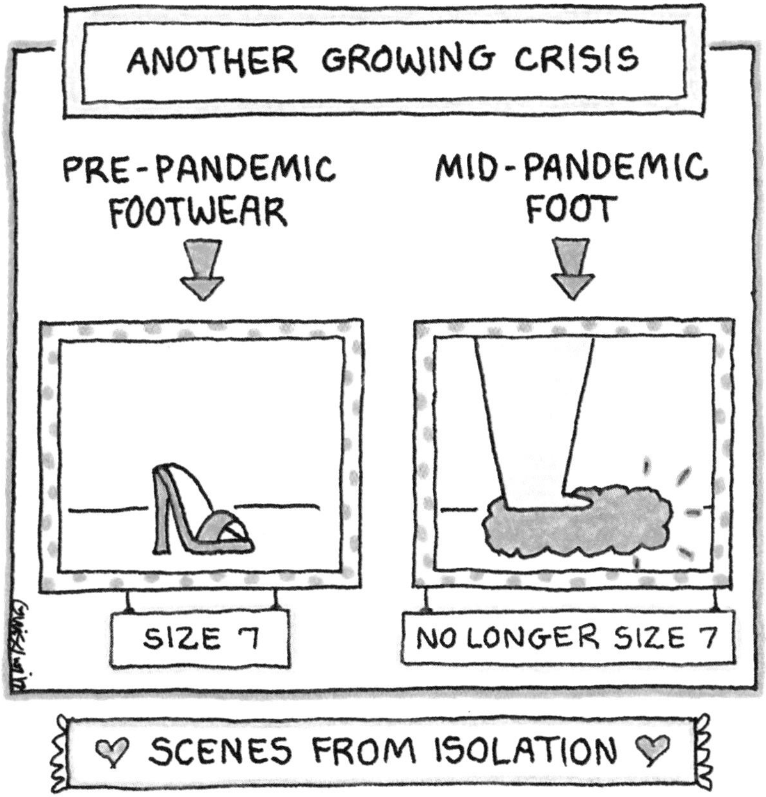
ANOTHER GROWING CRISIS
PRE-PANDEMIC FOOTWEAR
MID-PANDEMIC FOOT
SIZE 7
NO LONGER SIZE 7
SCENES FROM ISOLATION

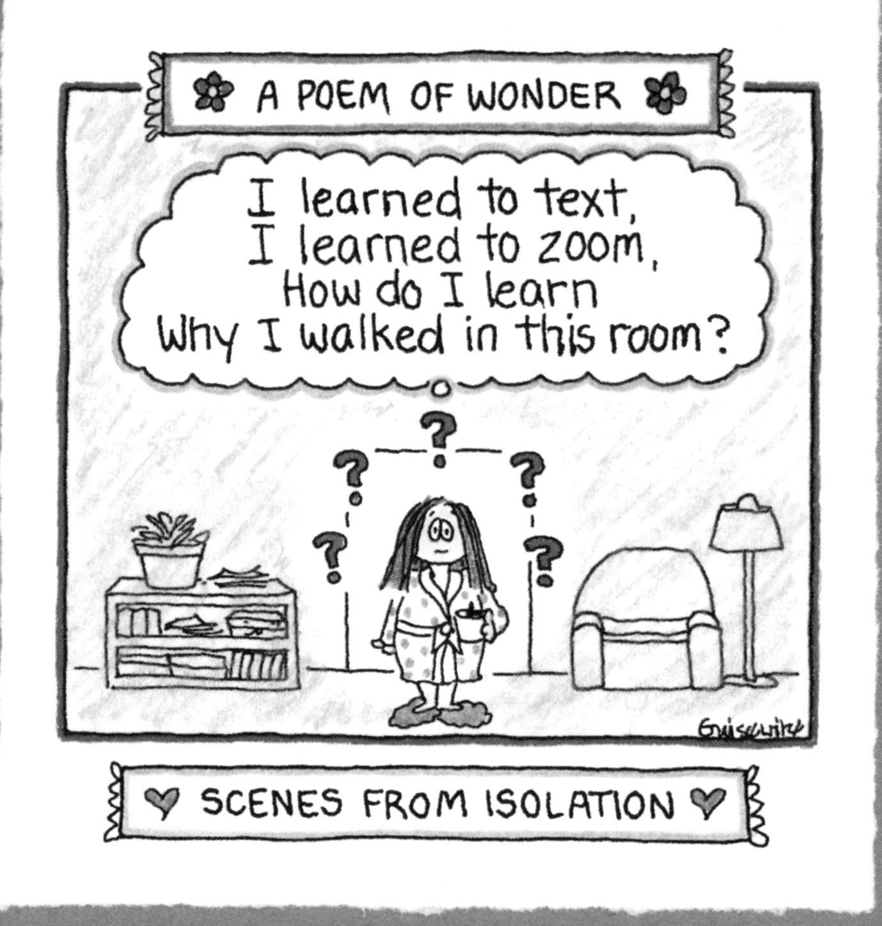
A POEM OF WONDER
I learned to text,
I learned to zoom,
How do I learn
Why I walked in this room?
SCENES FROM ISOLATION

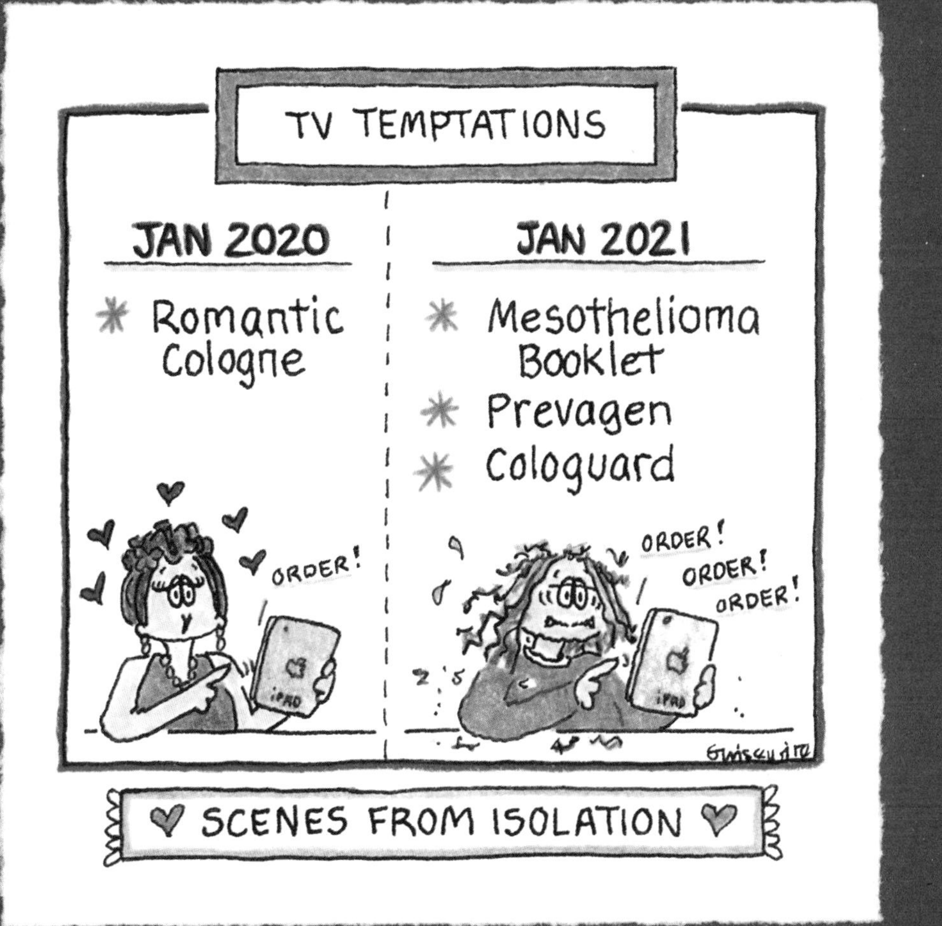

TV TEMPTATIONS
JAN 2020
* Romantic Cologne
ORDER!
JAN 2021
* Mesothelioma Booklet
* Prevagen
* Cologuard
ORDER!
ORDER!
ORDER!
SCENES FROM ISOLATION

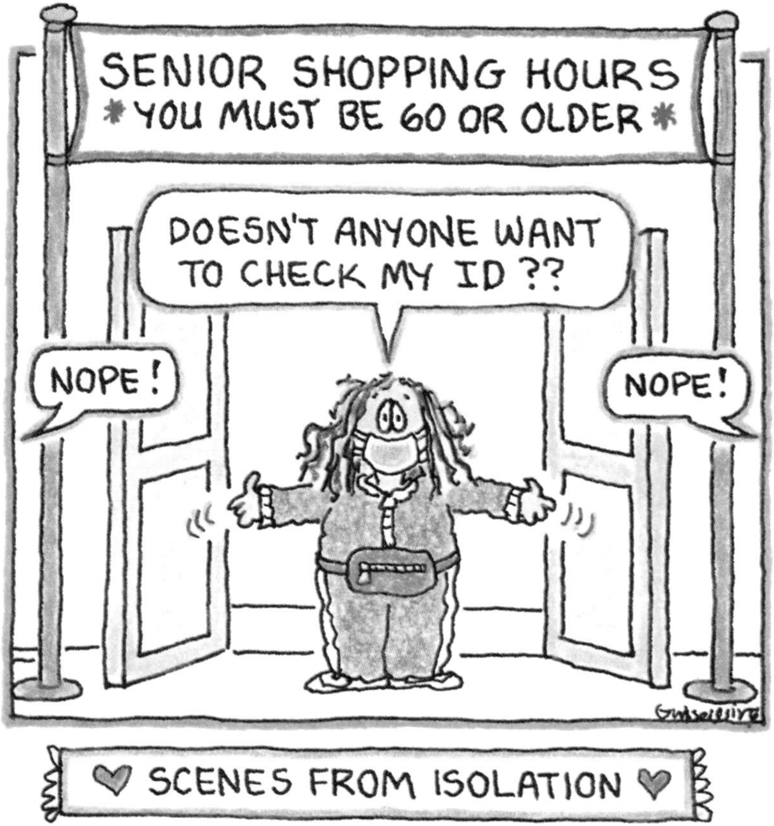
SENIOR SHOPPING HOURS
* YOU MUST BE 60 OR OLDER *
DOESN'T ANYONE WANT TO CHECK MY ID ??
NOPE!
NOPE!
SCENES FROM ISOLATION

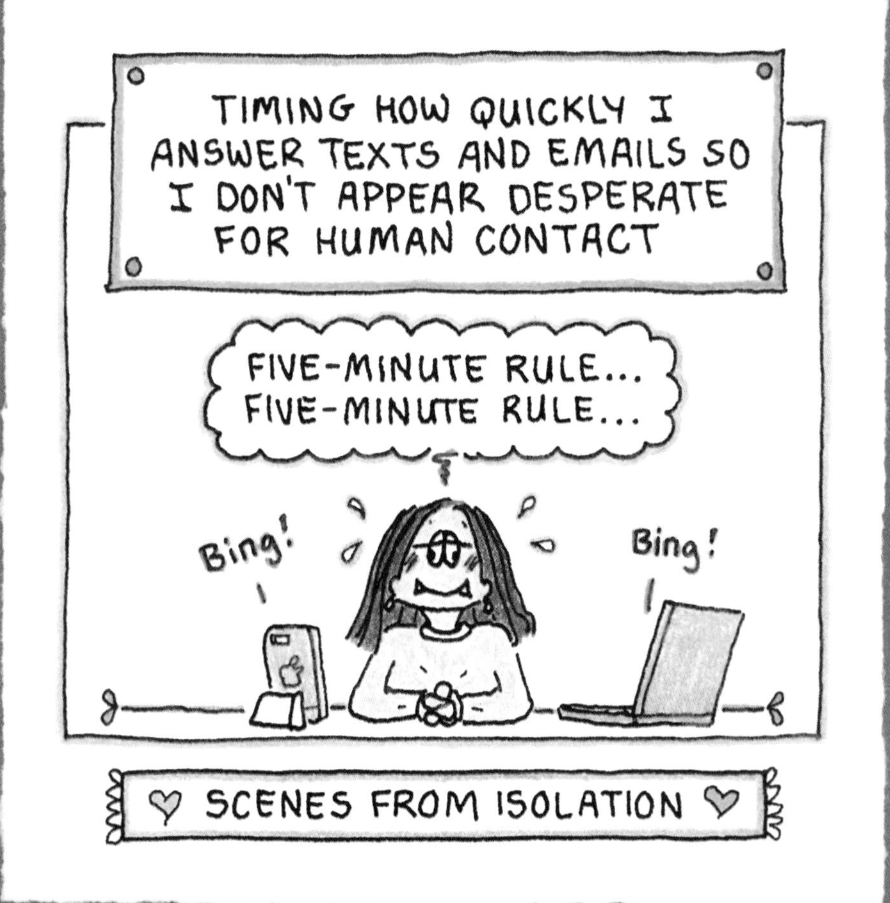
TIMING HOW QUICKLY I ANSWER TEXTS AND EMAILS SO I DON'T APPEAR DESPERATE FOR HUMAN CONTACT
FIVE-MINUTE RULE... FIVE-MINUTE RULE...
Bing!
Bing!
SCENES FROM ISOLATION

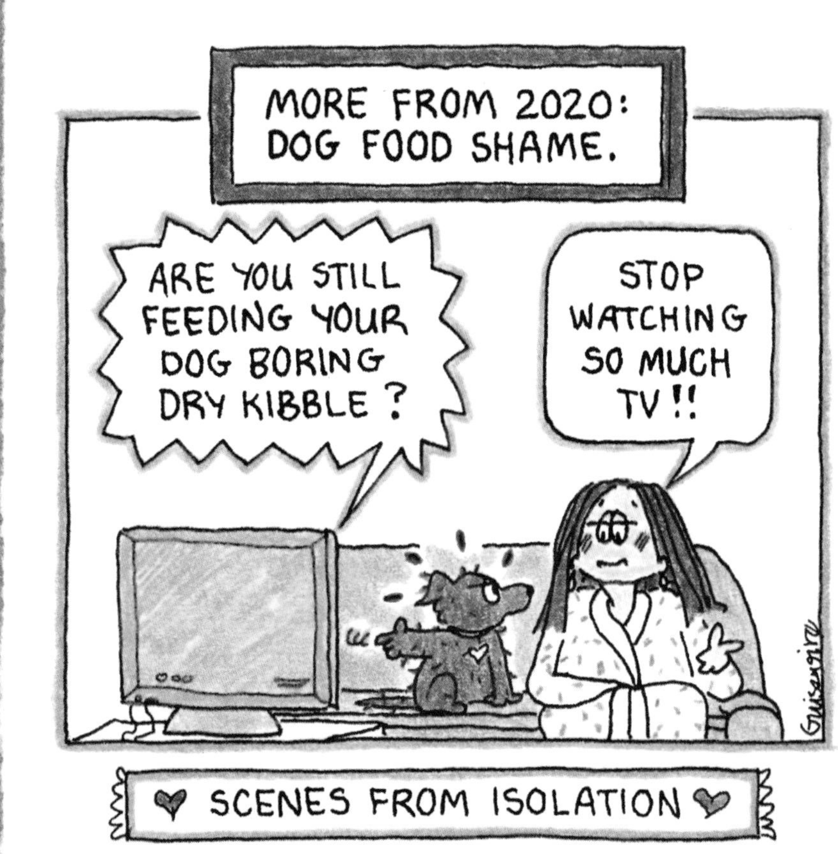
MORE FROM 2020:
DOG FOOD SHAME.
ARE YOU STILL FEEDING YOUR DOG BORING DRY KIBBLE?
STOP WATCHING SO MUCH TV!!
SCENES FROM ISOLATION

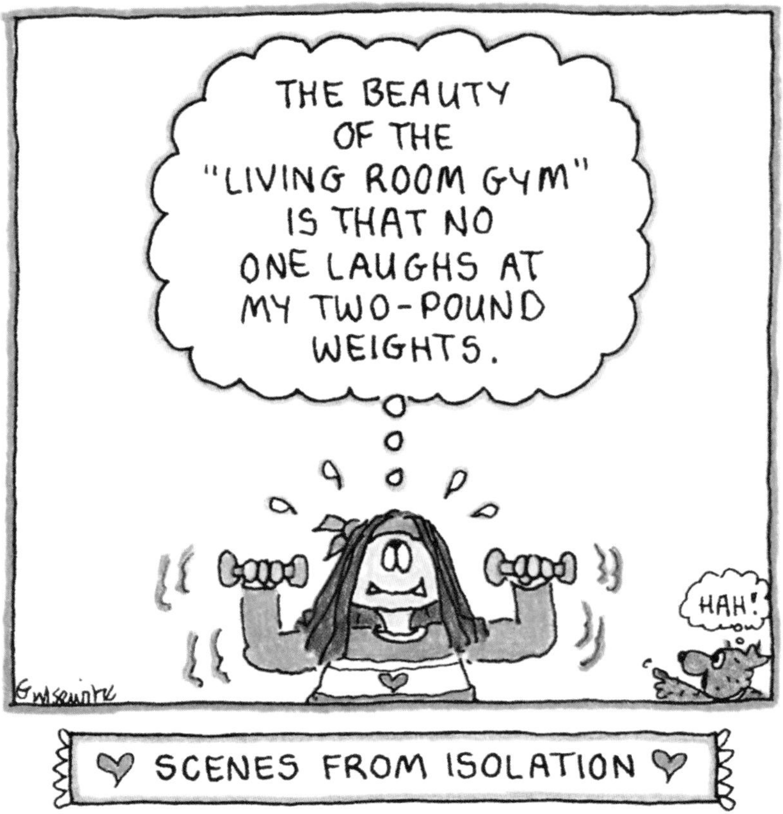
THE BEAUTY OF THE "LIVING ROOM GYM" IS THAT NO ONE LAUGHS AT MY TWO-POUND WEIGHTS.
HAH!
SCENES FROM ISOLATION

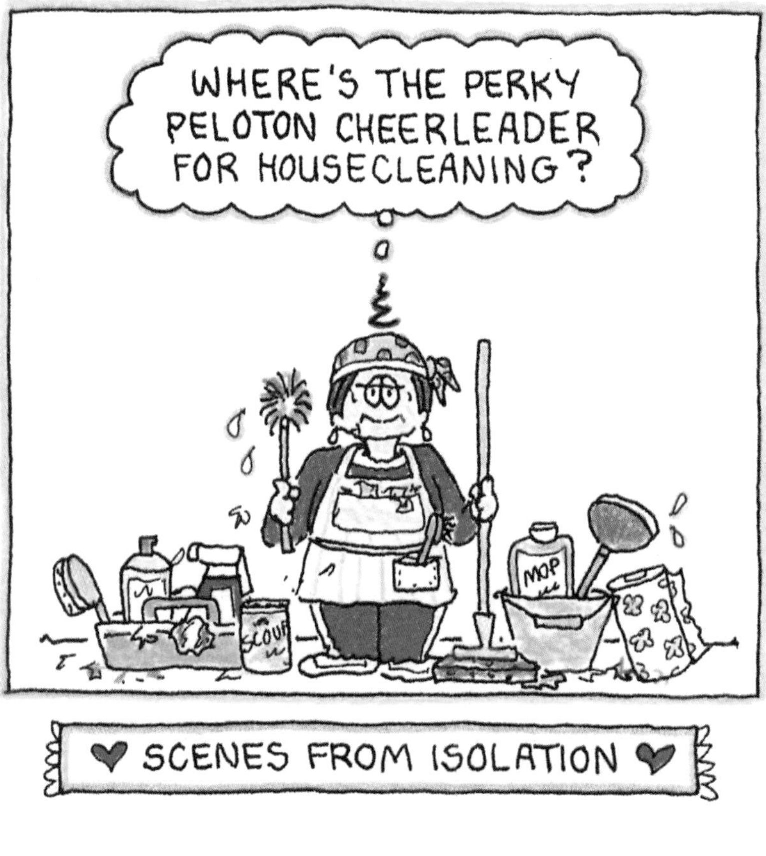
WHERE'S THE PERKY PELOTON CHEERLEADER FOR HOUSECLEANING?
SCOUR
MOP
SCENES FROM ISOLATION

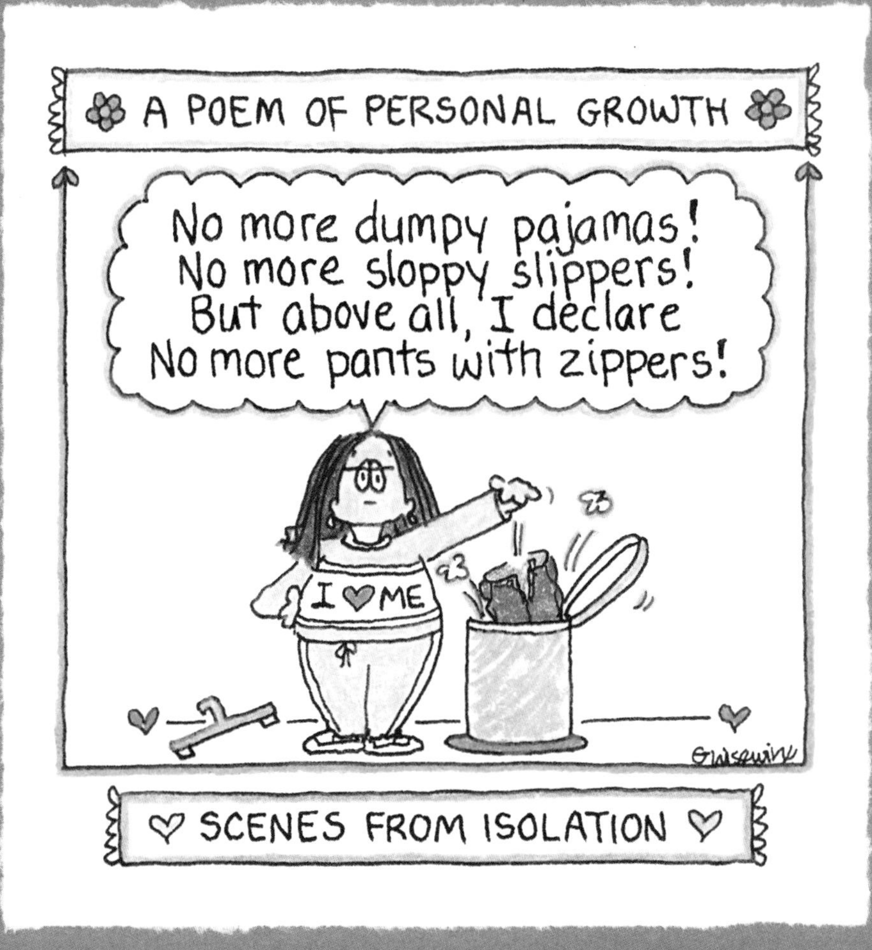
A POEM OF PERSONAL GROWTH
No more dumpy pajamas!
No more sloppy slippers!
But above all, I declare
No more pants with zippers!
I ♥ ME
SCENES FROM ISOLATION

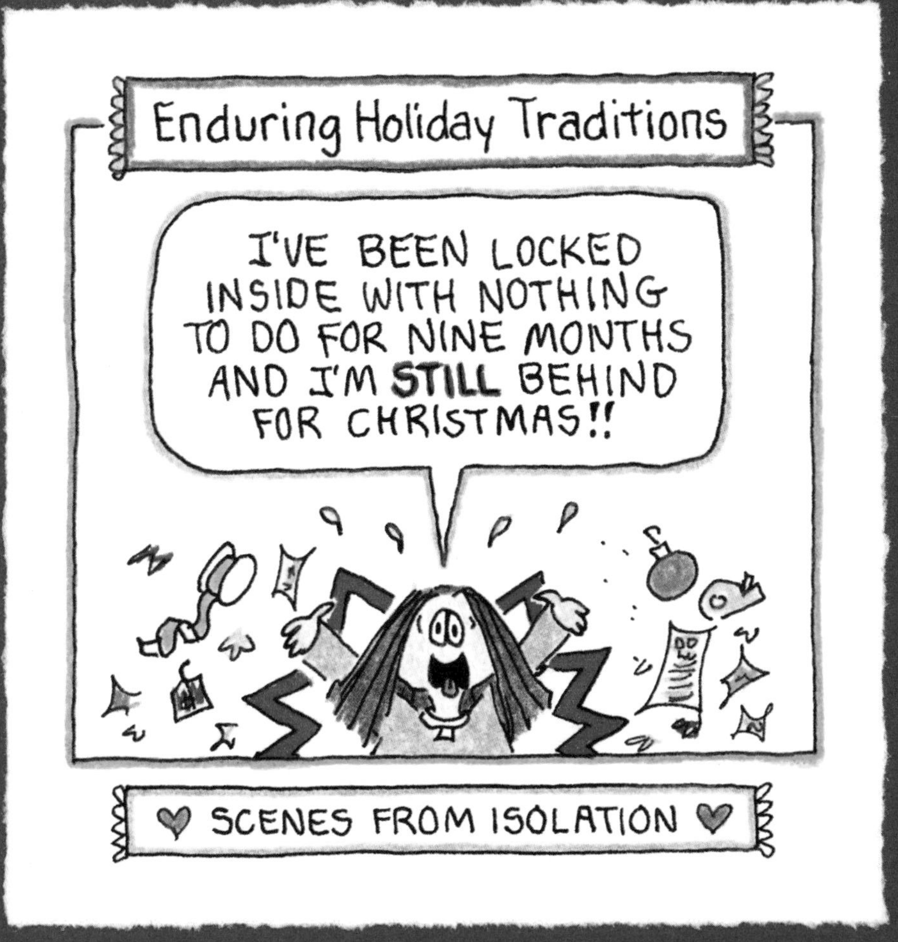
Enduring Holiday Traditions
I'VE BEEN LOCKED INSIDE WITH NOTHING TO DO FOR NINE MONTHS AND I'M STILL BEHIND FOR CHRISTMAS!!
SCENES FROM ISOLATION

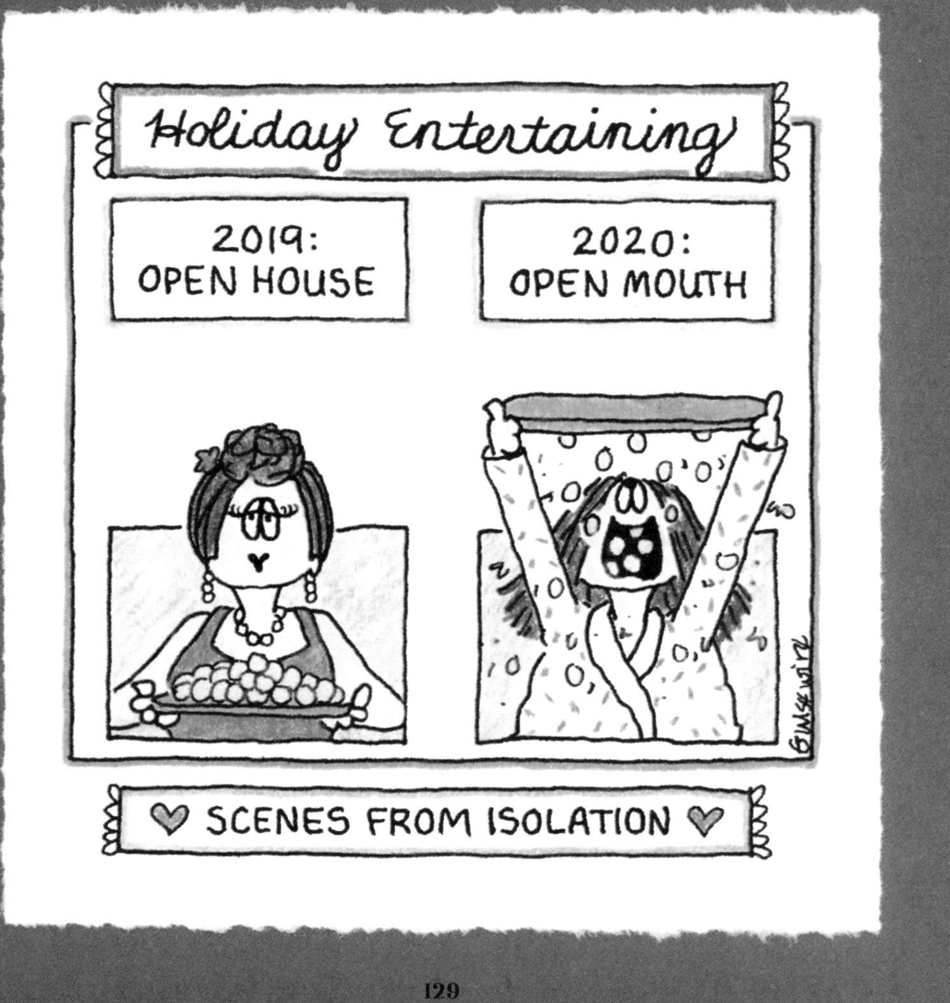
Holiday Entertaining
2019:
OPEN HOUSE
2020:
OPEN MOUTH
GINSBURG
SCENES FROM ISOLATION

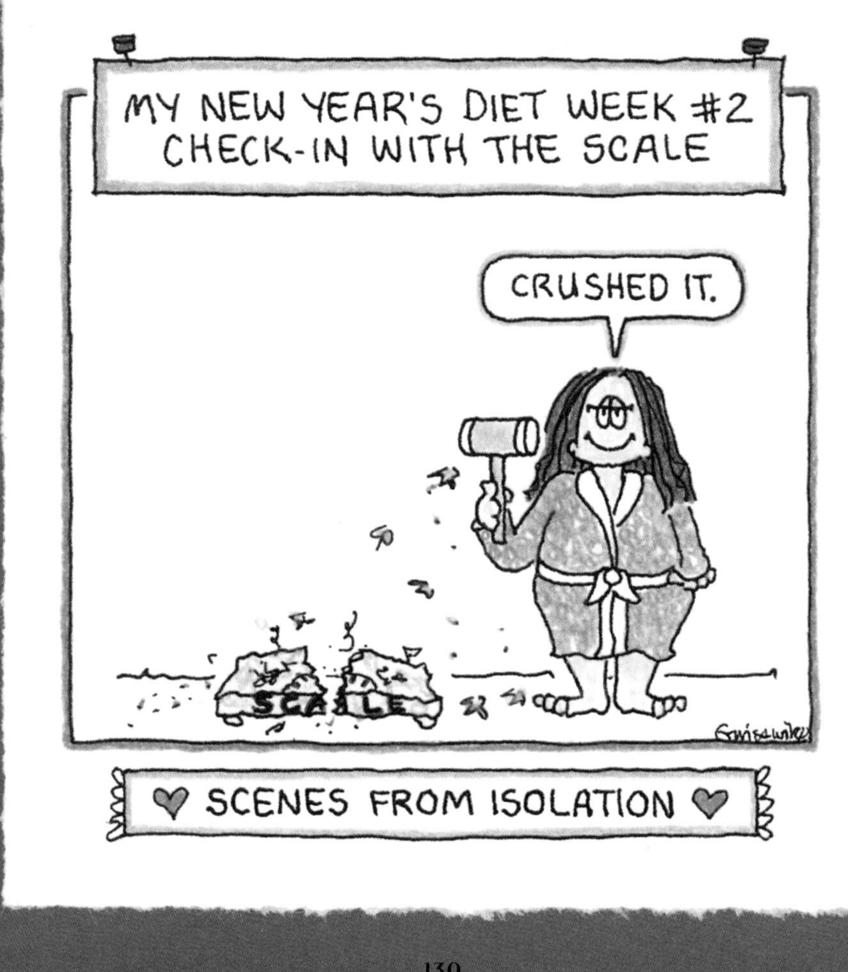
MY NEW YEAR'S DIET WEEK #2
CHECK-IN WITH THE SCALE
CRUSHED IT.
SCALE
SCENES FROM ISOLATION

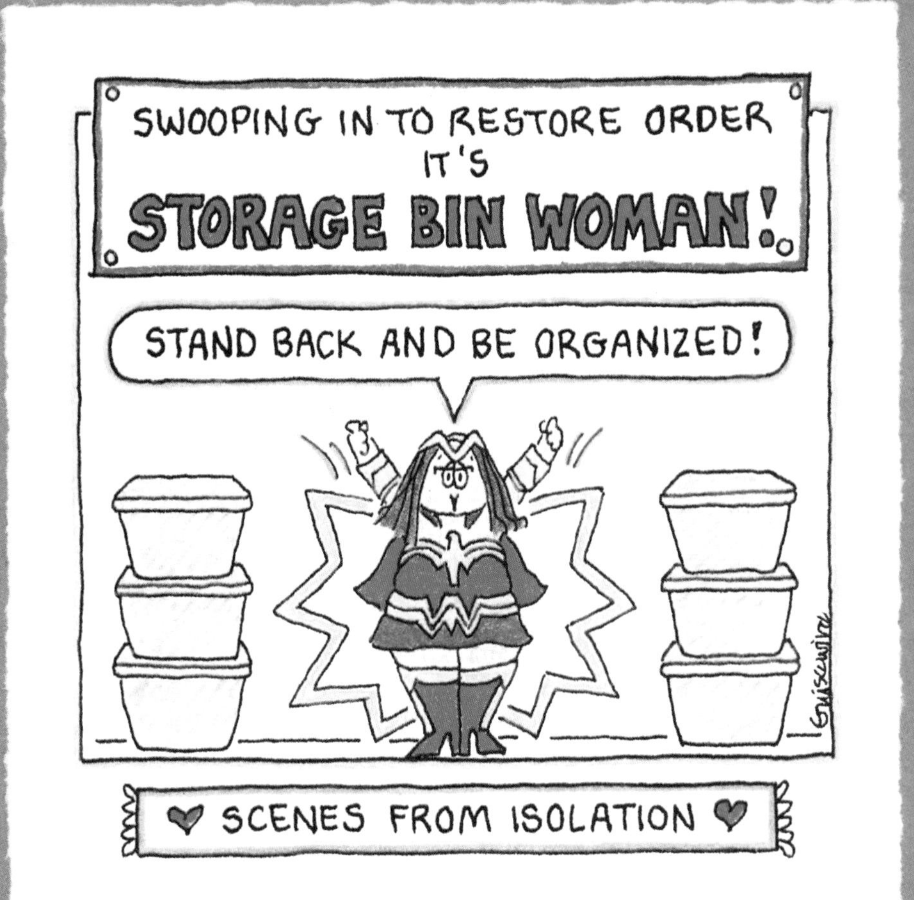
SWOOPING IN TO RESTORE ORDER
IT'S
STORAGE BIN WOMAN!
STAND BACK AND BE ORGANIZED!
SCENES FROM ISOLATION

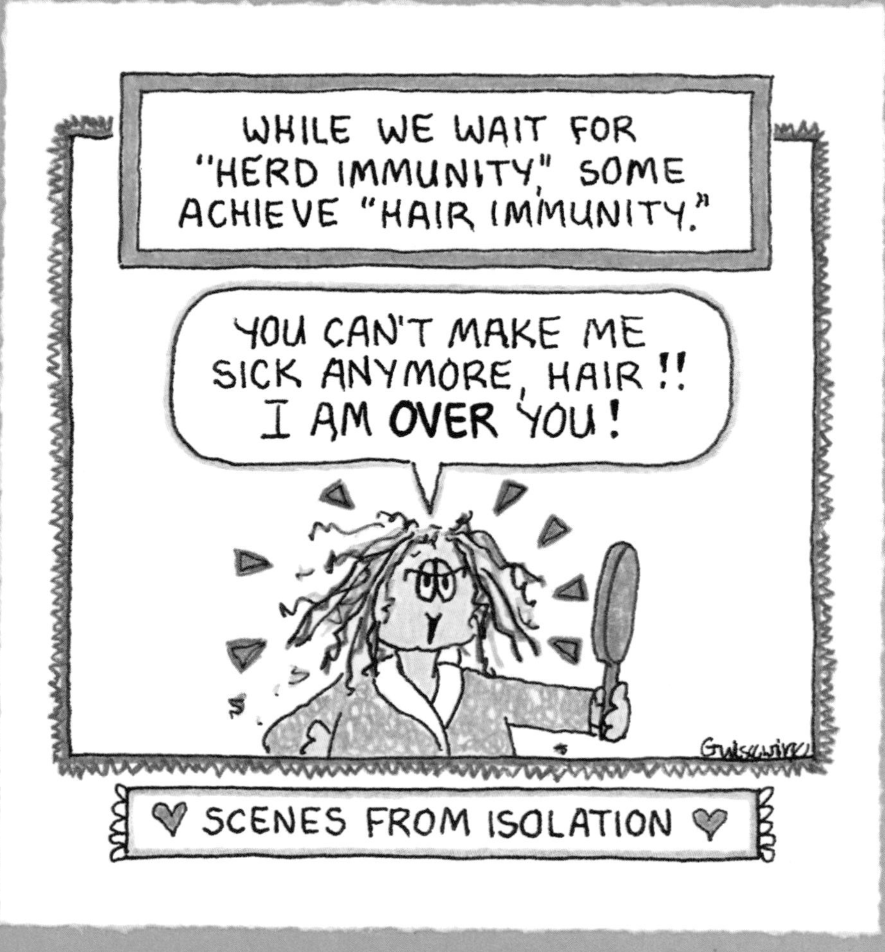
WHILE WE WAIT FOR "HERD IMMUNITY," SOME ACHIEVE "HAIR IMMUNITY."
YOU CAN'T MAKE ME SICK ANYMORE, HAIR!! I AM **OVER** YOU!
SCENES FROM ISOLATION

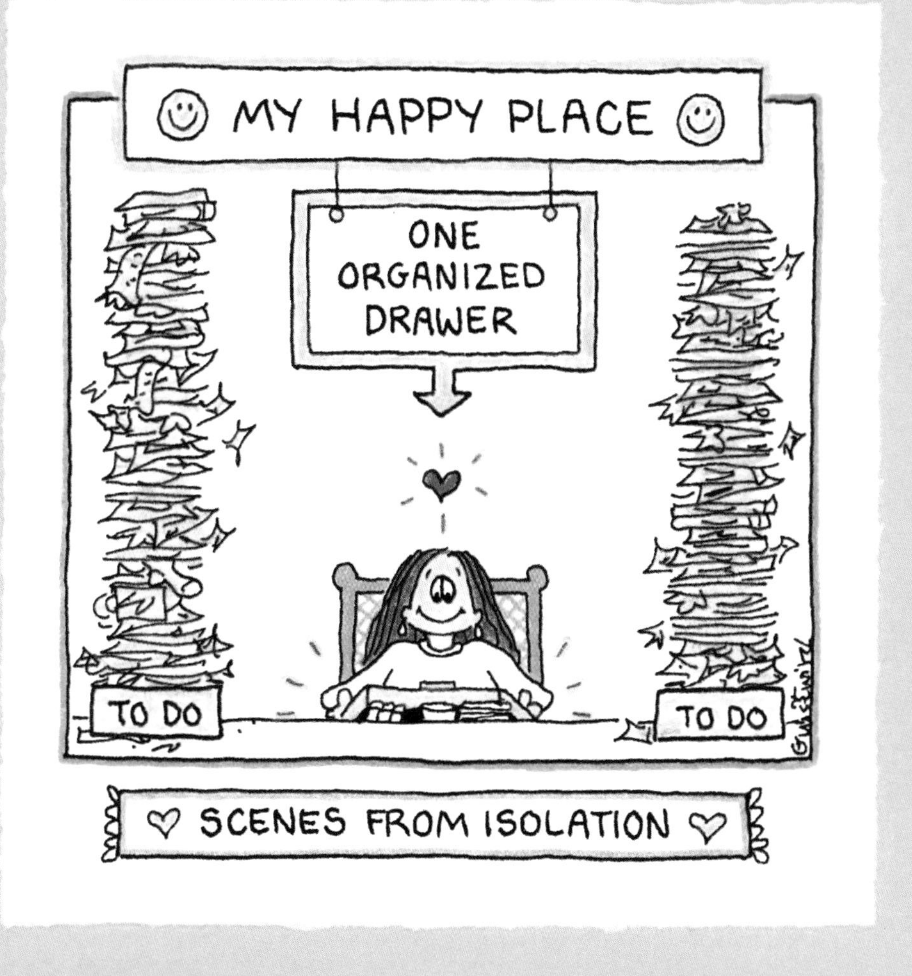
MY HAPPY PLACE
ONE ORGANIZED DRAWER
TO DO
TO DO
SCENES FROM ISOLATION

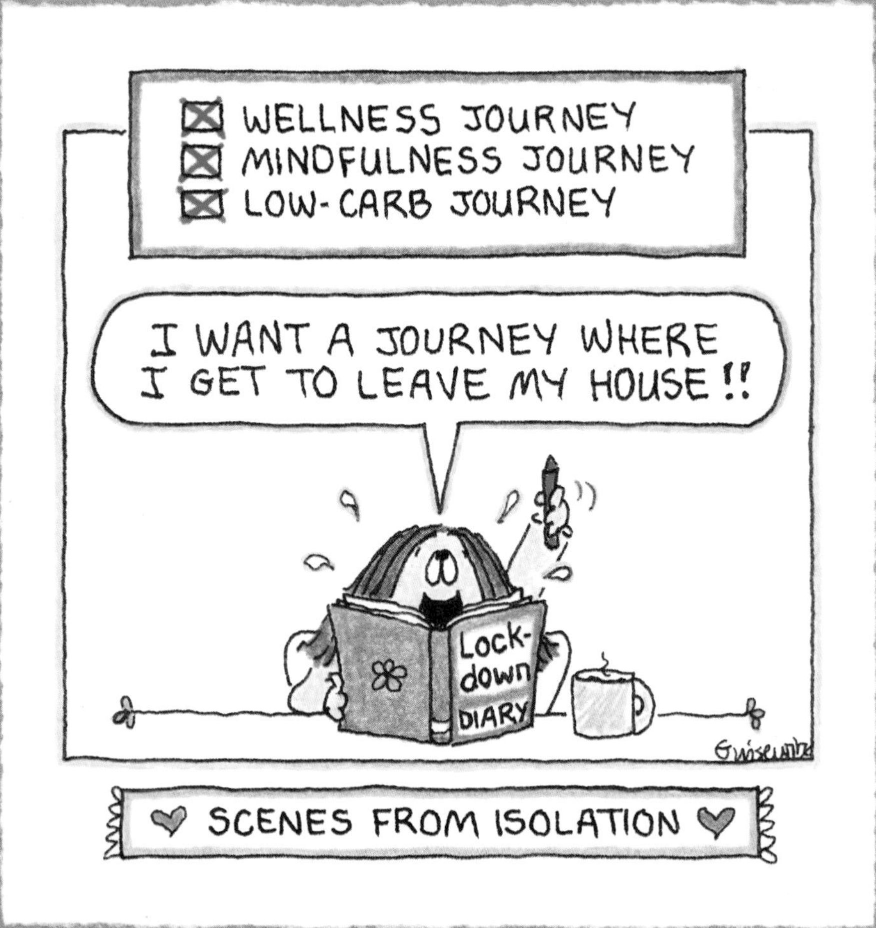
WELLNESS JOURNEY
MINDFULNESS JOURNEY
LOW-CARB JOURNEY
I WANT A JOURNEY WHERE I GET TO LEAVE MY HOUSE!!
Lock-down DIARY
SCENES FROM ISOLATION

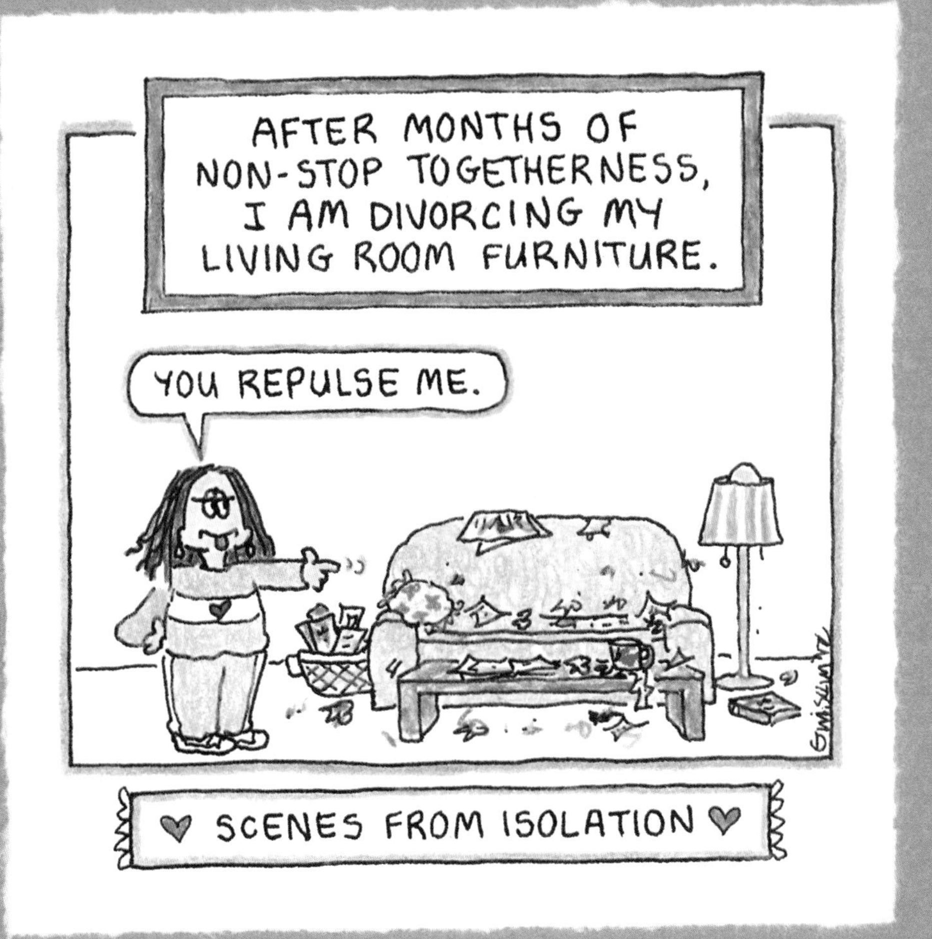
AFTER MONTHS OF NON-STOP TOGETHERNESS, I AM DIVORCING MY LIVING ROOM FURNITURE.
YOU REPULSE ME.
SCENES FROM ISOLATION

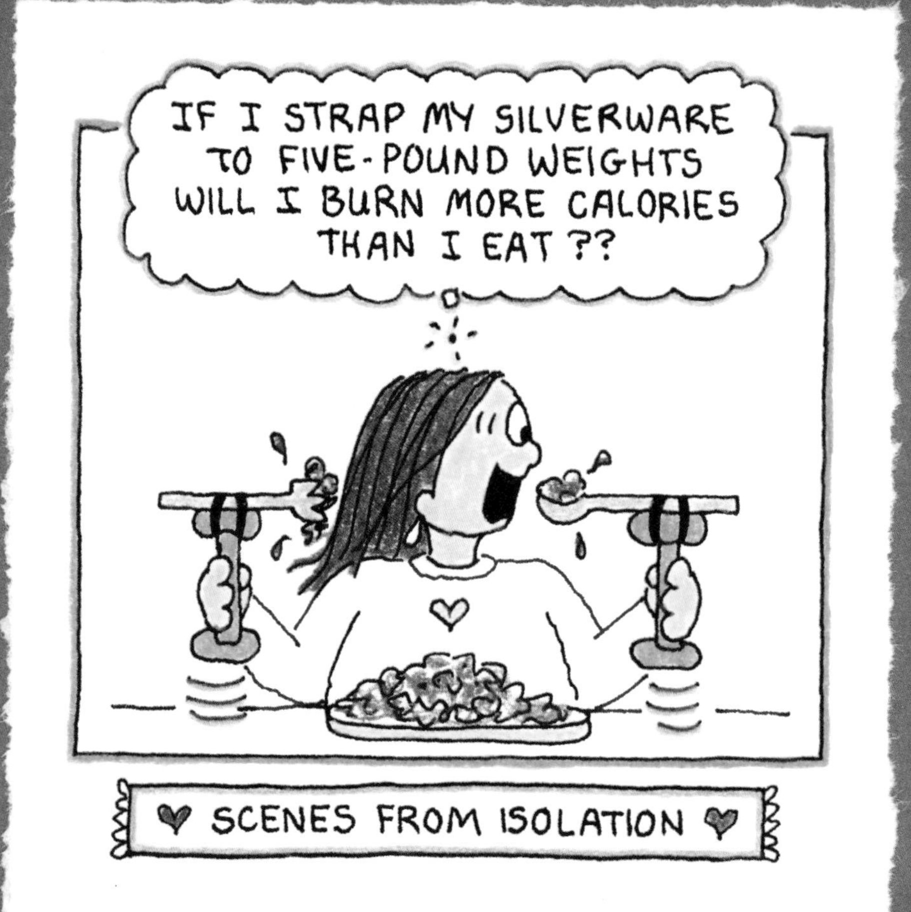
IF I STRAP MY SILVERWARE TO FIVE-POUND WEIGHTS WILL I BURN MORE CALORIES THAN I EAT ??
SCENES FROM ISOLATION

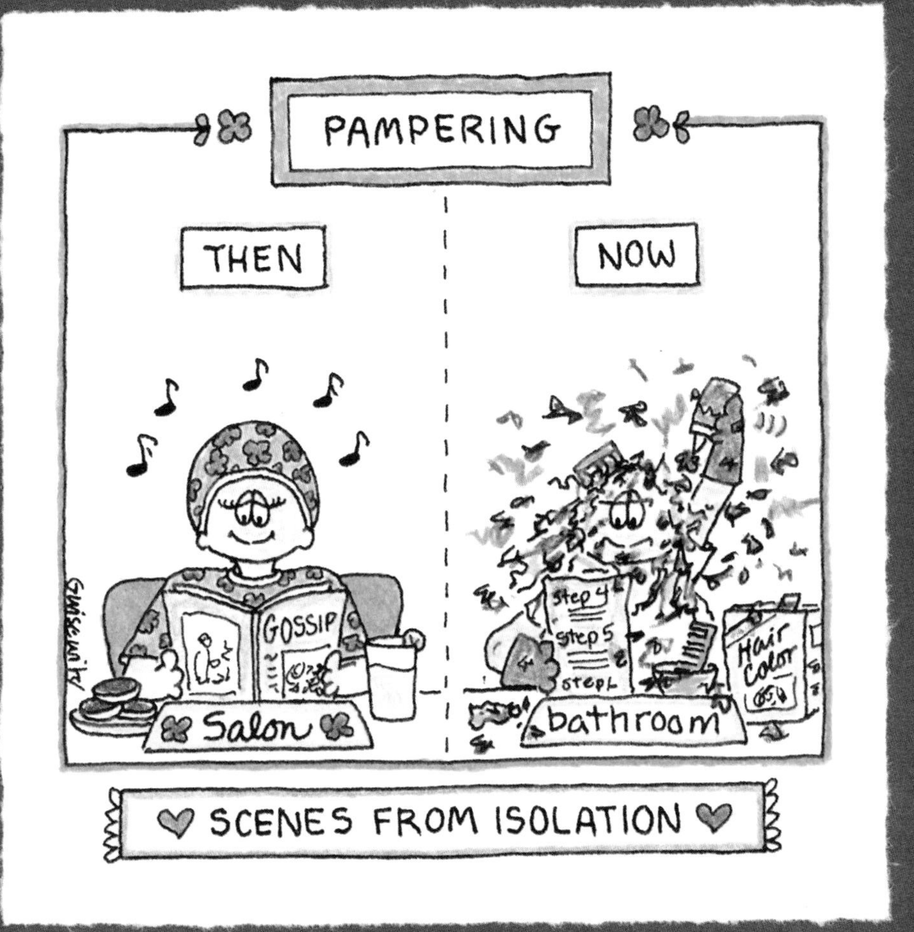

PAMPERING
THEN
NOW
GOSSIP
Salon
Step 4
Step 5
Step 1
Hair Color
bathroom
SCENES FROM ISOLATION

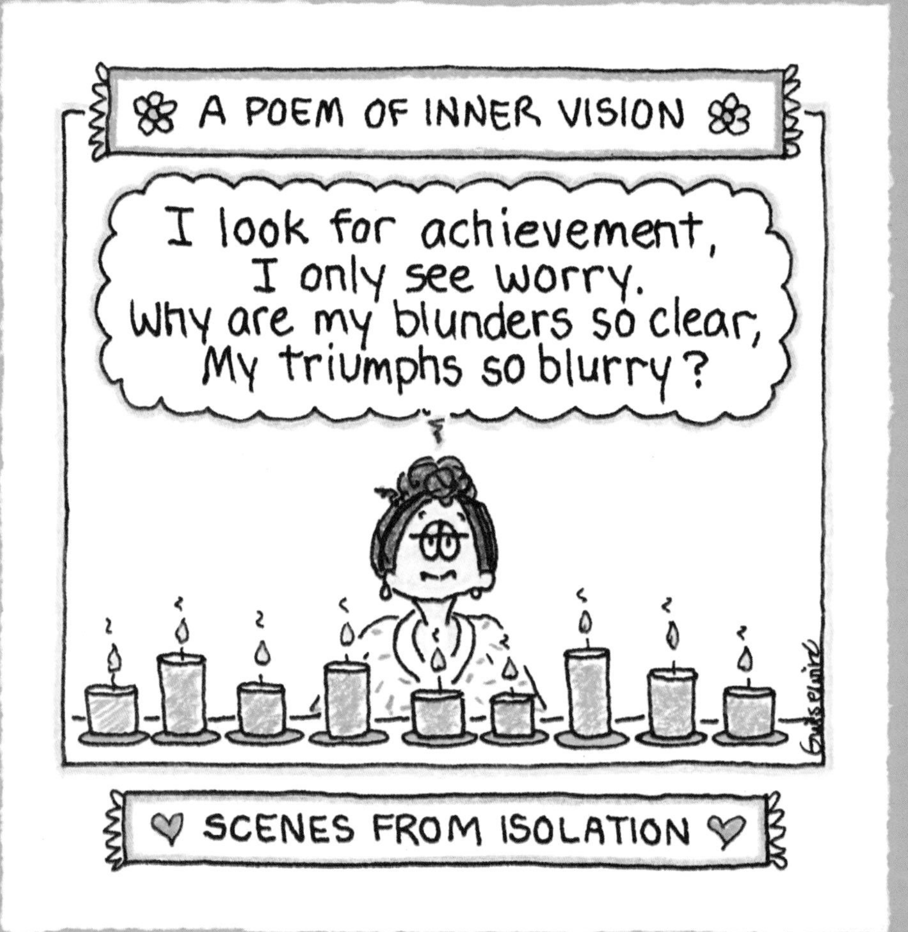
A POEM OF INNER VISION
I look for achievement, I only see worry. Why are my blunders so clear, My triumphs so blurry?
Guisewite
SCENES FROM ISOLATION

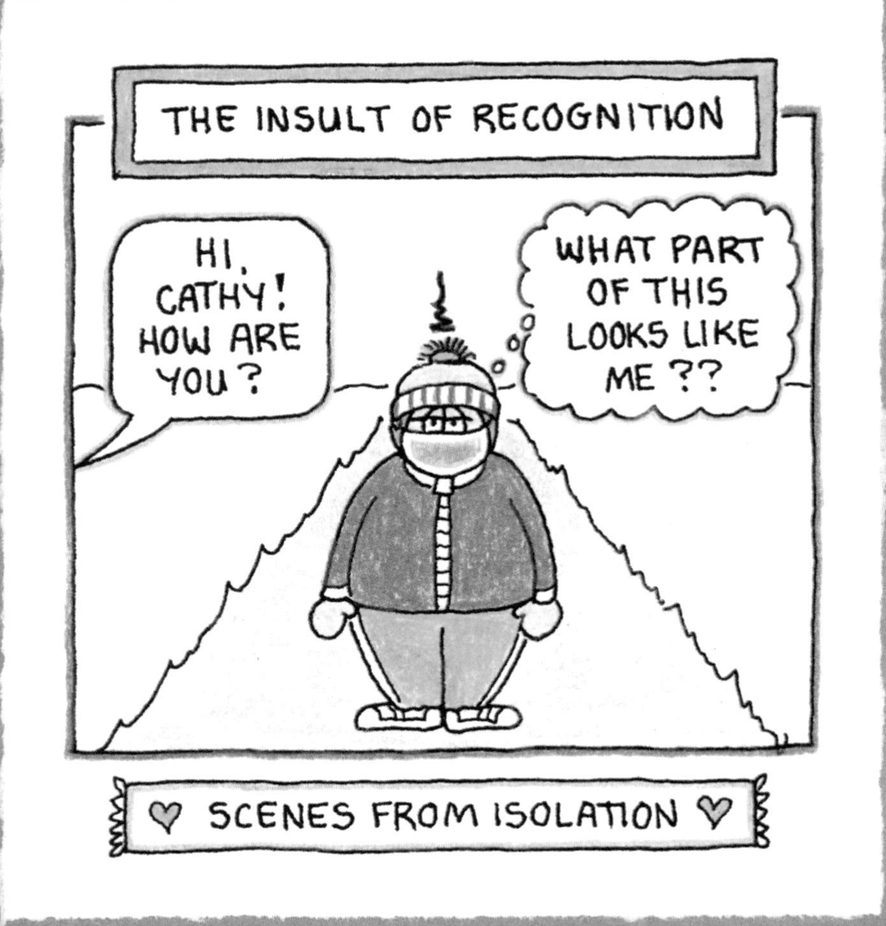
THE INSULT OF RECOGNITION
HI, CATHY! HOW ARE YOU?
WHAT PART OF THIS LOOKS LIKE ME??
♡ SCENES FROM ISOLATION ♡

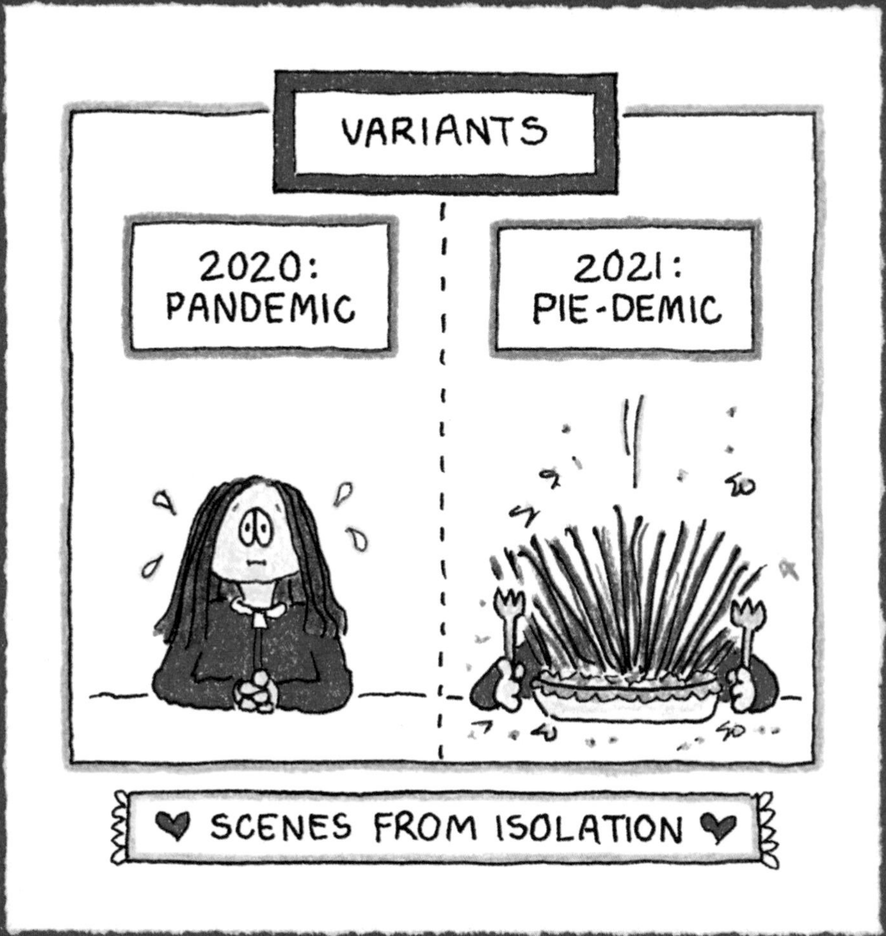
VARIANTS
2020: PANDEMIC
2021: PIE-DEMIC
SCENES FROM ISOLATION

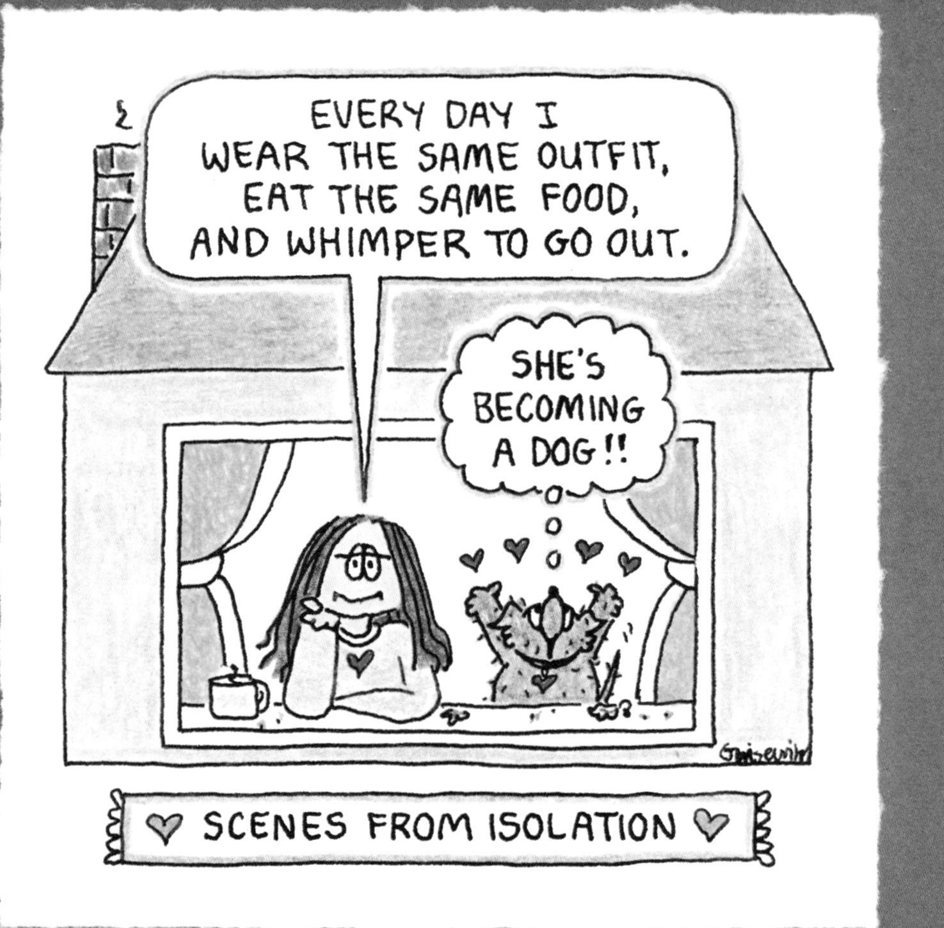
EVERY DAY I WEAR THE SAME OUTFIT, EAT THE SAME FOOD, AND WHIMPER TO GO OUT.
SHE'S BECOMING A DOG!!
SCENES FROM ISOLATION

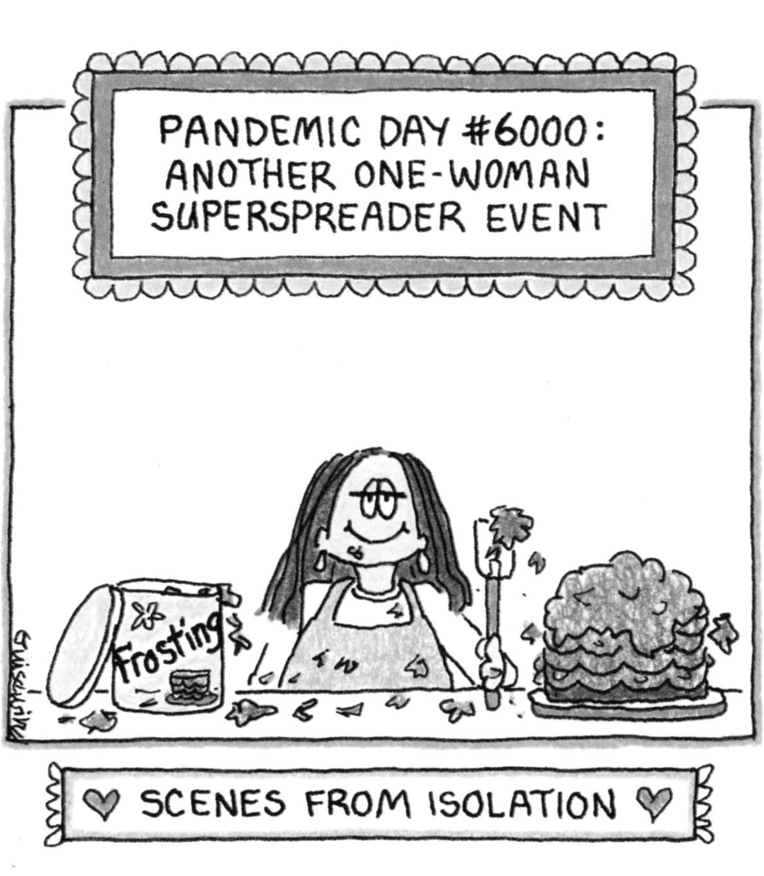
PANDEMIC DAY #6000:
ANOTHER ONE-WOMAN
SUPERSPREADER EVENT
Frosting
GUISEWITE
SCENES FROM ISOLATION

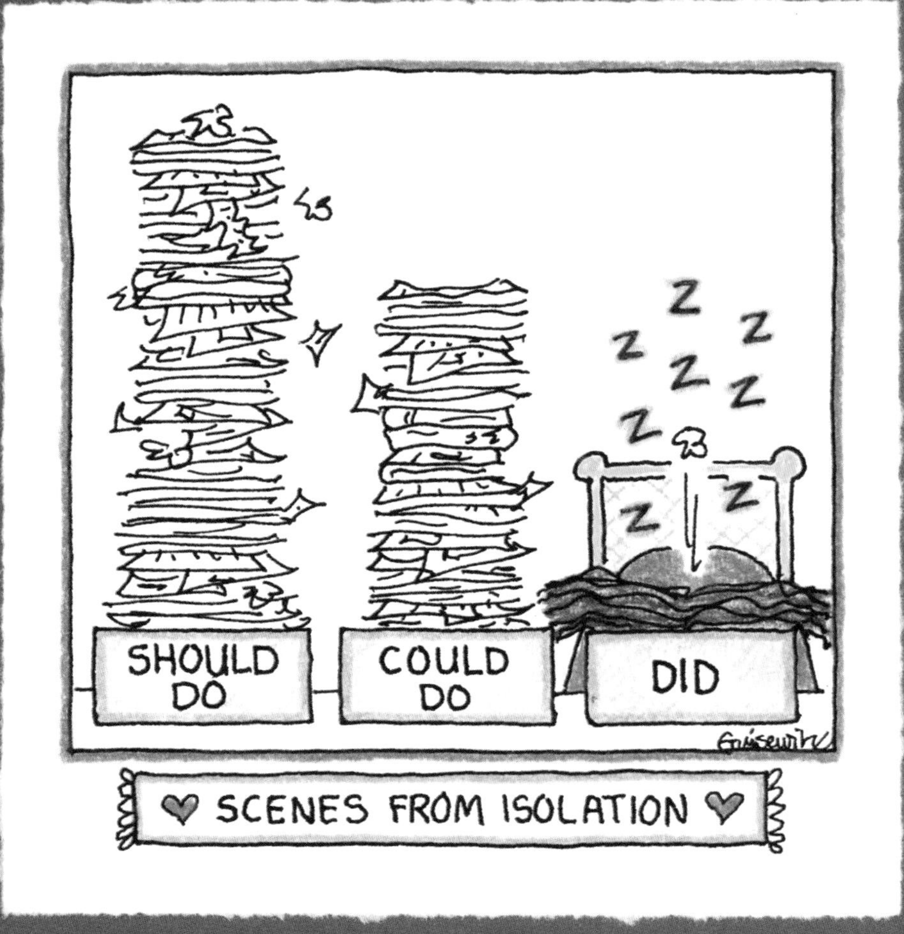
SHOULD DO
COULD DO
DID
Z
Z
Z
Z
Z
Z
Z
Z
Z
SCENES FROM ISOLATION

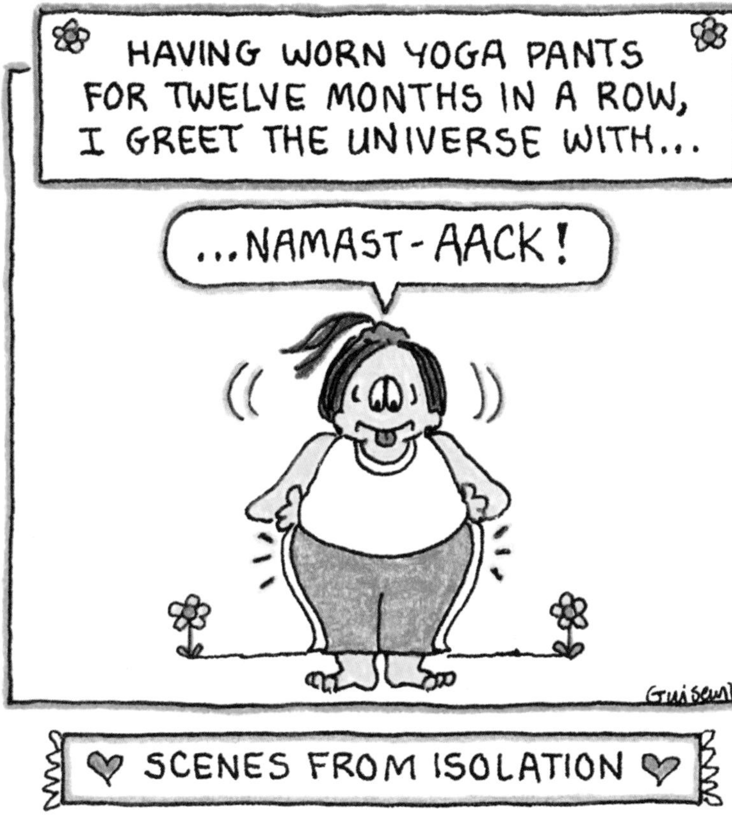
HAVING WORN YOGA PANTS FOR TWELVE MONTHS IN A ROW, I GREET THE UNIVERSE WITH...
...NAMAST-AACK!
SCENES FROM ISOLATION

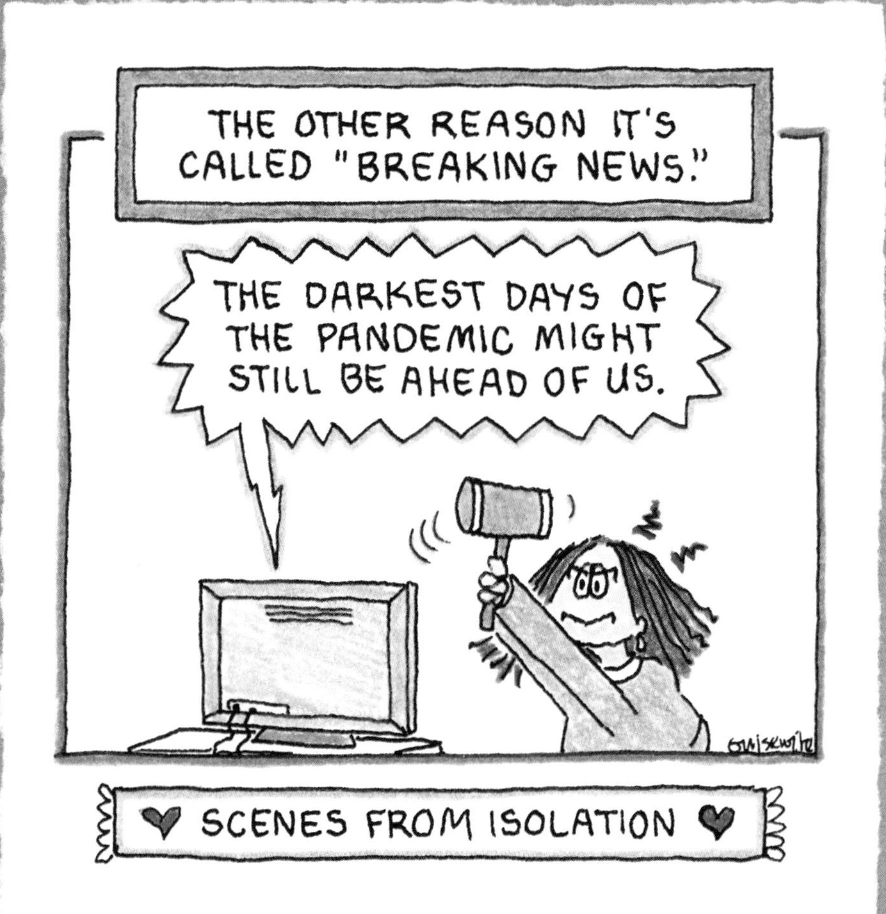
THE OTHER REASON IT'S CALLED "BREAKING NEWS."
THE DARKEST DAYS OF THE PANDEMIC MIGHT STILL BE AHEAD OF US.
SCENES FROM ISOLATION

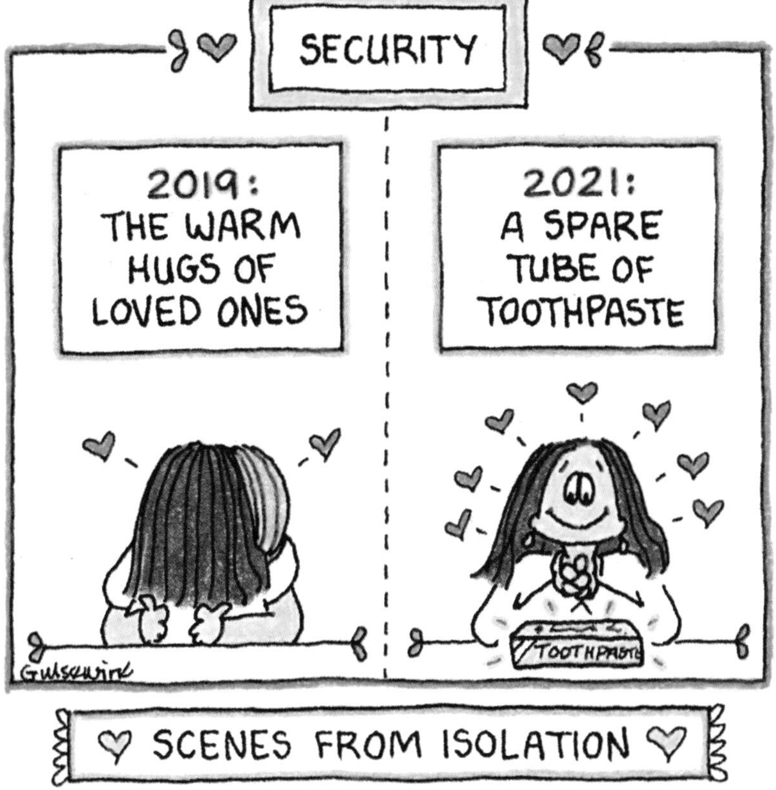
SECURITY
2019: THE WARM HUGS OF LOVED ONES
2021: A SPARE TUBE OF TOOTHPASTE
TOOTHPASTE
GUISEWITE
SCENES FROM ISOLATION

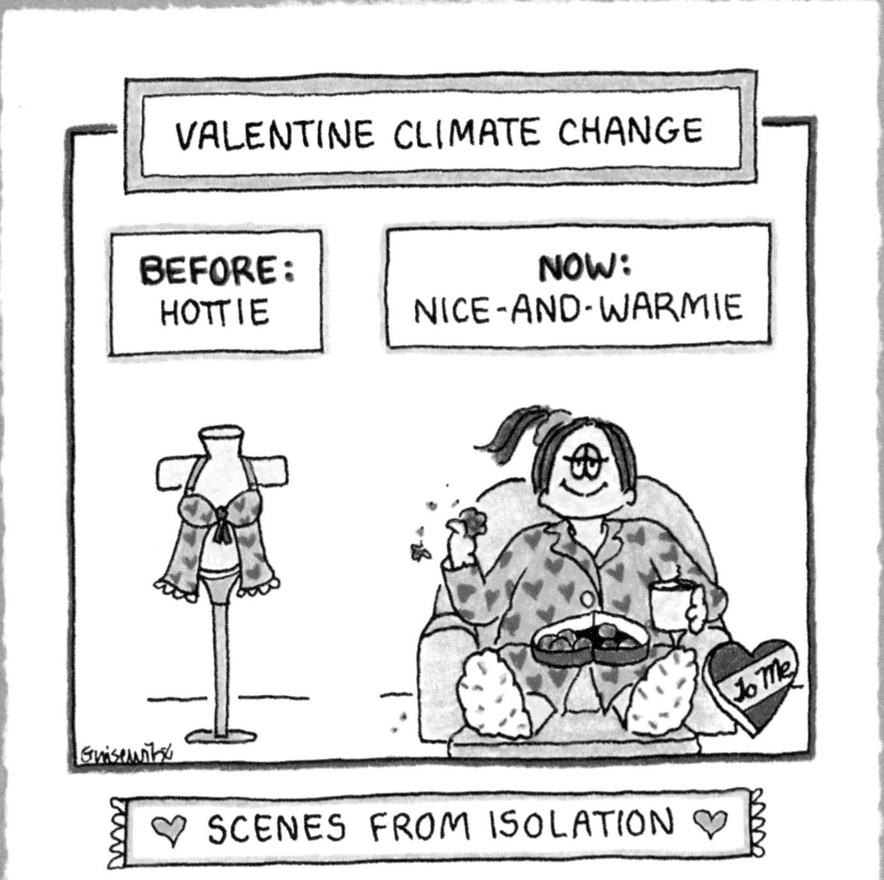
VALENTINE CLIMATE CHANGE
BEFORE:
HOTTIE
NOW:
NICE-AND-WARMIE
To Me
SCENES FROM ISOLATION

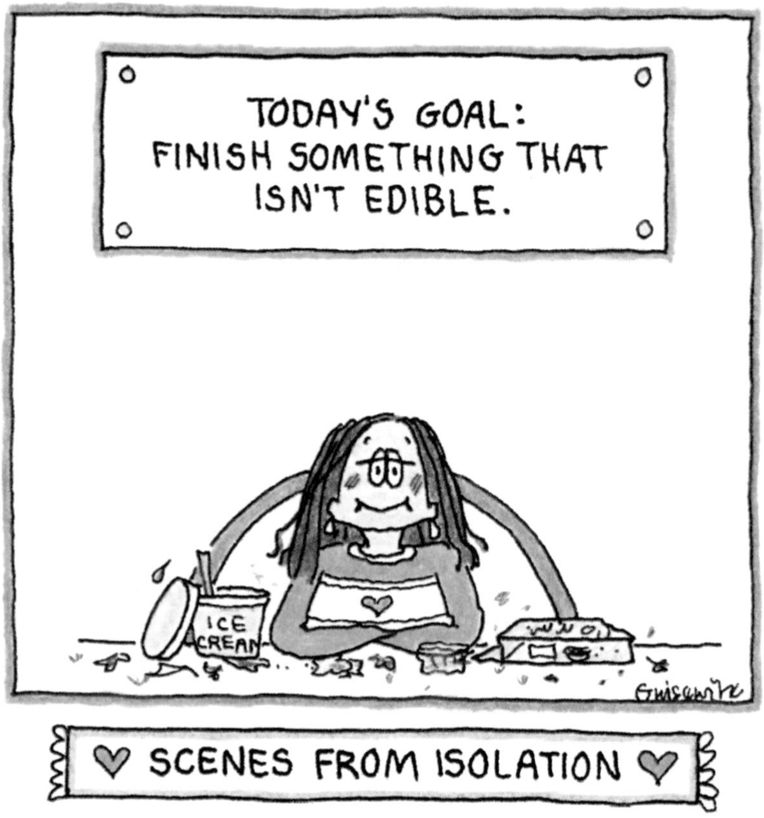
TODAY'S GOAL:
FINISH SOMETHING THAT
ISN'T EDIBLE.
ICE
CREAM
SCENES FROM ISOLATION

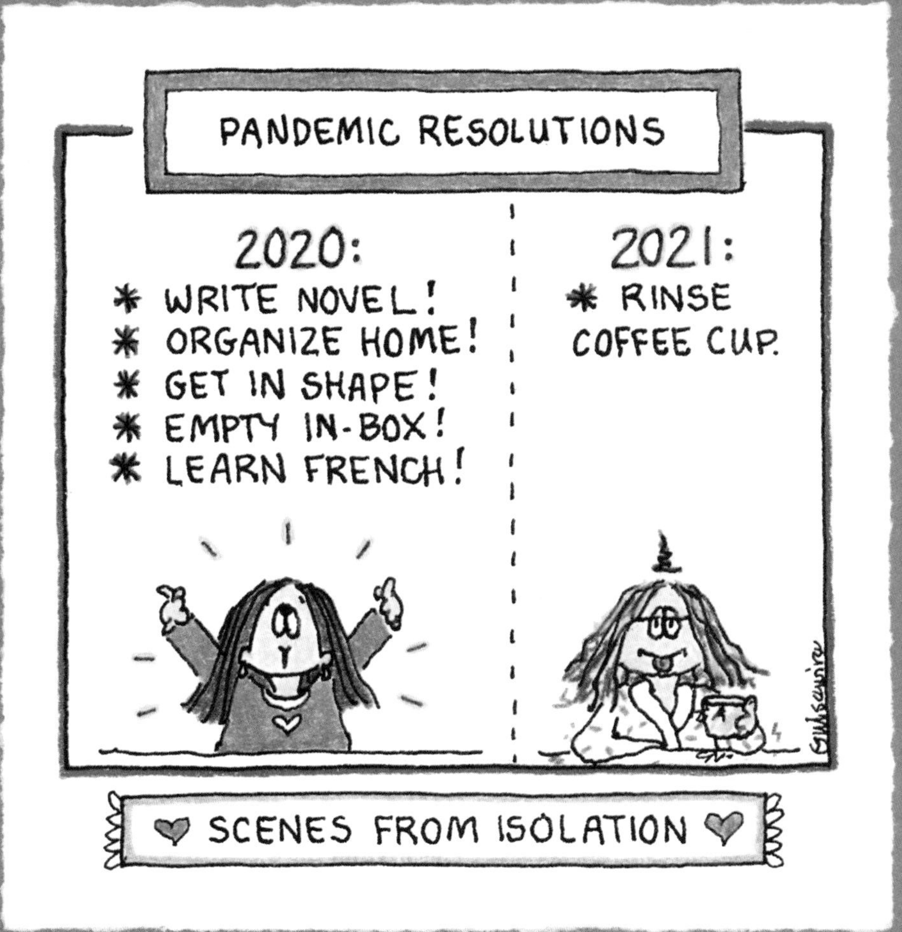
PANDEMIC RESOLUTIONS
2020:
* WRITE NOVEL!
* ORGANIZE HOME!
* GET IN SHAPE!
* EMPTY IN-BOX!
* LEARN FRENCH!
2021:
* RINSE COFFEE CUP.
SCENES FROM ISOLATION

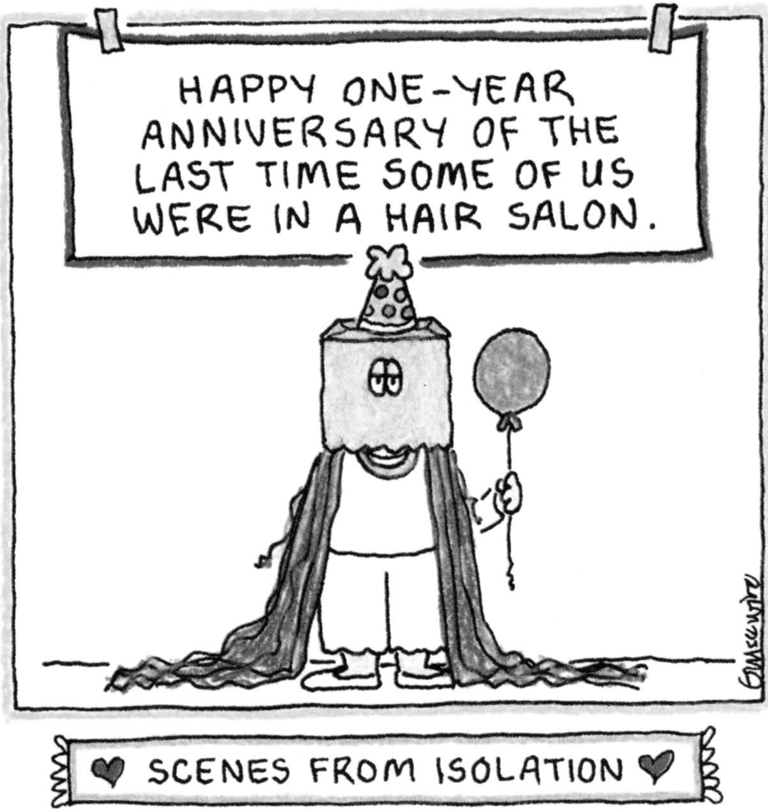
HAPPY ONE-YEAR ANNIVERSARY OF THE LAST TIME SOME OF US WERE IN A HAIR SALON.
SCENES FROM ISOLATION

A POEM OF GRATITUDE
I add up complaints,
I calculate stressings,
But today, for a change,
I'm counting my blessings.
SCENES FROM ISOLATION

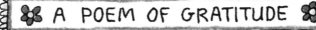

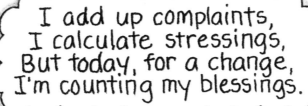

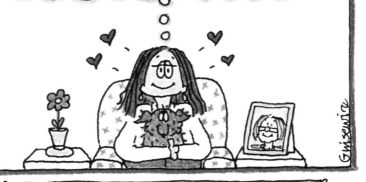

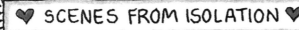

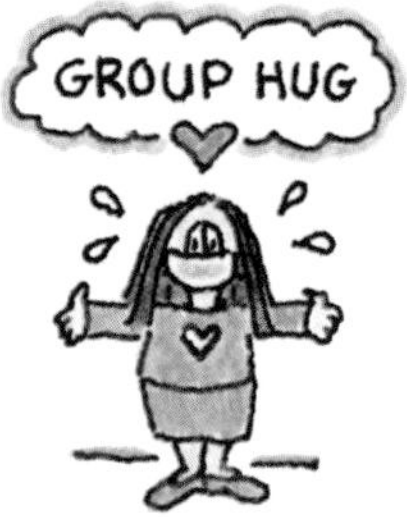
GROUP HUG

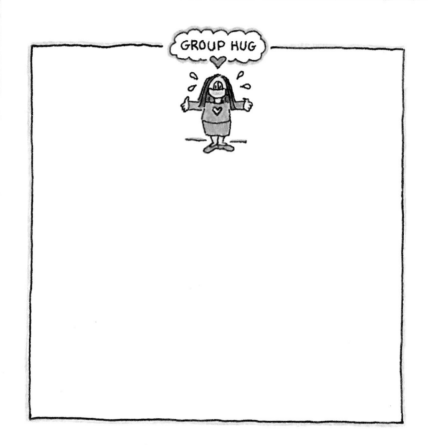

Scenes from Isolation

Andrews McMeel Publishing
a division of Andrews McMeel Universal
1130 Walnut Street, Kansas City, Missouri 64106

www.andrewsmcmeel.com

21 22 23 24 25 TEN 10 9 8 7 6 5 4 3 2 1

ISBN: 978-1-5248-7104-8

Library of Congress Control Number: 2021938190

Editor: Patty Rice
Art Director/Designer: Holly Swayne
Production Editor: Dave Shaw
Production Manager: Tamara Haus

Attention: Schools and Businesses

Andrews McMeel books are available at quantity discounts with bulk purchase
for educational, business, or sales promotional use. For information, please e-mail
the Andrews McMeel Publishing Special Sales Department:
specialsales@amuniversal.com.